Praise for *Georgia Irvin's Guide to Schools*

"Simply put, no one knows more about schools in the Metro Washington area than Georgia Irvin. And no one can better lead a family through the school search and application maze. *Georgia Irvin's Guide to Schools* will be an invaluable resource to families . . . and a critical reference source for all educational professionals working in the national capital area."

— **Mark H. Sklarow,** executive director,
Independent Educational Consultants Association

"The key to educational success is finding a school that is the right match for each child. Every parent needs this book! Georgia Irvin combines a wealth of information and years of experience with DC schools. What shines through most, however, is her wisdom about children, which helps families find their way through the confusion to a happy ending."

— **Susan Piggott,** former director, National Child Research Center

"Georgia Irvin is a skillful and seasoned educational consultant who knows the schools and students of metropolitan Washington, DC. Her guide takes the mystery out of the admissions process by aiding parents and prospective students in understanding what to expect and how to choose a public or independent education."

—**Bruce Stewart,** head of school, Sidwell Friends School

"Georgia Irvin is a most knowledgeable source for information on schools in the Washington area. Her advice to parents is right on target."

—**Dr. Regan Kenyon,** president,
Secondary School Admission Test Board

Georgia Irvin's Guide to Schools

Georgia Irvin's Guide to Schools
METROPOLITAN WASHINGTON

SELECTED INDEPENDENT SCHOOLS AND PRESCHOOLS

THIRD EDITION

Georgia K. Irvin

TAYLOR TRADE PUBLISHING
Lanham • New York • Boulder • Toronto • Plymouth, UK

Published by Taylor Trade Publishing
An imprint of The Rowman & Littlefield Publishing Group, Inc.
4501 Forbes Boulevard, Suite 200, Lanham, Maryland 20706
http://www.rlpgtrade.com

Estover Road, Plymouth PL6 7PY, United Kingdom

Distributed by National Book Network

British Library Cataloguing in Publication Information Available

Library of Congress Cataloging-in-Publication Data
Irvin, Georgia K., 1932–
    Georgia Irvin's guide to schools : selected independent schools and preschools /
Georgia K. Irvin. — 3rd ed.
      p.   cm.
    ISBN 978-1-58979-461-0 (pbk. : alk. paper)
    1. Private schools—Washington Metropolitan Area—Directories. 2. Public schools—Washington Metropolitan Area—Directories. 3. Education—Parent participation—Washington Metropolitan Area. I. Title. II. Title: Guide to schools.
L903.W27I79 2010
371.02025'753—dc22   2009029682

∞ ™ The paper used in this publication meets the minimum requirements of American National Standard for Information Sciences—Permanence of Paper for Printed Library Materials, ANSI/NISO Z39.48-1992.

Printed in the United States of America

For Kate, Stuart, and Carrie
and
Molly, Elizabeth, and Isabelle

Contents

Preface

A s a parent, you want the best possible education for your child. The process of determining which preschool or independent school best meets your family's needs can be daunting. This is particularly true in metropolitan Washington, DC, where more than 450 independent schools (also known as *private schools*) and a number of public school districts serve the nation's capital and its vicinity. Excellent preschools and daycare centers abound.

This book is designed to help alleviate the anxiety associated with the school search process. It was written in response to the many clients who encouraged me to develop a guide. This book is the culmination of four decades of experience as a parent, grandparent, public school teacher, independent school admission officer, and educational consultant.

Here, you will find:

- In-depth profiles of over one hundred independent schools in greater Washington, DC
- An overview of the independent school admission process: how to apply and what to expect

- In-depth profiles of ninety-three preschools, fifty-four of which are programs for the youngest children within a larger school; thirty-nine are preschools listed in a separate section of the book, most of which end at five years; however, a few continue through first grade or are non-graded
- An overview of the preschool admission process
- A chapter on charter schools and home schooling
- Answers to frequently asked questions on education and parenting in a chapter called "A Conversation with Georgia"

In previous editions, I included public schools in the District of Columbia and seven districts surrounding Washington. Although my commitment to public education is as strong as ever, and I would like to continue to have these schools in my book, the section on independent schools has been received much more enthusiastically than the section on public schools. This reflects the difficulty of acquiring consistent, useful information from seven public school systems and hundreds of individual schools. The demand for basic information on preschools has led me to include a section on selected preschools and general information about applying.

As you use this book, please keep in mind that:

- This book is designed to serve as a neutral source. None of the schools has paid to be included, and the book is not intended to be an advertisement for schools or preschools.
- Information on each school and preschool was provided by the school. Daycare centers are not included.
- Consistent with my philosophy that no one school is best for all students and that the best school for a child is the one that fits his or her unique needs, I have neither rated, ranked, nor critiqued the institutions.
- No two schools have identical admission procedures. The overview of the application process is just that. **It is important that you observe the specific policies of the schools or preschools to which you apply.**

A word about the independent schools and preschools chosen for inclusion: one of the hallmarks of the schools in this area is variety. I include schools that represent a broad range of educational options and vary in size, philosophy, methodology, and student composition. As in previous editions, I sent questionnaires to schools and preschools with which I have had some engagement over the years. Those that returned the forms are included. Please note that a preschool's or school's presence or absence from the book represents neither an endorsement nor censure.

It may prove useful to look at the defining characteristics of some broad types of schools:

- *Public schools* are open to all students, funded by tax dollars, governed by an elected board of education, and require teachers to be certified in an area of expertise.
- *Independent schools* are nonprofit, tax-exempt institutions that receive income from tuition, endowments, foundations, and gifts. They are governed by a self-perpetuating board of trustees, and can select faculty, students, and curricula consistent with their mission. Teacher certification is not required.
- *Religious schools* were the primary source of a formal education before state and federal governments established schools. Many faith-based organizations continue to educate the children of members of their denominations. In recent years, many of the schools have become much more inclusive of those of other faiths.

    There are two types of religious schools. *Parochial schools* are nonprofit, tax-exempt religious institutions serving all grade levels. They are similar to other independent schools; however, they are under the jurisdiction of a local diocese or other faith-associated governing body. The school facility is usually located adjacent to the church or temple, which provides a subsidy. Children in the associated congregation usually have a priority in admission, and the parish priest, minister, or rabbi and members of the congregation are actively involved in the school. Catholic parochial schools are often called *parish schools.*

Religious orders or groups of committed members of a denomination also have established schools within the same faith. This is especially true of Roman Catholic schools and colleges. These schools tend to have a more selected enrollment than parochial schools and are funded independently of a specific congregation. In the Washington, DC, area, most parochial schools are Roman Catholic, and all Catholic schools in this book are considered independent schools.

Almost every religious group has a school in metropolitan Washington. There are many Episcopal and Jewish schools and a significant representation of the Society of Friends (also known as *Quaker* or *Friends Schools*). There is an Islamic school and a growing number of schools that call themselves *Christian* without a specific denominational affiliation.

- *For-profit* or *proprietary schools* are owned by individuals or corporations, privately financed, managed as if they were commercial businesses, and required to pay taxes. Each state sets standards for these schools. They are free from many of the regulations governing public and nonprofit institutions. These are also included in the section on independent schools.

- *Alternative educational options* are included in this edition in a chapter called "Alternatives" in which I give basic points on charter schools and home schooling.

A word about the use of the words *private* and *independent*. *Private* is still used to describe most nursery schools, but *independent* is used for most schools for older children. The different words refer to the source of funding. *Private* and *independent* both indicate that parents pay the tuition and the institutions are *independent* of federal funds. (*Private* is still used to describe nonpublic colleges and universities, but schools enrolling younger students consider the word elitist, so these precollegiate schools often call themselves *independent* as a statement of access to all races and socioeconomic levels.)

All of the schools in this book comply with state and local health and safety regulations and applicable laws regarding discrimination.

Most independent schools offer need-based financial aid; a few also offer merit scholarships.

Accreditation for independent schools varies by state. Membership in the National Association of Independent Schools (NAIS; www.nais.org) indicates compliance with high standards of governance and academic excellence and accreditation by an NAIS-approved organization. Membership in regional organizations, such as the Association of Independent Schools of Greater Washington (AISGW; www.aisgw.org), the Association of Independent Maryland Schools (AIMS; www.aimsmd.org), and the Virginia Association of Independent Schools (VAIS; www.vais.org), indicates compliance with standards established by the respective organizations. For additional information on these organizations, consult their websites.

The Middle States Association of Colleges and Schools (MSA; www .middlestates.org) provides accreditation to many public and independent elementary and secondary schools in Maryland and the District of Columbia. Schools in Virginia may be accredited by the Southern Association of Colleges and Schools (SACS; www.sacs.org). Many of the schools in this book are accredited by either the Middle States or the Southern Association of Colleges and Schools. Accreditation, however, was not a condition for inclusion in this book.

It is my hope that this book will strengthen your understanding of the many fine educational opportunities available in metropolitan Washington, DC, and enable you to make important decisions with greater confidence and ease.

PRESCHOOL INFORMATION:
HOW TO MOST EFFECTIVELY USE THIS BOOK

Data on ninety-three preschools can be found in two sections of this book. Most of the thirty-nine schools in the "Preschools" chapter end at five years, the age at which compulsory education begins; however, a few continue through first grade or are non-graded. The fifty-four preschools in the "Independent Schools" chapter have grades that extend beyond kindergarten. A table on pages 370–375 lists all ninety-three preschools with page numbers.

In addition, for a broader understanding of admission policies, it is useful to read the "Independent Schools" chapter. This is especially helpful if you are considering one of the preschools that continues beyond age four, or if you are considering an independent school after preschool.

The final chapter, "A Conversation with Georgia," contains a section on kindergarten readiness. This will be important as you consider kindergarten.

The information in this book was first gathered in the fall of 2002 and updated in the spring of 2005 and again in the winter of 2009. The data from schools change frequently and parents should rely only on information they have received directly from a school. In particular, parents should seek specific information from schools on deadlines for applications and application criteria. Throughout the school directories, the abbreviation N/A is used to indicate information that is either not applicable or not available for a particular school.

This book is sold on the terms and understanding that the publisher, author, consultants, and editors are not responsible for the results of any actions taken on the basis of information in this book or for any error in or omission from this book. The publisher and the author, consultants and editors, expressly disclaim all liability and responsibility to any person, whether a purchaser or reader of this book or not, in respect of anything, and of the consequences of anything, done or omitted to be done by any such person in reliance, whether wholly or partially, upon the whole or any part of the contents of this book.

GEORGIA IRVIN
Georgia K. Irvin and Associates, Inc.
Educational Consultants
Chevy Chase, MD
www.gkirvin.com
301-951-0131

Acknowledgments

I t is gratifying to know that the first and second editions of this book have been useful to countless families. I have received many expressions of appreciation from students, parents, heads of schools, admission officers, members of boards of trustees, and families from all over the world who have moved to metropolitan Washington, DC.

The cooperation of all the independent schools and preschools listed herein has been heartwarming. I want to express my deep gratitude, again, to each school for its support of the original book and its subsequent revisions. I have tried to faithfully represent the information they provided.

Too many friends and colleagues contributed directly or indirectly to the work on all three editions for me to even begin to acknowledge all of them. In earlier editions special credit was given to Nicole Chardavoyne and Edith Furber Zhang for their effort and expertise in every detail. For this edition, Susan Piggott, former director of the National Child Research Center, provided her insights on preschools. This update would not have been possible without Kathleen Herman, a knowledgeable former admission officer and colleague. Nancie McManus contributed her editorial expertise and delicious treats when they were most needed. I want to give endless thanks to my associate, Jennifer Gucwa, who once more has worked tirelessly over weekends and late evenings to make the corrections reflected in these pages and provide her superb editing skills. With her cheerful, can-do attitude, she made all the data come together. Pamela Tedeschi, an extraordinarily talented educational consultant and my associate and dear friend, is always active in all areas of everything we do in our office and especially in writing this edition. Helen Colson, a beloved friend and mentor, supplied perspective and encouragement. Stuart Irvin, my son, contributed legal expertise and was also an insightful reader and critic, while Carrie Chimerine Irvin, my daughter-in-law, gave valuable time to critique and edit early drafts. And, most importantly, to my daughter, Kate, goes endless love and gratitude for her wisdom throughout these projects. To each of you and many more, my profound "thank you."

About the Author

Georgia K. Irvin, a certified educational planner, is considered one of the premier educational consultants in the country. She specializes in day schools in metropolitan Washington, DC, and boarding and therapeutic schools nationwide.

Since 1984, as founder, president, and CEO of Georgia K. Irvin and Associates of Chevy Chase, Maryland, she has helped thousands of students and families from all backgrounds and from all over the world select the educational option that best meets each child's needs.

For fifteen years, Ms. Irvin was director of admission and financial aid at Sidwell Friends School in Washington, DC. She has served on numerous boards, including the Black Student Fund, the School and Student Services for Financial Aid, the Independent Educational Consultants Association, the advisory board of a public school, and as a trustee of an independent school. She is a frequent lecturer at schools and conferences. The Secondary School Admission Test Board honored her with the prestigious William B. Bretnall Award for "exemplary contribution to the field of independent school admissions."

Independent Schools

Applying to an independent school is a process that can involve a considerable commitment of time. However, it is time well spent when, in the end, you make an informed decision on behalf of your child. This chapter provides the following: a timetable and detailed explanation of the steps in the process and what to expect; profiles of more than one hundred independent schools; maps that show the schools' locations; a chart that indicates the location by state, grade range, and gender makeup of the students enrolled; and a worksheet to organize your information as you submit applications.

WHY ATTEND AN INDEPENDENT SCHOOL?

In metropolitan Washington, DC, many parents attended public schools, at least through high school, and are unfamiliar with independent schools; more parents attended private colleges. Although there are significant differences between independent schools and independent colleges, in addition to the age of the students enrolled, some similarities are notable.

1

Many public schools share the following attributes, but among the reasons commonly cited for attending independent elementary and secondary schools are:

- An independent school's total enrollment is smaller in comparison to most public schools and there are fewer students in each class.
- A selected enrollment allows teachers to focus on individual students and reduces disciplinary issues.
- The "No Child Left Behind" Act does not apply to independent schools, and teachers have more autonomy to be innovative and creative in their classes.
- Excellence in the subject area is the primary credential for employment, as distinguished from state certification.
- Curriculum and teaching methods can be established by each school.
- Arts and physical education classes are offered with more frequency.
- Schools have more control over their financial resources.
- Tenure is established by the school. Teachers and administrators are not subject to being moved to another school location.
- Activities that may be more competitive in larger schools allow students in smaller schools to participate and have leadership positions.
- Religious beliefs and traditions can be observed and taught.
- Rich academic and nonacademic opportunities and personal relationships with teachers can enhance a student's abilities, interests, and confidence, and can provide advantages that maximize potential and improve future educational options.

Parents, grandparents, and alumni may provide leadership and serve on the governing boards.

At a minimum, all independent schools must adhere to state and federal health and safety regulations and applicable laws regarding discrimination.

HOW TO APPLY TO AN INDEPENDENT SCHOOL

This section is designed to demystify the admission process and enable you and your child to pursue your school options with less stress and greater confidence as you select a school that will maximize your child's potential.

A Message for Parents

Keep in mind that applying to an independent school is not about getting into the most prestigious school. It is about matching your child's abilities with a school that will maximize his or her potential and in which he or she will also feel happy and rewarded. An independent school will have a major influence on the future of your child; it is also a significant financial investment. As parents, you should consider your options and conduct research as carefully as you would when making any other major decision or investment.

Schools with widespread name recognition have track records that reflect their reputations, but they are not the only excellent schools in the area. In fact, often the less-well-known schools meet the needs of some students better than the well-known ones. The "best" school is the one at which *your child* will succeed.

In recent years, the number of applications for many of the area's independent schools has far exceeded the available places. If your child is not accepted into your first-choice school, it is important to realize that this does not necessarily reflect any inadequacies on his or her part or on yours, but more likely is a consequence of the intense demand for a relatively limited number of places in some schools. There are enough schools in the area that a fine and appropriate one is nearly always an option.

Begin the process of researching, visiting, and applying to independent schools after Labor Day and continue through the fall and early winter of the year before your child will enter. The chronological receipt of an application (prior to the deadline) is rarely a determining factor in admission. It is wise to submit applications early enough to allow ample time to complete each step in the process and reschedule visits or tests that may be delayed by snow days or illness.

Herein you will find a timetable and checklist to use as you apply to independent day schools. This is followed by a detailed discussion of the application process. Some families move to the area after deadlines have passed and other families become interested in options later in the year. For those families, it is possible to adapt this schedule to the extent that school deadlines and space constraints allow. Older students applying to boarding schools also may use this schedule.

Being organized helps. Many families use the worksheet on page 272 as a model to create their own spreadsheet, adapting it to include the points pertinent to their child's age.

If You Miss the Deadlines

Many families move to the area after all the schools' deadlines have passed or after the school year has started. Local families may be unaware of how early the admission process begins. In any case, some schools can be flexible; others are unable to accept additional applications after stated deadlines. Fire marshals, zoning regulations, and health officials set firm limits on the number of students that can be enrolled; therefore, schools that are at capacity cannot "make a place." By calling different schools, parents may be fortunate enough to find a space. If you are moving, one parent might commute until appropriate schools can be found for the children.

Parents may decide to consult with an educational consultant. (See pages 9–10 for information on finding an educational consultant.) After meeting a student, consultants can advise families of possible options, may call appropriate schools to determine if there is a place for a student with the skills and interests of the child (or children), assist with short- and long-term plans, and provide useful information about the transition.

APPLICATION PROCESS CHECKLIST

Begin one year or more prior to enrollment

I. **September or Earlier: Do Your Homework**
- ✔ Consider your child's strengths and needs.
- ✔ Gather information on schools through websites and publications available from the admission offices.
- ✔ Identify schools you and your child want to visit.
- ✔ Consider working with an educational consultant and scheduling an appointment.
- ✔ If you are eligible, contact the Black Student Fund, the Latino Student Fund, or other sources of financial aid.

II. **October–January: Prepare to Apply**
- ✔ Arrange to attend open houses, school tours, information sessions, or shadow days.
- ✔ Narrow your list of schools to those to which you will apply.
- ✔ Determine deadlines for the receipt of applications.
- ✔ Determine due dates for all materials pertinent to each application.

III. **Before the Deadlines**
- ✔ Submit the applications; supporting recommendations, test results, and transcripts can follow.
- ✔ Arrange test dates, interviews, or play dates.
- ✔ Distribute recommendation forms to current teachers.
- ✔ Request that a transcript be sent directly to each school by the applicant's current school.
- ✔ Submit financial aid forms.

IV. **February: Follow Up**
   ✔ Contact each school or check online to confirm the
      receipt of all application materials.
   ✔ Continue to schedule or follow through with appoint-
      ments for tests, interviews, or play dates.
   ✔ Submit recent reports, if available.

V. **If You Miss the Deadlines**
   ✔ Evaluate your options.

VI. **March and April: Admission and Enrollment Decisions**
   ✔ Schools notify parents of acceptance, denial, or a place
      on the waiting list in March.
   ✔ If your child is accepted by the school of your first
      choice, read the contract carefully, sign, and return it
      immediately to the school. Be aware that the terms of
      the contract may make it difficult to withdraw without
      significant penalties.
   ✔ If you are unsure which school to accept, revisit the
      school or schools and encourage older students to revisit
      before making a decision. Attend meetings and programs
      designed for accepted students and families. Consult
      with current parents and other professionals if necessary.
   ✔ After accepting a place in a school, notify the other
      schools to which your child applied that your child will
      not enroll. Doing this with dispatch allows those on the
      waiting list to gain a place.
   ✔ If you wish to have your child's name remain on waiting
      lists, contact each school immediately. In April, after
      those who were accepted have responded, the admis-
      sion officers can inform parents more accurately of the
      likelihood of places becoming available.

VII. **May–August: Show Continued Interest**
  ✔ Keep schools advised of your continued interest in remaining on the waiting list; send your child's final report card and notify the schools of any recent achievements.
  ✔ If your child was denied, you may call the school to discuss the reasons for denial and the wisdom of reapplying.

Applicants from Out of Town

Most schools require parents who are moving to the area to bring their children for a play date or interview, even if it requires a long trip. If possible, try to arrange to be in the area at the time of a regularly scheduled play date or group visit. Sometimes several schools have a scheduled group visit for applicants that your child can join; more often special arrangements will have to be made to accommodate you while you are in the area. Plan in advance. Try to make these arrangements before winter weather, when snow days can disrupt schedules. Do not schedule more than two schools in one day; even the most resilient child will have a meltdown when over-scheduled. It is best to arrive in the area early enough that your child can have a weekend to recover from travel fatigue or jet lag.

There are advantages to having admission tests administered in the familiarity of one's hometown. If this is not an option and a test must be scheduled when you come for the visits and interviews, it is wise to arrange the testing to follow the school visits. Not only is the child apt to be less tired for the test, he or she may be more motivated to do well after seeing the schools.

Most schools communicate with families via e-mail, but international families may want to specifically request that final decisions be e-mailed. It is most unwise to buy a house before you know where your children will go to school.

DO YOUR HOMEWORK

Start doing your homework by assessing the developmental level of your child. Research schools and select those that interest you most.

Birthday Cut-Off Dates

It is not unusual for schools to require that applicants be three, four, or five years old by a specific date before enrolling. This date varies from school to school, but the date can be as early as July 1 before a fall enrollment, with September 1 as the most frequently used date. Schools that are firm about their birthday cut-off dates for admission to the early grades also realize that they must not put an "intellectual lid" on a child's head, and they try to keep each child appropriately challenged in every subject area. The goal is to maximize the child's academic potential while remaining in a chronological age group that is socially appropriate and emotionally healthy.

The birthday cut-off dates are usually less rigid at seventh grade and above because the maturation pace has stabilized; the late bloomer's skills have caught up with those of the early bloomer, and indications of maturity other than age are given more consideration in admission decisions.

It can be difficult to discern the best grade placement for children with summer birthdays. There are many advantages to being among the oldest, but each child's readiness for the program in a specific school must be considered. Students in Washington, DC-area independent schools generally are chronologically older than students in the same grade in other parts of the country.

Consider Your Child's Strengths and Needs

Begin your school search by honestly assessing your child's development. In comparison with contemporaries, consider the following:

- Language development: receptive and expressive skills, articulation, vocabulary, intonation, understanding the nuances of language, ability to expand on a topic

- Organization of known information or ability to recount a story or event in sequence
- Short- and long-term memory for facts and events
- Attitudes toward school, specific subjects, and homework
- Attention span, organizational skills, tenacity, and frustration level
- Pace at which work is accomplished
- Motor skills: fine and gross
- Problem-solving skills
- Ability to initiate appropriate activities
- Curiosity (which involves not only asking questions, but a genuine interest in finding answers)
- Physical stamina
- Social skills
- For young children, the ability to separate from parents
- Relationships with peers, teachers, and other adults
- Use of leisure: reading, playing team sports, music, playing with technological toys, drawing, writing
- A passion, interest, or commitment to a subject or activity
- Sources of self-esteem
- Maturity: physical, intellectual, social, and emotional
- Medical conditions that may affect the selection of a school (wheelchair accessibility, presence of a nurse to administer medications, etc.)

Consider an Educational Consultant

Certified Educational Planners (CEP) are full-time, experienced, professional educational consultants who have gained extensive knowledge of educational options through personal visits and frequent contact with many schools. They may specialize in day schools, boarding schools, therapeutic programs, colleges, or a combination of these. Most consultants meet personally with the student and family to help clarify a child's educational needs and to identify his or her strengths and talents, as well as to assist parents in understanding what to look for in a school. The consultant provides a customized list of options and information that can inform parents as they go through the process and in making decisions. This includes but is not limited to knowing each school's admission criteria, test requirements, academic rigor, extracurricular opportunities, and student population. Often consultants provide insights into learning style, and recommend activities that the student may enjoy or need. Consultants receive no compensation from any educational institution or other professional or make any guarantees for admission. For a list of certified educational planners, contact the Independent Educational Consultants Association at www.iecaonline.com or 703-591-4850.

Parents interested in long-term planning may begin working with a consultant several years before admission; others start during the spring or summer before the application process begins—or later.

Gather Information about Schools

Go to the websites. Each year the sites are improved, and for some schools, all of the steps in the application process, including making appointments, submitting the application, and learning the admission committee's decision, can be accessed online. If any part of the application process is not online, contact the admission office. A few schools ask parents to visit before providing an application. As you review materials, remember that there is no perfect school—or perfect child!

Ask yourself:

- What is important to me?
- What is important to my child?
- Are my interests consistent with my child's needs and style?
- Which schools are a reasonable commute?
- What transportation options are available?
- Which schools will enhance my child's strengths?
- Which schools uphold and reinforce my family's values?
- Which schools have the appropriate level of challenge, pressure, or competition?

- Which schools will maximize my child's potential?
- While my child's needs are paramount, can I see myself as a parent in this school?

In addition to each school's website, the following are especially helpful for more general information:

National Association of Independent Schools (NAIS)	www.nais.org
Association of Independent Schools of Greater Washington (AISGW)	www.aisgw.org
Virginia Association of Independent Schools (VAIS)	www.vais.org
Association of Independent Maryland Schools (AIMS)	www.aimsmd.org
The Association of Boarding Schools (TABS)	www.boardingschool.org
Secondary School Admission Test (SSAT)	www.ssat.org
Independent School Entrance Exam (ISEE)	www.iseetest.org
High School Placement Test (HSPT)	www.ststesting.com

Understand Schools' Academic Demands and Characteristics

I group schools into four broad categories based on the general characteristics of their teaching style and their students. Each group includes schools that may be considered preppy, traditional, or structured, as well as those considered progressive, innovative, flexible, and informal. This characterization provides a general guideline for the culture of the school as well as the likelihood of admission; however, there is a degree of overlap of students enrolled in each group.

- Some schools are highly selective and look for students who already have a record of achievement, high test scores, and evidence enthusiasm for learning and a disciplined approach to new ideas and activities. Instruction moves quickly and is geared to students who are inquisitive and receptive to consistently high expectations. Older applicants have good grades and a commitment to extracurricular interests.

- Some schools look for potential, even if the child may not have fully demonstrated it. These schools see their primary task as nurturing and assisting students as they acquire skills and identifying talents that will allow them to advance in ways consistent with their ability. Students who want to learn and are willing to work and become engaged in the life of the school are selected.

- A third group of schools recognizes that for many children, school is not easy. These students may have experienced disappointments, be immature and unsure of themselves, or need to be nurtured and appreciated for who they are in less traditional ways. The classes are smaller and the pace of instruction may be slower, but there are challenges and opportunities.

- Some schools are designed to meet the needs of children with specific learning difficulties. Typically, teachers in these schools have advanced degrees in special education and expertise in using nontraditional methods and materials. Class sizes are small and emphasis is on remediation and learning compensatory skills. In addition to a patient and skilled faculty, these schools offer other support services, such as occupational and speech therapy.

Independent schools do not always have honors or gifted and talented programs like public schools. Enrichment opportunities, including grouping the most sophisticated students in advanced classes and providing independent study as well as Advanced Placement (AP) classes, are designed to meet the needs of students who want maximum challenges. A few schools participate in the International Baccalaureate Programme (IB).

Most schools provide additional services for those who need support in a subject area, but the level of help varies enormously from school to school, with the least amount of support offered in schools that have the most competitive admission.

No school wants to enroll a student who will be more frustrated than rewarded; parents should share that perspective. Parents sometimes like to think a child will rise to the occasion and stretch and reach in order to master a challenging program. However, the child who has not shown a propensity for stretching and reaching is rarely prepared for vigorous academic work and typically will not be successful in more rigorous programs. Look for schools in which you have reasonable confidence that your child will be challenged and enjoy success.

Schools begin and end at different grade levels. Schools that end at second and third grades are usually called *primary schools*. Those that continue through fifth or sixth grades are called *elementary schools*, and those that end at eighth grade are often called *junior schools*. (See the chart at the end of this chapter.)

The Washington, DC, area differs from some other metropolitan areas in that there are relatively few *feeder schools*, meaning the graduates are expected to continue their education at specific schools. Although some religious schools, especially Episcopal and Catholic schools, may give special consideration in admission to children enrolled in other schools of the same denomination, there are only a few formal feeder-school relationships. Do not presume that enrolling your child in a specific nursery, elementary, or junior school will guarantee future enrollment in any other school or college.

Schools that are associated with a religious denomination may give priority in the admission process to those who share the school's religious tenets, but most are receptive to applicants from different religious heritages as well as those from nonreligious backgrounds; some religious schools have enrolled a significant number of families from different faiths or who are unaffiliated with any religion. Parents often volunteer to share their customs, culture, or worship traditions with the class.

Understand Costs

Many parents sacrifice to send their children to independent schools; however, tuition does not cover the entire cost of educating a child in most schools. Nonprofit schools need philanthropy. Parents are encouraged to participate in fund-raising activities and, whenever possible, donate money to the school's causes.

In the past, the tuition increased as a student advanced through the grades. Recently, some schools have established tuitions with fewer differentials between the lower grades and the upper grades. Tuition also increases annually by a percentage of the current tuition. This fee is typically announced each spring with the enrollment or reenrollment contract. Parents should inquire about the following, even if they are not recipients of financial aid:

- What are the options for paying tuition?
- When and in what amount are tuition payments due?
- How much is the average annual increase in tuition by grade?

Financial Aid, Grants, Scholarships, and Payment Plans

Financial aid is the term used most frequently to describe the financial assistance provided to students on the basis of need. *Grants* refer to a sum of money awarded that does not require repayment. A few schools offer *merit scholarships* that are based on academic or nonacademic achievement and personal qualities instead of financial need, but merit aid in independent schools is not comparable to college opportunities. Most schools take the position that, to the extent that a family is able, they are responsible for paying tuition and other fees. Schools are committed to having a socioeconomically diverse student body and want to provide as much assistance as their resources allow. Sources of funds for financial aid include the school's endowment, gifts, fundraising events, and a portion of the annual operating budget. A number of schools offer no-interest payments over a ten-month period. A few schools have an agreement with an outside company to which parents may apply for an extended payment plan. Some families whose children are enrolled in schools that meet special needs are reimbursed by the public school system if it is proven that the public school cannot meet the child's needs.

Determining Eligibility

The service most widely used to determine financial need is the School and Student Service for Financial Aid (SSS) in Princeton, New Jersey. The SSS application form is available online (https://sss.ets.org) and from schools, and

Table 1.1 How Much Might I Have to Pay for Day School?

	Per-Child Contribution	
No. of Children	Net Worth: ≤$100,000	Net Worth: ≤$200,000
1	$19,862	$24,362
2	$9,931	$12,181
3	$6,621	$8,121

Source: Mark J. Mitchell, vice president, Financial Aid Services, National Association of Independent Schools.

Note: Assumptions used in calculations: parents' age 43, each earning $75,000; three children in family; net worth includes home equity, investments, bank accounts, other resources, and liabilities; average state and other taxes for District of Columbia; standard federal income tax deduction (no itemization); no student contribution.

should be submitted in January. Small schools often have their own methods of determining need. Catholic schools in the Archdiocese of Washington use the Private School Aid Service. Applications are available online (www.adw.org/education) and from the Catholic schools and should be submitted in December. Visit the websites for detailed information on each service, and be sure to know and comply with each school's specific instructions.

Schools may request a current tax return; it is important to prepare and file your tax return as soon as possible if you intend to apply for aid.

In recent years, the SSS has adjusted its methods of computing financial need to make independent schools more affordable to middle-income families. In addition, a geographic index represents the higher cost of living in metropolitan areas. The above table is based on methodology used by SSS for the 2009–2010 academic year. Financial aid is not just for poor children anymore. With tuitions at the current level, it does not hurt to ask if you qualify.

Sources of Financial Aid

In addition to aid from the school in which a student is enrolled, there are organizations that contribute financially to the school following a student's acceptance. The Black Student Fund (BSF) and the Latino Student Fund (LSF) provide a wide range of services to students attending pre-kindergarten through twelfth grades in selected independent schools. Each organization has an annual school fair at which representatives from many different schools are available to discuss their programs and enrollment options.

The BSF, founded in 1964, provides grants and essential support services to black students of modest means in Maryland, Virginia, and the District of Columbia. The BSF works toward creating an equitable learning experience for all students. During the 2008–2009 school year, 220 students received $240,000 in financial aid. For further details call 202-387-1414 or visit www.blackstudentfund.org.

The LSF, founded in 1994, provided $108,000 in financial assistance to about eighty-four students of Hispanic descent in the 2008–2009 school year. The LSF also provides a bilingual school directory and bilingual assistance, tutoring, and mentoring. For more information call 202-244-3438 or visit www.latinostudentfund.org.

Since 1993, Capital Partners for Education (CPE; www.cpfe.org), in conjunction with the school to which the student has been admitted, has provided low-income youth up to $4,500 annually toward the school's tuition, plus adult mentors, academic support, and enrichment opportunities.

The Washington Scholarship Fund (WSF; www.washingtonscholarshipfund.org) has two programs that enable low-income families within the District of Columbia to have a choice in where they send their children to school. WSF is the largest kindergarten-through-twelfth-grade scholarship-granting organization in the District, having distributed nearly $63.2 million in privately and publicly funded scholarships to more than 6,800 students attending nearly one hundred local private schools in fifteen years.

The Opportunity Scholarship Program (OSP) is federally funded and is often referred to as *school vouchers*. The Signature Scholarship Program (SSP) is privately funded and is designed for families who may not qualify for the OSP.

Because schools and organizations that offer aid have limited funds, some families may qualify for more aid than these institutions can afford to provide. Financial aid officers work closely with families to explain financial assistance and to offer aid to as many students as possible. As of January 2009, schools are continuing their commitment to economic diversity in spite of an economic downturn.

Independent schools and families are grateful for the work of these organizations as they assist in preparing all children for life in a multicultural world.

Identify Schools to Visit

After reviewing the websites and other materials, create a list of the schools you want to visit and make appointments. You may wish to include a variety of schools—single-sex and coeducational, religious and secular, large and small. As you visit each school, look for evidence that it lives up to its stated mission and goals.

Not all schools accept new students at every grade level. Determine at which grades each school accepts applications and how difficult it may be to gain admission at each grade. If possible, find out how many places are usually available to families new to the school. Each school's admission procedure is different. Make note of the differences. (See the worksheet on page 272.)

PREPARE TO APPLY

The purpose of the initial research is to identify schools to which you want to apply. You may not learn everything you wish to know in your initial research, but the schools to which your child is admitted will welcome your questions before you sign a contract. Do not apply to a school with a philosophy or culture that is not compatible with your family's values or whose program is not right for your child's learning needs. However, be open to learning about schools with which you are unfamiliar.

Visit the Schools

Each school has a different system for introducing parents to the school and getting to know applicants, but in general the application process includes one or more of the following on-campus visits:

- Open house, tour, or information session—Designed to provide a group of prospective parents and older students an opportunity to tour the campus and meet faculty, enrolled students, and their parents. Some visits are by appointment. No application or fee is required.
- Pre-application visit—Required by a few schools. Parents make an appointment to meet with a school official and tour the campus before receiving an application form.
- Play date—The visit of an applicant or group of applicants to pre-kindergarten through, usually, fourth grade. An application and fee must be submitted in advance.
- Student visit or interview—Typically for students in fifth grade and above, it includes a campus tour followed by meeting individually with a teacher or admission officer, participating in activities with a small group of other applicants, or spending a portion of the day in the classroom. An application and fee must be submitted in advance.
- Visit following acceptance—Parents and older students who have been accepted are invited to return to the campus to learn more about the school. This is a time to ask lingering questions.

Open Houses, Tours, or Information Sessions

Opportunities to see the school are scheduled throughout the year, but most occur in the autumn. These visits take about two hours and are usually optional. They include a chance to meet faculty and students, see the facilities, and learn about the school's programs from admissions personnel or parents. Ideally, classes are in session, and you can observe methods of instruction and teacher–student interaction during a normal school day; however, some schools hold these events only on weekends and evenings. Student interviews or play dates, which are scheduled after you submit the application, provide an opportunity for all applicants and parents to visit the school.

If you know you want to apply to a school, you may submit an application before an optional tour. Unless attendance by the student is required, students younger than ten years old should not attend tours.

Remember: know the directions to the school and where to park before the appointment. Be on time. *Turn off your mobile phones and all technological gadgets.* Do not chew gum or bring food or drink. Make every effort to keep scheduled appointments.

What to Look for During Your Visit

You will want to observe and inquire about the grades in which your child will be enrolled in the next few years. If you are applying for a young child to a school that continues to higher grade levels, when possible, observe the upper grades as well. Often the differences between schools are more visible in the middle and upper schools.

The qualities or characteristics listed here are meant to be as comprehensive as possible. Not all apply or will be available in each school. You must determine which features are most important to you. Some of the answers are available in published materials and on websites. Remember: schools are human institutions and none are perfect.

As you visit, be sensitive about the tone of your inquiry. You want to establish a relationship with the school based on mutual understanding and trust.

School Community

- Size of school, grade levels included
- Religious affiliation; mandatory courses, prayers, chapel; religious holidays that are celebrated; spiritual climate; moral values
- Governance: role of the board of trustees, head of school, principals, other administrators; if for-profit, who makes final decisions

- School accreditation and memberships, license (if applicable)
- Urban or suburban location
- School calendar, holidays, policy on snow days
- Length of school day
- Availability of before- and after-school care
- Availability of school transportation, carpools, access to Metro
- Culture, climate, personality, atmosphere, formal or informal style, general ambiance of the institution
- Demeanor of the students
- School traditions, school spirit
- Supervision of playgrounds and free time
- Additional personnel (nurse, community service coordinator, resource teachers, media specialist, etc.)
- Counselors: academic, college or next-school placement, psychologist
- Colleges or schools typically attended upon graduation
- Opportunities for and evidence of parent involvement
- Rate of attrition (number of students who do not return annually: local average in 2007–2008 was about 9.5 percent; source: Mark Mitchell, vice president of Financial Aid Services, NAIS)
- Property: owned or leased, terms of lease
- Future plans for programs or facilities
- Financial stability of the institution; endowment, if any

Student Body

- Age at which a student is eligible for admission (schools have different birthday cut-off dates)
- Single-sex or coeducational; if coed, boy/girl ratio
- Range of academic abilities
- Racial diversity or multiculturalism
- Percentage of families who receive financial aid
- Mutual respect among students

- Evidence that your child will be comfortable in the social setting
- Evidence of the values that you want in your child's friends

Faculty

- Academic background
- Background security check
- Age range, experience, average years of service
- Male/female ratio
- Racial diversity or cultural diversity
- Average class size and total teaching load
- Responsibilities: classroom and extracurricular
- Professional mentoring and development opportunities
- Evidence of excitement and commitment
- Camaraderie among teachers
- Rapport with students

Facilities

- A safe, hospitable, and student-centered climate in the halls, around the lockers, and in classrooms
- Clean and cheerful inside and outside
- Wheelchair accessibility
- Equipment and supplies that are appropriate to the grade and age
- Classrooms: arrangement of desks, maps, and other furniture; content and format of bulletin boards; organization and quality of science labs; availability of space for the arts
- Gymnasium, playground, and playing fields that are well maintained, safe, and age appropriate
- Other space: faculty room and supplies, conference room, tutoring space, nurse's office, library or media center
- Food service: optional, required, additional expense; nutritional value; ability to accommodate special diets; atmosphere of dining room or eating area

Curricular Offerings and Teaching Methods

- Curriculum: specific texts and materials used to meet yearly goals and objectives; courses that are required, available electives
- Methods of teaching math, reading, and writing
- Current textbooks, maps, and other teaching tools
- Advanced courses: availability of AP courses (www.collegeboard.com/student/testing/ap), including number and frequency of courses offered; IB program (www.ibo.org); honors and gifted programs; consortium courses; independent study
- Character/religious education
- Technology: course requirements and electives; integration of computers and the Internet into the curriculum; availability, location, sophistication of equipment; faculty training
- Teaching styles:
  - Teacher-directed courses in a traditional setting
  - Student-initiated activities with experiential learning
  - A combination of styles
- Foreign languages: grades introduced, courses offered, requirements
- Fine and performing art requirements and opportunities to participate
- Athletic requirements, options at each grade level, level of competition, opportunities to participate
- Availability of elective courses listed in the program of studies; frequency offered; prerequisites; if popular, ability to accommodate all interested students
- Clubs, publications (e.g., look for a student newspaper), other activities that reflect students' interests and school endorsement of them
- Homework expectations at each grade level
- Unique courses or programs such as Arabic, Asian-family, classical or other languages; orchestra; filmmaking; internships; travel or

study abroad; distinguished speakers' forum; other enrichment
opportunities

- Accommodation of special learning needs: tutoring, study skills,
extra help, extended time on tests, use of laptop computers or calculators, waiver of a foreign language requirement, reduced
course load, optional math courses, and so on
- Remediation of learning differences through specialized instruction, qualifications of special ed teachers
- Counseling and support for college or next-school placement

School Policies

- Tuition, availability of financial aid (see "Financial Aid, Grants,
Scholarships, and Payment Plans" earlier in this chapter)
- Hidden costs: books, activity fees, field trips, athletic equipment
- Safety issues: measures in place to handle emergencies
- Requirements for graduation
- Community service opportunities or requirements
- Advisor–advisee or mentoring system
- Dispensing of medications, if needed
- Dress code or uniform
- Disciplinary measures
- Policy on drugs, smoking, and sex education, if age-appropriate
- "Open campus" or freedom to leave campus during school hours
- Students' cars: allowed on campus, use during the school day,
parking
- In single-sex schools, opportunities to meet the opposite sex
- Method and frequency of communicating grades and progress
- Use of standardized tests and other forms of assessment

You may understand more about the culture of a school if you attend a
middle or upper school athletic or arts event. Listen to students and talk
to parents. This can be especially helpful if your child has an interest in a
specific sport, artistic endeavor, or other activity.

SUBMIT APPLICATION

A completed application may include a student essay, parent essay, or both, and a photograph of the student. Test scores and transcripts (if appropriate) and teacher recommendations must be submitted separately. In addition, a visit or interview must be scheduled and attended.

Finalize the list of schools to which you will apply and comply with each school's requirements in submitting the application. In general, submit applications to a maximum of six schools, but if attendance at an independent school is important to you, apply to more than just the most highly selective schools. The number of applications submitted is dependent upon your comfort with alternatives.

Working with the Office of Admission

Admission office personnel are gracious and grateful for your interest in their school; however, sometimes the pressure of numbers limits their ability to respond immediately to questions and requests. There are times when your patience is necessary. Keep your calls and e-mails to a minimum and your communication focused and organized.

Most schools allow time for parents to speak in private with an admission officer at the time of the visit or interview. Sometimes faculty members conduct interviews and often the head of school or a division principal will greet families when they visit. If a meeting with a representative of the admission office is not scheduled, use your judgment about a special request to speak to someone.

Timetable

Learn the deadlines for each school, some of which are as early as November. Try to submit applications no later than January 1, even if the deadlines are later. Applications must be submitted before the student's interview or play date is scheduled.

Format

Schools that are equipped for online applications prefer that you use the Internet. For others, write legibly, in ink.

Student Essay or Writing Sample

Older students may be asked to submit a paper that has been graded by a teacher. Most schools ask that the applicant write an essay. This should be the student's work, and unless the school indicates that using the computer is acceptable, it should be in his or her own handwriting, in ink. Parents may discuss the topic with the student, but editing is not appropriate: admission tests often include an essay, and if there is a discrepancy in quality and style between that essay and one written at home, it may raise questions. There never seems to be a good time to write these essays, but it is probably best to do it during the Thanksgiving holiday, because it does not get easier to find the time later. The essay questions often ask for a student's personal opinion on a subject that reveals an interest, attitude, insight, or passion. Examples are "What is an event that changed the way you think or feel?" or "What is important in a friendship?" or "What makes a teacher interesting?"

Parent Comments

Some schools provide a questionnaire for parents to complete. Most can now be submitted online, often with a limited number of words or characters. Under any circumstances, be mindful of the length. Schools do not want an exhaustive family history or your curriculum vitae. Stick to the questions. Too much information is not as helpful as a few relevant, insightful comments about your child. If the school does not provide a questionnaire and you want to convey information that is pertinent to your child's application, include your comments in a brief letter.

Photograph

A photograph should be recent and appropriate. Silly gimmicks to gain attention are not appreciated.

Recommendations

Most recommendation forms are online and can be downloaded and distributed to the appropriate teachers. Some schools mail forms and instructions after receipt of the completed application. Follow the instructions from each school. Some want recommendations to be completed after January 1 by current teachers. For older students, schools usually require a form from the English and math teachers and from one other person. A few schools want a former teacher's recommendation as well. Write the student's name in the appropriate blank before giving it to the teachers and supply stamped envelopes addressed to the schools. Be sure the teacher knows the due date. Giving teachers ample time to complete the forms is not only a courtesy, it may enhance the quality of the recommendation. Parents are not privy to these comments and should not request a copy. Remember to thank the teachers because writing these recommendations usually is not in their job description.

Recommendations from personal friends are useful when they tell the admission officers something they may not otherwise know. The most useful letter is from someone who knows both the applicant and the school well. Letters on fancy letterheads from celebrities or others who do not know the school or the student are not helpful to an admission committee. Members of the board of trustees are usually asked to write on behalf of numerous students, and schools are unable to accept every student recommended by a board member. If you do not know someone well enough to know where his or her children go to school or if he or she serves as a trustee, it is reasonably safe to assume that a recommendation from that person may not be effective.

Letters from coaches and other extracurricular instructors can be useful. Be selective; having too many letters is inappropriate. There is an old adage among admission officers: "The thicker the file, the thicker the child!"

Transcript

Schools ask for reports for all grade levels at which they are available. Some schools' application materials include a card for parents to sign requesting a transcript from the current school. If this is not available, parents should provide the current school with the name and address of each school where an application has been submitted, and request in writing that a transcript be sent directly to each school. For older students, the transcript should include standardized test results and grades. It is acceptable to ask the current school for an unofficial copy for review; on occasion, mistakes have been detected and corrected.

Schools will not release a transcript until outstanding bills have been settled.

Tests

Parents must make arrangements for the appropriate test or tests to be administered. General comments about testing are difficult because schools in this area use many different tests and some schools accept existing test results. Read each school's information to determine what is required at each grade level, the dates on which the test will be administered, and how to register or make an appointment to take the test.

Some schools do not require formal tests for any of their applicants. Instead, they conduct an informal assessment, often on the day of the interview. Applicants to nursery programs are not tested. Usually they accompany their parents for a brief visit to the school. (See chapter 2, "Preschools.")

The following tests are administered to groups of students on specified Saturdays at designated schools. They contain sections on mathematics, reading, vocabulary, and writing, and last about two and a half hours.

- **High School Placement Test (HSPT)** is published by Scholastic Testing Service, Inc. (www.ststesting.com). It is used by Roman Catholic schools in the Archdiocese of Washington (Maryland and the District of Columbia) and the Diocese of Arlington (Virginia) for admission to ninth grade. It is administered in December. For applicants to other grades, existing test data is used. For additional information, visit www.adw.org/education or call 301-853-5304.

- **Secondary School Admission Test (SSAT)** is accepted by most independent schools for applicants to sixth through eleventh grades. The lower level is for applicants to sixth through eighth grades and the upper level is for ninth grade and above. (PSAT scores may be used for twelfth-grade applicants, although schools rarely admit new seniors.) It is administered one Saturday each month from November through April at local schools or by appointment at various locations. The test can be taken more than once in an academic year, but be aware that schools to which scores are reported will have access to all test results from the academic year. While using the practice booklet published by SSAT can be beneficial, and some tutoring or mentoring may familiarize students with test-taking skills and increase self-confidence, many educators question the effectiveness of prolonged tutoring for the purpose of prepping for specific questions that might be on the test. For registration information, consult www.ssat.org or the *Student Registration Guide,* available at the schools that require the test.

- **Independent School Entrance Exam (ISEE)** is used exclusively by some independent schools and accepted by most others for applicants to fifth through eleventh grades. Three levels of the test address the age and grade of the applicants and measure similar skills as the SSAT. It can be taken only when making a formal application to a school accepting the ISEE and only once in a six-month period. The test is administered from November through March on various Saturdays at several schools. Consult the *ISEE*

Student Guide, available at schools that accept the test, or visit
www.iseetest.org for registration and the practice book, *What to
Expect on the ISEE*, which includes a practice test.

In certain circumstances, special arrangements can be made for students
to be tested individually or have extended time for the SSAT and ISEE. For
more information, contact individual schools, the SSAT at www.ssat.org or
609-683-4440, or the ISEE at www.iseetest.org or 800-446-0320.

The following tests are administered by a qualified diagnostician to an
individual student. In general, these tests provide an objective assessment
of development, comparing children of the same age range. *According to
the protocols for these tests, students cannot take the test more than once in a
twelve-month period.* For that reason, and to avoid over-testing, many of the
schools have an understanding with various testers to send the test results
to more than one school. You need to arrange to have the test administered
and instruct the administrator to send a copy to each school that requires
it. Schools that do not require this type of testing often appreciate receiving a copy, which you deliver.

In this category, the following are the most commonly used tests:

- **Wechsler Preschool and Primary Scale of Intelligence, Third
  Edition (WPPSI-III)** is used primarily for applicants to pre-
  kindergarten through first grade or for children who are younger
  than six years old. Children younger than age four are given a
  lower level form (preschool) and children four years and older are
  given a higher level (primary). It is a structured test that evaluates
  a child's verbal and nonverbal skills. The test takes about an hour
  and is administered individually.

  Children learn through visual, tactile, and auditory stimulation. The only test preparation for young children is playing, reading, and talking with them. Playing with puzzles, blocks, and
  other toys; participating in activities that are musical or have
  rhythm and patterns or that require following sequential directions, observing differences, stringing beads, throwing soft balls,
  physical exercise through gymnastics, riding tricycles or bicycles,

or running are all play activities from which children enjoy learning the skills that promote success in school. Pedantic teaching of numbers and letters is not as important or effective as experiencing the meaning of quantities or exploring the power of words.

- **Wechsler Intelligence Scale for Children, Fourth Edition (WISC-IV)** is used primarily for students older than age six or entering grades two through five. It is administered the same way as the WPPSI and takes about an hour and fifteen minutes. Verbal comprehension, perceptual reasoning, working memory, and processing speed are assessed.

- **Woodcock-Johnson Tests of Achievement, Third Edition (WJ-III)** can be used for applicants to first grade and above. This individually administered test takes several hours to complete and measures achievement in reading, math, written language, and general knowledge. It determines the level of mastery a student has achieved in specific subject areas. This type of testing is requested less frequently than the intelligence tests.

The results of other tests the student has taken may also be considered. Please keep in mind that test results for young children are subject to many variables and are not always an indicator of future performance. Scores may vary over time, but often certain patterns of strengths or deficiencies are discernable from an early age.

Some schools place a greater emphasis on test scores than others, but all schools look beyond the performance on one test in determining acceptance. Admission tests can be a "gate keeper," with good reason. Schools want their students to be happy and successful. They know the scores of the students who have been successful and the scores of those who have been more frustrated than rewarded. Therefore, when scores appear to be below those that predict success in their program, schools are cautious about offering a place. However, it should be noted that all schools admit students with a range of test scores and do not always admit those with the highest scores.

Preparing Students for a Test or Interview

The best preparation for a test or interview is a good night's sleep, breakfast, and an on-time, unhurried arrival. In an age-appropriate way, explain the process to your child. Explain that there are lots of wonderful schools and some will not have enough space for everyone, but they are still worth investigating. Make sure your attitude and conversation do not convey anxiety or pressure.

Familiarize the older child with the schools you intend to visit by going to websites and reviewing school materials. It is best to tell young children about the visit only a few days in advance. If the campus or test site is unfamiliar, ride by the location and speculate about the visit by asking questions like, "I wonder which room is the one you will go to meet the nice person who is going to be with you while I wait for you?" or "I wonder if there are toys like yours here?" Let the child know that this is a friendly place.

Parent and Student Interviews and Play Dates

School personnel like to meet both parents. Since scheduling can be difficult, plan well in advance. If it becomes impossible for both parents to attend, it is often better for one parent to keep the appointment because rescheduling can be an even greater challenge. Parents with a predetermined first-choice school often ask if that school should be scheduled first or last. Although you know your child's response to new situations better than anyone else, I do not believe that the sequence of the visits makes a difference. It is often best to try to arrange the visits over a period of time rather than in rapid succession. Most schools provide specific information on what the children can expect at a play date or interview.

The parent interview allows you to ask specific questions and to share anything of significance. Do not feel you have to be profound or dynamic; most interviewers ask a few straightforward questions. A conversation may go like this:

- "How did you learn about our school?"
- "Did you observe anything today that interested you?"
- "Do you have any questions about our school?"
- Parents might want more information about lunch programs or teacher training.
- Please do not feel the need to have a rehearsed group of questions or information to share.
- Be natural. Most parents enjoy the conversation.

If your child is ill, reschedule. If your child gets sick following an interview or play date (with a fever or other symptoms), advise the admission office of the condition.

Dress

Look at pictures of students in the school materials and on the website and encourage your child to dress similarly. In general, boys wear shirts with collars and girls wear a simple dress, skirt, or pants. Young children wear comfortable play clothes and shoes. Hair should be kept out of the child's face. Do not overdress. Parents usually dress in business casual.

Advice for Students Entering Fourth Grade and Above

Some schools will invite you to spend part of the day at school and have lunch. A student guide often gives a tour, which includes participating in or observing a class. Other schools' visits or interviews last about two hours. Those generally include a school tour and a conversation with a teacher or admission officer. The interview serves two purposes. One is to give you an opportunity to get to know more about the school, and the other is for the school to learn more about you. Your goal is to be thoughtful and confident during your conversations. Most students have a wonderful time.

Depending upon your age, remember to do the following:

- Review the website and school materials before your visit.
- Be on time. *Turn off all cell phones and technological gadgets.* Do not chew gum or bring food or drinks.

- Present a firm handshake, if it seems appropriate to shake hands.
- Relax and be yourself.
- Maintain eye contact.
- Take an active role in the conversation; give more than "yes" or "no" answers.
- Talk freely about yourself and your interests.
- Keep focused on the topic.
- Ask questions: a good interview will be a mutual exchange of ideas and information.

Examples of questions you might ask a middle or high school interviewer:

- How much homework is there every night? Over the weekend?
- What's the average size of an English class, or other favorite subject?
- Is playing a sport required?
- On what days are games played? What other schools do you play?
- Can I play sports and also be in a school play?
- How good do I have to be to play on a team, act in a play, be in the band, or participate in any other activity?
- What do kids do on the weekend? Are there school parties?
- Is extra help or extra-credit work available?
- Will I have a "buddy" or someone to help me when school begins?
- Do kids have advisors?
- Do you have community service projects?
- Ask about anything that is important to you.

Examples of questions you might ask the student guide:

- What do you like the best about this school? What do you like the least?
- Which courses are the most interesting? The hardest?
- How much homework do you have on an average night? Over the weekend?
- What are your extracurricular activities? How much time do they take?

Examples of questions a middle or high school interviewer might ask you:

- How would your teachers describe you?
- Can you name a book or magazine that you would recommend to a friend? Why?
- If you were in charge of your school, what would you change?
- What do you like to do in your free time?
- What were your impressions of the tour? Were there any surprises?

Advice for Parents of Children Entering Third Grade and Below

Many schools invite small groups of children to visit on a weekday or Saturday morning. Age-appropriate activities are used to evaluate skills a student needs in order to succeed in the school's program and to assess reading, writing, and math skills, when appropriate. Children generally have a good time. Do not try to prep your child. Let him or her know that other children and parents will be there too, and assure him or her that nice teachers will have interesting things to do. Say something reassuring such as, "I'll be here when you finish." It may be helpful to say, "Remember to follow directions!" Resist saying there will be "games," because younger children may interpret that as meaning they can make up their own rules.

FOLLOW UP

Once the application has been submitted and steps in the process completed, continue to be engaged. Consider what you have learned about the school and ways to enhance the application.

Questions to Ask Yourself after the Visit or Student Interview

Your answers to the following questions may be useful when you make final decisions:

- Can I envision my child in this setting?
- Can I see myself as a parent in this school?
- Whose needs am I considering? Mine? My child's?

- Will my child be sufficiently challenged?
- Will my child be more frustrated than rewarded?

Children do not like to be asked a lot of questions after a visit. Let them tell you their impressions. Do not try to impose your ideas. For an older student, suggest that he or she make a few notes on what seemed interesting or different, or on any questions that remain.

Neither you nor your child should become invested in any one school to the exclusion of others. If admission to that school is denied, your child might feel personal failure or that he or she has disappointed you. This is not only unhealthy, it could preclude his or her ability to be happy in another equally fine institution.

Many schools will inform you when your child's file is complete or tell you what is missing. Others have this information on their websites. If in doubt, call or e-mail the school when you think the application should be complete.

Enhancing the Application

While you do not want the application file to be overly thick, sending selected copies of awards, artwork, published articles or any applicable information is appropriate. Be your child's advocate, but be honest. If you provide an aggrandized description of your child, the school may question whether you are realistic. As I have stated previously, it is unwise for a family to become deeply committed to only one school, but you may advise *one* school of the seriousness of your application by indicating that it is your first choice and, if your child is admitted, you will accept. This does not guarantee acceptance and should be done only when you will honor your commitment. Students sometimes write a letter expressing a keen desire to attend. Be cautious about this because, if the student is not admitted, it may add to his or her disappointment.

ADMISSION DECISIONS AND PARENTS' RESPONSES

Admission committees labor over decisions. The committee membership varies according to the size of the school. In larger schools, the head of school, possibly a departmental principal, admission officers, and selected faculty might review the files and make the final decisions. The committee may meet over the course of several weeks to carefully consider all of the information on each child. The decision to accept or deny is not based on a single item in the file. Each school uses different criteria for making final decisions. The school's mission and the committee's judgment about who "complements the class" contribute to the selection from among those who are qualified. "Complements the class" means enrolling a diverse group of students who can contribute to the school's academic and nonacademic programs and, in coeducational schools, enrolling an equal number of boys and girls. Schools weigh various factors differently, but depending upon the age of the applicant, among the considerations are the student's character, evidence of self-discipline, problem-solving skills, and extracurricular interests or activities. In addition to test results, consideration is given to the interview or play date, teacher recommendations, grades, parent comments, student essays, and any other pertinent information in the file.

No school wants to admit a child who is likely to fail. However, when possible, schools may accept a student with some questionable qualifications in the hope that with extra attention, he or she will succeed. Adding to the complexity of the decision-making process is the fact that teachers can manage only a limited number of "time-intensive" students in a class. The needs of each child in the class must be considered. Making admission decisions can be a complicated and often emotionally difficult process for the committee members.

This is a basic fact about admission: it is not an even playing field.

- Schools usually state in their admission materials that qualified siblings of current or former students, children of alumni and faculty, and members of the school's religious denomination are given preference. Cousins, stepchildren, and half- or stepsiblings may also be given special consideration. While schools genuinely want to keep families together, sometimes there are not enough available spaces at a specific grade to accommodate all priority applicants.

- In the belief that we learn from each other and that our children are growing up in a global community, the quest for economic, racial, ethnic, and cultural diversity allows some underrepresented groups of children to have an advantage.
- Schools located within the city often have a larger applicant pool because they are accessible to parents who work downtown even if they live in the suburbs, while suburban schools may serve a more limited geographical area and have fewer applicants simply because of their location.

Every year, families new to the school are admitted. If you have recently moved to the area or are a family new to independent schools, please know that *there are places for your child in many fine schools.* Admission to some schools is simply more competitive than to others, and it is well to have expectations based on that reality.

What about Priority Candidates?

All schools want to be responsive to the families who are already a part of the school community; however, schools that receive the most applications may have twice as many priority applicants as the number of available places in a grade. When applying to schools with highly competitive admission, parents should recognize that siblings might not be guaranteed a place.

When I was a director of admission, I was acutely aware of the school's dilemma. If the committee took a family new to the school, we might have denied a sibling. The new family was thrilled with the policy until they applied for a sibling who might not be admitted. Should schools be places that are loyal only to those families who are already in the school? How great is the responsibility to accept those without "connections" who go through an admission process expecting some degree of equality? These are tough questions for all schools with competitive admission, including colleges and universities.

If your child is denied admission, realize that it could simply be due to the lack of space. Fire marshals and zoning boards dictate maximum enrollment and schools cannot exceed those limits. Class size must be controlled; even one more student for a teacher may diminish his or her ability to do the best for everyone. If space is the only factor precluding acceptance, be patient and reapply at a later date.

There are occasions when not all the children in a family would be well served in the same school. You should look at each child's learning profile and determine what is right for that child. You might use the admission process to determine whether a sibling's school is appropriate, but be sure to include other potential schools. Remember, you do not want your child to be somewhere he or she will be more frustrated than rewarded, even if others in the family are successful there.

School Notification and Parent Response

Letters advising parents of a decision are mailed or e-mailed as early as February, but most schools notify parents in March. Letters indicate that the child has been accepted (usually a thicker envelope containing a contract), denied, or placed on a waiting list.

Acceptance

Your family may receive one or more thick envelopes! Parents and older students are often invited to revisit the schools to which they have been admitted. It is especially important for older students to take advantage of this opportunity. It helps determine the compatibility of the student and the school, and it enhances the student's confidence about entering in the fall. Because friends are particularly important to older students, having an opportunity to meet future classmates and teachers allows newly admitted students to begin to feel comfortable. Previously unanswered questions can be asked. Admission officers are pleased to provide assistance to facilitate the decision for those who have been accepted. Current parents are available to answer questions.

Information about a financial aid award is usually provided at the time of acceptance. You do not have to sign an enrollment contract until the school advises you of the size of the grant.

The role that older students play in the final decision is important. If you have established some parameters for the selection within a narrow range of schools, your child can be trusted to make the final decision.

Read your school enrollment contract carefully. When you decide upon a school, submit the contract and enrollment fee promptly. Notify other schools of your decision not to accept their offers of admission, and withdraw from other waiting lists. A prompt response may allow another student on the waiting list to be admitted.

Denial

Denial is often the result of the large number of well-qualified applicants relative to the total number of places. Some schools may have more than two hundred applications for twenty places. Neither you nor your child should feel any sense of failure. Some children may be advised to reapply at a later date. Although often no single factor can be identified as the reason for not being accepted, on occasion the committee feels that the school cannot meet the student's specific needs. Admission officers will discuss decisions with parents, and may refer them to an educational consultant who can direct them to schools with spaces or a more appropriate program.

Denial of your child is hurtful to parents and can be hurtful even to young children who do not get what they think they want. That is among the reasons that parents should submit applications wisely. Throughout the process, advise students who are old enough to understand that some schools have many more applications than spaces available. It is a time to learn some of life's lessons, like "Nothing ventured, nothing gained" and "The school would have been lucky to have you, but space was a problem." Talk to your child about occasions in your life when a lack of space prevented you from enjoying an opportunity and how you handled it. For some young children, unless they inquire, it may not be necessary to mention the decision. Above all, do not let your child feel that he or she is a disappointment to you.

Waiting List or Waiting Pool

The waiting list indicates that your child is qualified and, if space permits, will be admitted. If you want to remain on the list, notify the school immediately and convey your enthusiasm. Schools rarely rank students on the waiting list; selection from the list depends upon many factors, including the number of students who accept the places already offered and the withdrawal of currently enrolled students. Schools may admit more students than the exact number of places available with the expectation that not all families will accept the places offered; therefore, when an accepted student refuses a place, it may not immediately create a place for someone on the waiting list. After the deadline for parents to respond to an acceptance, admission officers can better "guesstimate" the odds of getting in from the waiting list. Continue to keep the school informed of your interest, and forward recent grades or evidence of recent achievements. First-semester tuition is usually due in July, and, on occasion, spaces become available at that time; however, a place can become available as late as the beginning of the school year.

When you no longer wish to remain on the waiting list, immediately inform the school of your decision to withdraw. Waiting lists usually cease to exist after the school year begins, and students must reapply for future consideration. Some schools modify the process for a reapplication.

If you have signed a contract with one school and your child is accepted from a waiting list at another school, you should know that if you break the contract with the first school, you are apt to be held responsible for the tuition according to the contract terms.

Enrolling in a New School

Rejoice over the selection of your child's new school! Even though this is a significant milestone, you must continue to be vigilant and actively involved in his or her education. No school is perfect, nor does any one school meet the needs of every child equally well every year. Even the best teachers may have a bad year, and the chemistry of a class may or may not be ideal. Parents have a right to high expectations—but they must be realistic. Monitor your child's academic progress, know the teachers, know your child's friends and their parents, be available to support school programs, and attend parent meetings and as many of your child's activities as possible. Remember, you and the school are coeducators or partners in education, and by working together, the common goal of your child's success and happiness can best be achieved.

ACRONYMS USED IN SCHOOL PROFILES

ADW	Archdiocese of Washington
AIMS	Association of Independent Maryland Schools
AISGW	Association of Independent Schools of Greater Washington
AMI	Association Montessori Internationale
AMS	American Montessori Society
ASCD	Association for Supervision and Curriculum Development
AWSNA	Association of Waldorf Schools of North America
BSF	Black Student Fund
CAPE	Council for American Private Education
CASE	Council for Advancement and Support of Education
CBSA	Catholic Boarding Schools Association
CDSHA	Country Day School Heads Association
CEC	Council for Exceptional Children
CES	Coalition of Essential Schools
CHADD	Children and Adults with Attention Deficit/Hyperactivity Disorder
CIS	Council of International Schools
CITA	Commission on International and Trans-Regional Accreditation
CRIS	Council for Religion in Independent Schools
CSEE	Council for Spiritual and Ethical Education
DCPS	District of Columbia Public Schools
ECIS	European Council of International Schools

ELEA	Evangelical Lutheran Education Association
ERB	Educational Records Bureau
ESHA	Elementary School Heads Association
ESP	Emerging Scholars Program
FCE	Friends Council on Education
HMAE	Head Mistresses Association of the East
IBSC	International Boys' Schools Coalition
IDA	International Dyslexia Association
IMC	International Montessori Council
JSEA	Jesuit Secondary Education Association
LDA	Learning Disabilities Association of America
LSF	Latino Student Fund
MAESA	Mid-Atlantic Episcopal Schools Association
MANSEF	Maryland Association of Nonpublic Special Education Facilities
MSA	Middle States Association of Colleges and Schools
MSDE	Maryland State Department of Education
NACAC	National Association for College Admission Counseling
NAES	National Association of Episcopal Schools
NAEYC	National Association for the Education of Young Children
NAGC	National Association for Gifted Children
NAIS	National Association of Independent Schools
NAMTA	North American Montessori Teachers' Association
NAPSEC	National Association of Private Special Education Centers
NAPSG	National Association of Principals of Schools for Girls
NAREA	North American Reggio Emelia Alliance
NASSP	National Association of Secondary School Principals
NCEA	National Catholic Educational Association
NCGS	National Coalition of Girls' Schools
NCISR	National Center for Independent School Renewal
NECPA	National Early Childhood Program Accreditation
NIPSA	National Independent Private Schools Association
NMSA	National Middle School Association

NSHS	Network of Sacred Heart Schools
NVAEYC	Northern Virginia Association for the Education of Young Children
PCW	Parents Council of Washington
PEN	Progressive Education Network
PJLL	Partnership for Jewish Life and Learning
RAVSAK	The Jewish Community Day School Network
SACS	Southern Association of Colleges and Schools
SAIS	Southern Association of Independent Schools
SBSA	Small Boarding School Association
SSATB	Secondary School Admission Test Board
SSS	School and Student Service for Financial Aid
TABS	The Association of Boarding Schools
VAIS	Virginia Association of Independent Schools
VAISEF	Virginia Association of Independent Specialized Education Facilities
VCPE	Virginia Council for Private Education
WACCC	Washington Association of Child Care Centers
WCDC	Washington Child Development Council
WSSA	Washington Small Schools Association

Independent
School Directory

THE ACADEMY OF THE HOLY CROSS   est. 1868

Dr. Claire M. Helm, President
4920 Strathmore Avenue
Kensington, MD 20895
301-929-6442 x442
www.academyoftheholycross.org

Louise Hendon, Director of Admissions
lhendon@academyoftheholycross.org

Girls: 9th–12th
Limited wheelchair access

Governance: Nonprofit
Accredited by: MSA, MSDE
Memberships: AISGW, CASE, NCEA
Religious affiliation: Roman Catholic

PROFILE
Total enrollment: 600
Graduating class size: 160
Average class size: 25
Number of faculty: 61
Boarding option: No
School day: 7:55–2:30
Extended day hours: 7:55–3:30
Schools three or more graduates have attended over the past five years: Catholic University, Salisbury University, Towson, University of Maryland, University of South Carolina, Virginia Tech

APPLICATION PROCESS
Grades with openings (approximate): 9th (150)
Birthday cutoff: N/A
Deadline: December 15
Fee: $50
Testing required: HSPT (9th)
Steps: Visit/open house, application, student-parent interviews

COSTS
Tuition: $15,550
Average additional fees: $500
Financial aid budget: $800,000+
Average grant size: N/A
% of students receiving aid:
Endowment: No

NOTE: This data applies to the 2009–2010 school year.

CURRICULUM
Languages and grades offered: French, Latin, Spanish (9th–12th)
AP classes/IB program: 15 AP classes
Tutors/learning specialists: 5
Other resource specialists: Academic support teacher
Art programs: Art fundamentals, art history, art studio (portfolio), ceramics, design, drawing, independent study, painting, photography, publications design, sculpture, studio art, web page design
Sports: Basketball, crew, cross-country, equestrian, field hockey, golf, lacrosse, soccer, softball, swimming & diving, tennis, track, volleyball
Special features and activities: Performing arts program and co-curricular activities
Summer programs: Enrichment courses, sports camps

CAMPUS LIFE
Transportation available: None
Lunch options: Cafeteria
Food allergy policy: None
Uniform: Yes

CAMPUS
Facilities: 28-acre campus with 4 athletic fields, gym, 400-seat theater
Long-range plans: Candidate school for the IB Diploma Programme

HISTORY AND MISSION STATEMENT
The Academy of the Holy Cross, a Catholic college preparatory school sponsored by the Sisters of the Holy Cross since 1868, is dedicated to educating young women in a Christ-centered community which values diversity. The Academy is committed to developing women of courage, compassion and scholarship who responsibly embrace the social, spiritual and intellectual challenges of the world.

NOTE: This data applies to the 2009–2010 school year.

THE AIDAN MONTESSORI SCHOOL   est. 1961

Kathy Minardi, Head of School
2700 27th Street, NW
Washington, DC 20008
202-387-2700
www.aidanschool.org

Christine Kranz Smith
c.smith@aidanschool.org

Coed: N–6th
Wheelchair accessible

Governance: Nonprofit
Accredited by: AIMS, AMI
Memberships: AISGW, NAIS
Religious affiliation: Nonsectarian

PROFILE
Total enrollment: 200
Graduating class size:
Average class size: 25 (1st–6th)
Number of faculty: 16 (plus assistants)
Boarding option: No
School day: 8:40–3:00 (1st–3rd), 8:15–3:30 (4th–6th)
Extended day hours: 8:00–6:00
Schools three or more graduates have attended over the past five years: N/A

APPLICATION PROCESS
Grades with openings (approximate): See table, plus attrition
Birthday cutoff: N/A
Deadline: January 20
Fee: $60
Testing required: N/A
Steps: Open house, application, interview, school visit, informal assessment

COSTS
Tuition: $19,817 (1st–6th)
Average additional fees: $500; $1,800 one-time registration fee
Financial aid budget: $140,000
Average grant size: $5,900
% of students receiving aid: 12%
Endowment: No

NOTE: This data applies to the 2009–2010 school year.

PRESCHOOL PROGRAM

Age	Days	Hours	Tuition	Openings	Class size	Teachers per class	Food provided
18 mo.–3 years	5	8:15–11:15	$14,320	8–10	12	3	
3–4 (Primary)	5	8:40–12:00	$14,320	30	28	1	
5	5	8:40–3:00	$19,366	30	28	1	

CURRICULUM
Languages and grades offered: Chinese (1st–6th), Spanish (Primary–6th)
AP classes/IB program: N/A
Tutors/learning specialists: 1 at an additional fee
Other resource specialists: School counselor
Art programs: Art, music
Sports: None
Special features and activities: Montessori curriculum, outdoor games, creative arts. After-school enrichment program includes Mandarin Chinese
Summer programs: None

CAMPUS LIFE
Transportation available: None
Lunch options: N/A
Food allergy policy: Peanut-free
Uniform: No

CAMPUS
Facilities: Montessori-designed environment with library, playground
Long-range plans: N/A

HISTORY AND MISSION STATEMENT
Aidan Montessori was founded by a group of parents who based the school's curriculum on the philosophy of Dr. Maria Montessori. At Aidan, we respect the individual child's needs and strive to meet those needs by providing a child-centered learning environment. We offer an education for the development of the whole child. Our student body, faculty and staff provide a rich cultural diversity, which contributes to an enriching educational experience.

NOTE: This data applies to the 2009–2010 school year.

ALEXANDRIA COUNTRY DAY SCHOOL   est. 1983

Alexander Harvey IV, Head of School
2400 Russell Road
Alexandria, VA 22301
703-548-4804
www.acdsnet.org

Rebecca Teti, Director of Admission
admissions@acdsnet.org

Coed: K–8th
Wheelchair accessible

Governance: Nonprofit
Accredited by: VAIS
Memberships: AISGW, BSF, ERB, LSF, NAIS
Religious affiliation: Nonsectarian

PROFILE

Total enrollment: 235
Graduating class size: 28
Average class size: 12–15
Number of faculty: 50
Boarding option: No
School day: 8:30–2:45 (K–2nd); 8:15–3:00 (3rd–8th)
Extended day hours: 7:00–6:00
Schools three or more graduates have attended over the past five years: Bishop Ireton, Episcopal High, Field, Potomac, St. Stephen's & St. Agnes

APPLICATION PROCESS

Grades with openings: K (24), plus attrition
Birthday cutoff: September 30
Deadline: January 31
Fee: $75
Testing required: WPPSI-III/WISC-IV (K–4th), ISEE (5th), ISEE or SSAT (6th–8th)
Steps: Parent visit, application, student visit

COSTS

Tuition: $19,300 (K–3rd), $20,860 (4th–8th)
Average additional fees: $350 new student enrollment fee
Financial aid budget: $590,000
Average grant size: $11,500
% of students receiving aid: 21%
Endowment: Yes

NOTE: This data applies to the 2009–2010 school year.

CURRICULUM
Languages and grades offered: Spanish (K–8th)
AP classes/IB program: N/A
Tutors/learning specialists: 4 instructional specialists
Other resource specialists:
Art programs: Students in lower school have art 1–2 times a week and music 1–2 times a week. Middle school students have intensive 6-week programs in art and music.
Sports: Basketball, cross-country, soccer, softball, swimming, tennis
Special features and activities: Small classes, challenging academic program, variety of extracurricular options, strong performing and visual arts program, award-winning faculty, safe and supportive environment, all students in one building together, buddy program, character education program, excellent high school placement, outdoor education program, public speaking component
Summer programs: Six one-week sessions. In past years, camps have included academic (math, science, writing), artistic (both visual and performing), athletic, community service, and culinary options.

CAMPUS LIFE
Transportation available:
Yes, for an additional fee
Lunch options: Hot lunch program for an additional fee
Food allergy policy: Peanut-free school
Uniform: Yes

CAMPUS
Facilities: Art studio, athletic field, 2 computer labs and 3 laptop carts, gym, library, science lab, stage
Long-range plans: ACDS will break ground on a new gymnasium, cafeteria, and performing arts center in the near future.

HISTORY AND MISSION STATEMENT
Alexandria Country Day School is a dynamic community that values academic excellence, character, independent thinking, citizenship, and respect for others. We inspire in our students creativity, enthusiasm for leaning, and confidence through a stimulating academic program, athletics, the arts and community service.

NOTE: This data applies to the 2009–2010 school year.

THE AVALON SCHOOL   est. 2003

Kevin J. Davern, Headmaster
200 W. Diamond Avenue
Gaithersburg, MD 20877
301-963-8022
www.avalonschools.org

Kevin J. Davern
kevindavern@avalonschools.org

Boys: 3rd–12th
Wheelchair accessible

Governance: Nonprofit
Accredited by: MSDE
Memberships:
Religious affiliation: Catholic Inspiration

PROFILE
Total enrollment: 160
Graduating class size: 10
Average class size: 12–15
Number of faculty: 20
Boarding option: No
School day: 8:50–3:15
Extended day hours: 8:50–6:00
Schools three or more graduates have attended over the past five years: N/A

APPLICATION PROCESS
Grades with openings (approximate):
3rd (12), 4th (5), 5th (5), 6th (5), 7th (10), 8th (8), 9th (10), 10th (5), 11th (3)
Birthday cutoff: N/A
Deadline: Rolling
Fee: $50
Testing required: None
Steps: Application, student shadow visit, family interview

COSTS
Tuition: $10,950 (3rd–5th), $12,450 (6th–8th), $13,000 (9th–11th), $13,100 (12th)
Average additional fees: N/A
Financial aid budget: 19% gross tuition
Average grant size: $5,000
% of students receiving aid: 33%
Endowment: No

NOTE: This data applies to the 2009–2010 school year.

CURRICULUM

Languages and grades offered: Latin (7th–12th), Spanish (9th–12th)

AP classes/IB program: 7 AP classes

Tutors/learning specialists: N/A

Other resource specialists: N/A

Art programs: Actors Guild, drama

Sports: Baseball, basketball, cross-country, football, golf, lacrosse club, soccer, swim team

Special features and activities: Poetry recitation, yearly musical revue, student school newspaper

Summer programs: Baseball camp, Civil War, math camp, natural history, rocket science camp, sports adventure camp

CAMPUS LIFE

Transportation available: Shuttle to and from Shady Grove Metro station; shuttle from Gaithersburg, Darnestown, Germantown, Glenmont and Bethesda areas for an additional fee

Lunch options: Hot lunch program

Food allergy policy: N/A

Uniform: Dress code

CAMPUS

Facilities: N/A

Long-range plans: Campus will move to permanent location in Clarksburg, Maryland

HISTORY AND MISSION STATEMENT

The Avalon School, an independent school for boys, seeks to cultivate in its students intellectual freedom, personal responsibility, and a spirit of adventure in an atmosphere that allows boys to be boys. The distinctive learning characteristics of young men are addressed both in and out of the classroom through a curriculum steeped in the humanities and sciences, the arts and athletics. A faculty well-versed in the liberal arts serve as both teachers and role models. The school desires to form boys into men of faith and purpose who will help foster a more human, more vital society through their daily lives as husbands, fathers, professionals and citizens.

NOTE: This data applies to the 2009–2010 school year.

THE BARNESVILLE SCHOOL   est. 1969

John Huber, Head of School
21830 Peach Tree Road
Barnesville, MD 20838
301-972-0341
www.barnesvilleschool.org

Georganna Glen, Director, Admissions and Advancement
gglen@barnesvilleschool.org

Coed: N–8th
Wheelchair accessible

Governance: Nonprofit
Accredited by: AIMS
Memberships: AIMS, AISGW, NAIS
Religious affiliation: Nonsectarian

PROFILE

Total enrollment: 217
Graduating class size: 25–30
Average class size: 13
Number of faculty: 28
Boarding option: No
School day: 8:00–3:00
Extended day hours: 7:00–6:00
Schools three or more graduates have attended over the past five years: Bullis, Good Counsel, Landon, Mercersburg, Poolesville Global Ecology Public School, public magnet schools, Sandy Spring Friends, St. Andrew's Episcopal, St. John's (Frederick)

APPLICATION PROCESS

Grades with openings (approximate): All
Birthday cutoff: September 1
Deadline: January 15
Fee: $75
Testing required: In-house (N–4th), SSAT or ISEE (5th–8th)
Steps: Application, student visit/interview

COSTS

Tuition: $11,320 (K), $15,145 (1st–4th), $16,195 (5th–8th)
Average additional fees: $135 (1st–4th), $615 (5th–8th)
Financial aid budget: N/A
Average grant size: N/A
% of students receiving aid: N/A
Endowment: Yes

NOTE: This data applies to the 2009–2010 school year.

PRESCHOOL PROGRAM

Age	Days	Hours	Tuition	Openings	Class size	Teachers per class	Food provided
3	3	8:00–11:30	$3,925	10	10	2	None
3	5	8:00–11:30	$6,535	10	10	2	None
3	5	8:00–3:00	$11,320	10	10	2	None
4	5	8:00–11:30	$6,535	30	13	2	None
4	5	8:00–3:00	$11,320	30	13	2	None

CURRICULUM

Languages and grades offered: Spanish (N–8th)
AP classes/IB program: N/A
Tutors/learning specialists: 2
Other resource specialists: Speech
Art programs: Art, drama, music
Sports: Basketball, cross-country, equestrian, lacrosse, mountain biking, soccer
Special features and activities: Mountain biking and equestrian team; after-school LAND Program—flora and fauna
Summer programs: Yes, 7 weeks

CAMPUS LIFE

Transportation available: Bus service
Lunch options: Provided at an additional cost
Food allergy policy: As necessary
Uniform: No

CAMPUS

Facilities: 50 acres with 3 buildings including museum building (N–1st) and main building (2nd–8th); full gym and stage, soccer field, cross-country course
Long-range plans: N/A

HISTORY AND MISSION STATEMENT

Founded as a primary school, Barnesville expanded to 8th grade in the 1990s with two classes of each grade and a student body of 250. Barnesville students are part of a nurturing community which cares for its greater community through service and learning as an integral part of the curriculum. Barnesville School is dedicated to providing a joyful and supportive learning environment for the development of excellence in each of us.

NOTE: This data applies to the 2009–2010 school year.

THE BARRIE SCHOOL   est. 1932

Michael Kennedy, Interim Head of School
13500 Layhill Road
Silver Spring, MD 20906
301-567-2800
www.barrie.org

Andrea Williams, Director of Admission and Financial Aid
admissions@barrie.org

Coed: N–12th
Wheelchair accessible

Governance: Nonprofit
Accredited by: AMS, MSA
Memberships: AIMS, AISGW, CASE, College Board,
ERB, NAIS, NACAC, SSATB
Religious affiliation: Nonsectarian

PROFILE

Total enrollment: 390
Graduating class size: 30
Average class size: 25 (1st–5th), 15 (6th–12th)
Number of faculty: 64
Boarding option: No
School day: 9:00–3:10 (1st–3rd), 8:10–3:20 (4th–12th)
Extended day hours: 8:10–6:00
Schools three or more graduates have attended over the past five years: Boston University, Brown, Carnegie Mellon, Dickinson College, Haverford, Oberlin, University of Chicago, University of Rochester, Virginia Tech, Wooster

APPLICATION PROCESS

Grades with openings: See table, plus attrition
Birthday cutoff: September 1
Deadline: January 15
Fee: $100
Testing required: WPPSI-III/WISC-IV (N–5th), SSAT or ISEE (6th–12th)
Steps: Parent tour/open house, application, applicant visit

COSTS

Tuition: $18,500 (1st–5th), $20,990 (6th–8th), $23,150 (9th–12th)
Average additional fees: $500
Financial aid budget: N/A
Average grant size: N/A
% of students receiving aid: 23%
Endowment: Yes

NOTE: This data applies to the 2009–2010 school year.

PRESCHOOL PROGRAM

Age	Days	Hours	Tuition	Openings	Class size	Teachers per class	Food provided
2	5	9–12:30	$11,300	4	28	2	
2	5	9:00–3:00	$16,200	24	28	2	
3	5	9:00–3:00	$16,200	Attrition	25	2	
4	5	9:00–3:00	$16,200	Attrition	25	2	
5	5	9:00–3:00	$16,200	Attrition	25	2	

CURRICULUM

Languages and grades offered: French (6th–12th), Latin (6th–8th), Spanish (N–12th)

AP classes/IB program: 8 AP classes

Tutors/learning specialists: 2

Other resource specialists: College counselor, Director of Student Services, guidance counselor

Art programs: Art history, choral, dance, drama, instrumental, music, studio art, technical theater

Sports: Baseball, basketball, cross-country, equestrian, golf, lacrosse, soccer, tennis, track & field, volleyball, wrestling

Special features and activities: Internships, community service, boat races, Middle and Upper School Retreats

Summer programs: Arts & crafts, canoeing, computer, counselor in training, drama, equestrian, nature study, sports, studio art, swimming, teacher training in Montessori education

CAMPUS LIFE

Transportation available: Bus service

Lunch options: Students bring lunch

Food allergy policy: Extensive, please visit website

Uniform: No

CAMPUS

Facilities: 45 wooded acres, 11 academic buildings; art cottage, 2 art rooms, athletic fields, computer labs, 2 gyms, stables, outdoor pool, black box theater, renovated Middle/Upper School

Long-range plans: Master plan completed in 2008

HISTORY AND MISSION STATEMENT

Founded in 1932, Barrie has a Montessori curriculum in the Lower School that provides the foundation for more traditional college preparatory programs in the Middle and Upper Schools. At all levels, there is an emphasis on student-centered instruction and experiential learning.

NOTE: This data applies to the 2009–2010 school year.

BEAUVOIR, THE NATIONAL CATHEDRAL ELEMENTARY SCHOOL   est. 1933

Paula J. Carreiro, Head of School
3500 Woodley Road, NW
Washington, DC 20016
202-537-6493
www.beauvoirschool.org

Margaret Hartigan, Director of Admissions and Financial Aid
mhartigan@cathedral.org

Coed: PK–3rd
Wheelchair accessible

Governance: Nonprofit
Accredited by: AIMS, MSA
Memberships: AIMS, AISGW, MSA, NAES, NAEYC, NAIS
Religious affiliation: Episcopal

PROFILE
Total enrollment: 386
Graduating class size: 78
Average class size: 21 with 2 faculty members
Number of faculty: 59
Boarding option: No
School day: 8:00–3:00
Extended day hours: 8:00–6:00
Schools three or more graduates have attended over the past five years: Bullis, Georgetown Day, Holton-Arms, Landon, Maret, National Cathedral, National Presbyterian, Norwood, Potomac, St. Albans, St. Patrick's Episcopal, Sidwell Friends

APPLICATION PROCESS
Grades with openings (approximate):
PK (63), K (21), plus attrition
Birthday cutoff: August 31
Deadline: January 8
Fee: $65
Testing required: WPPSI-III/WISC-IV (PK–3rd)
Steps: Tour, open house, application, student play date, evaluation

COSTS
Tuition: $25,970
Average additional fees:
Financial aid budget: $1M
Average grant size: $17,220
% of students receiving aid: 17%
Endowment: Yes

NOTE: This data applies to the 2009–2010 school year.

PRESCHOOL PROGRAM

Age	Days	Hours	Tuition	Openings	Class size	Teachers per class	Food provided
4	5	8:00–3:00	$25,970	63	21	2	Yes

CURRICULUM

Languages and grades offered: Spanish (PK–3rd)

AP classes/IB program: N/A

Tutors/learning specialists: 5

Other resource specialists: Librarian, performing arts, physical education, science, technology, visual arts

Art programs: Performing and visual arts

Sports: Physical education for all

Special features and activities: Enrichment After School classes: art, basketball, Chinese, drama, soccer

Summer programs: Multitude of half- and full-day programs for 3- to 10-year-old boys and girls, with full use of the Beauvoir pool

CAMPUS LIFE

Transportation available: None

Lunch options: Included in tuition

Food allergy policy: Full-time nurse on duty, faculty trained to use EpiPen

Uniform: No

CAMPUS

Facilities: Art studio, broadcasting center, children's garden, dining room, greenhouse, gymnasium, library, music & performing arts room, playdecks, playground

Long-range plans: N/A

HISTORY AND MISSION STATEMENT

Beauvoir, the National Cathedral Elementary School founded in 1933, is a primary school dedicated to educating a diverse student body within a caring and creative environment. Our program is designed to nurture the spiritual, ethical, intellectual, emotional, physical and social development of our children. We seek to foster a spirit of inquiry and a joy in learning.

NOTE: This data applies to the 2009–2010 school year.

BISHOP IRETON HIGH SCHOOL est. 1964

Timothy Hamer, Principal
201 Cambridge Road
Alexandria, VA 22314
703-751-7606
www.bishopireton.org

Peter Hamer, Director of Admission
hamerp@bishopireton.org

Coed: 9th–12th
Wheelchair accessible

Governance: Nonprofit
Accredited by: NCEA, SACS
Memberships: VCEA
Religious affiliation: Roman Catholic

PROFILE
Total enrollment: 800
Graduating class size: 190
Average class size: 24
Number of faculty: 65
Boarding option: No
School day: 8:00–3:00
Extended day hours: 7:00–4:30
Schools three or more graduates have attended over the past five years: Air Force Academy, Georgetown, James Madison, Notre Dame, University of Virginia, Virginia Tech, William and Mary

APPLICATION PROCESS
Grades with openings (approximate):
9th (200), plus attrition
Birthday cutoff: N/A
Deadline: End of January
Fee: $50
Testing required: HSPT
Steps: Application

COSTS
Tuition: $10,400–14,950
Average additional fees: $600
Financial aid budget: $350,000
Average grant size: $3,000
% of students receiving aid: 10%
Endowment: Yes

NOTE: This data applies to the 2009–2010 school year.

CURRICULUM
Languages and grades offered: French, German, Latin, Spanish (9th–12th)
AP classes/IB program: 16 AP classes
Tutors/learning specialists: N/A
Other resource specialists: N/A
Art programs: Acting class, art, chorus, drama club (co-curricular), symphonic wind ensemble
Sports: 41 different teams
Special features and activities: Academic Enrichment Program
Summer programs: Late June–early August

CAMPUS LIFE
Transportation available: Bus service to and from the King Street Metro/VRE stop
Lunch options: Optional
Food allergy policy: None
Uniform: Yes

CAMPUS
Facilities: State-of-the-art performance hall, turf field
Long-range plans: N/A

HISTORY AND MISSION STATEMENT

In the Catholic tradition and in the spirit of St. Francis de Sales, Bishop Ireton High School is a college preparatory high school that promotes spiritual, intellectual, creative, scientific, technological, social and physical development. As a Salesian community of learning, Bishop Ireton challenges students to recognize and respect the multicultural diversity within our global society. In addition, the school fosters Christian ethics, religious values and community service. A Bishop Ireton education teaches students to think critically and develops the whole person to meet present and future challenges and opportunities.

NOTE: This data applies to the 2009–2010 school year.

BLESSED SACRAMENT SCHOOL   est. 1923

Christopher M. Kelly, Principal
5841 Chevy Chase Parkway, NW
Washington, DC 20015
202-966-6682 x2320
www.bsstoday.org

Colleen O. Molloy, Director of Admissions
cmolloy@blessedsacramentdc.org

Coed: K–8th
Wheelchair accessible

Governance: Nonprofit
Accredited by: MSA
Memberships: NCEA
Religious affiliation: Roman Catholic

PROFILE
Total enrollment: 500
Graduating class size: 48
Average class size: 20
Number of faculty: 60
Boarding option: No
School day: 8:15–3:10
Extended day hours: 8:15–6:00
Schools three or more graduates have attended over the past five years: Georgetown Prep, Georgetown Visitation, Gonzaga, Holy Cross, Sidwell Friends, St. Albans, St. John's College High

APPLICATION PROCESS
Grades with openings (approximate): K (60), plus attrition
Birthday cutoff: September 1
Deadline: February 6
Fee: None
Testing required: In-house
Steps: Open house, application, student visit (4th–8th)

COSTS
Tuition: $7,450 (parish), $11,200 (non-parish)
Average additional fees: $200
Financial aid budget: N/A
Average grant size: N/A
% of students receiving aid: 4%
Endowment: Yes

NOTE: This data applies to the 2009–2010 school year.

CURRICULUM

Languages and grades offered: French, Spanish (3rd–8th)

AP classes/IB program: N/A

Tutors/learning specialists: 3

Other resource specialists:

Art programs: Band, chorus & cantors, school play, Shakespeare theater

Sports: Basketball, football, soccer

Special features and activities:

Summer programs: Kindergarten camp, art camp, DC at Your Doorstep, summer reading camp

CAMPUS LIFE

Transportation available: None

Lunch options: Hot lunch available

Food allergy policy: Precautions taken for nut allergies

Uniform: Yes

CAMPUS

Facilities: Auditorium, gym, playing field

Long-range plans: N/A

HISTORY AND MISSION STATEMENT

Blessed Sacrament is a parish, neighborhood school dedicated to excellence within an atmosphere of Christian love and concern. The curriculum incorporates a balance of basic educational needs and advanced materials. The school setting provides children with opportunities for the practice of Christian virtues and values as they deal with their own personal growth and development and their relationships with others.

NOTE: This data applies to the 2009–2010 school year.

BRITISH SCHOOL OF WASHINGTON   est. 1998

Peter Harding, Head of School
2001 Wisconsin Avenue, NW
Washington, DC 20007
202-829-3700
www.britishschool.org/washington

Katherine Wilson, Admissions Director
k.wilson@britishschool.org

Coed: N–12th
Limited wheelchair access

Governance: Proprietary
Accredited by: IB World Schools
Memberships: CIS, ECIS
Religious affiliation: Nonsectarian

PROFILE
Total enrollment: 375
Graduating class size: 18
Average class size: 15
Number of faculty: 40
Boarding option: No
School day: 8:30–3:30
Extended day hours: 8:00–6:00
Schools three or more graduates have attended over the past five years: Nottingham Trent University (UK)

APPLICATION PROCESS
Grades with openings (approximate): All
Birthday cutoff: September 1
Deadline: Rolling
Fee: $150
Testing required: None
Steps: Parent tour, application, student evaluation visit

COSTS
Tuition: $18,975 (K–5th), $20,475 (6th–10th), $22,475 (11th–12th)
Average additional fees: N/A
Financial aid budget: N/A
Average grant size: N/A
% of students receiving aid: N/A
Endowment: No

NOTE: This data applies to the 2009–2010 school year.

PRESCHOOL PROGRAM							
Age	Days	Hours	Tuition	Openings	Class size	Teachers per class	Food provided
3+	5	8:00–12:00	$10,440	30	40	1:8	Snack*
3+	5	8:00–3:30	$18,475	30	40	1:8	Snack*

*Brought by parents on a rota basis

CURRICULUM

Languages and grades offered: French (N–12th), Latin (3rd–10th), Spanish (3rd–12th)

AP classes/IB program: IB program

Tutors/learning specialists: 3

Other resource specialists: Librarian

Art programs: Art club, choirs, design technology workshop, musical activities, theater club

Sports: Basketball, rugby, soccer, track

Special features and activities: IB Film, International Primary Curriculum, Design and Technology

Summer programs: N/A

CAMPUS LIFE

Transportation available: Buses

Lunch options: Bring lunch or purchase hot lunch. 9th–12th may buy lunch off campus with parental permission

Food allergy policy: Nut-free tables

Uniform: Yes (through 10th)

CAMPUS

Facilities: Auditorium, design technology workshop, Early Years play area, fitness center, 2 libraries, multipurpose room, playing fields and gym, 3 science labs

Long-range plans: Expansion to 550 students, expansion of arts and modern language capability

HISTORY AND MISSION STATEMENT

The British School of Washington is now entering its second decade and celebrating our first anniversary in our new Georgetown facilities. The Mission of the British School of Washington is to provide a world class education by creating an open learning community in which the academic, social and personal needs of our children, pupils and students are recognized and nurtured in order to enable them to become lifelong learners and active contributors in a changing global society.

NOTE: This data applies to the 2009–2010 school year.

BROOKEWOOD SCHOOL   est. 2006

Joseph W. McPherson, Headmaster
10401 Armory Avenue
Kensington, MD 20895
301-949-7997
www.brookewood.org

Charmie Cruz Vince, Director of Admissions
brookewoodschool@verizon.net

Girls: 1st–12th
No wheelchair access

Governance: Nonprofit
Accredited by: ADW
Memberships: N/A
Religious affiliation: Catholic Inspiration

PROFILE
Total enrollment: 120
Graduating class size: First graduating class in 2010
Average class size: 12
Number of faculty: 17
Boarding option: No
School day: 8:30–3:15
Extended day hours: 8:30–5:15
Schools three or more graduates have attended over the past five years: N/A

APPLICATION PROCESS
Grades with openings (approximate): All
Birthday cutoff: N/A
Deadline: Rolling
Fee: $50
Testing required: None
Steps: Application, parent and student interview

COSTS
Tuition: $9,200 (1st–5th), $10,300 (6th–12th)
Average additional fees: None
Financial aid budget: 18% of tuition
Average grant size: $3,000
% of students receiving aid: 34%
Endowment: No

NOTE: This data applies to the 2009–2010 school year.

CURRICULUM
Languages and grades offered: Italian (1st–12th), Latin (6th–12th)
AP classes/IB program: None
Tutors/learning specialists: None
Other resource specialists: None
Art programs: Art, art history, choir, music appreciation, piano, violin
Sports: Cross-country, field hockey, lacrosse
Special features and activities: MathCounts competition, Model UN, tuition discount for siblings ($1,000)
Summer programs: Drama & literature, math camp, natural history

CAMPUS LIFE
Transportation available: Limited
Lunch options: Pizza Fridays
Food allergy policy: None
Uniform: Yes

CAMPUS
Facilities: Educational wing of St. Paul's United Methodist Church, use of nearby parks and fields
Long-range plans: N/A

HISTORY AND MISSION STATEMENT

Brookewood School seeks to help parents form their daughters into young women who are educated, cultured, pious, cheerful, adventurous, and generous. Brookewood seeks to take account of new studies and traditional wisdom to help girls develop their learning styles and interests in a single-sex setting. Brookewood is an academic place in the sense that teaching and learning are central. The curriculum is traditional because it is based on the heritage of human achievement in the True, the Good, and the Beautiful. Experiential learning through frequent field trips and excursions enriches classroom education. A religion program is conducted according to the *New Catechism of the Catholic Church*.

NOTE: This data applies to the 2009–2010 school year.

BROWNE ACADEMY   est. 1941

Margot Durkin, Head of School
5917 Telegraph Road
Alexandria, VA 22310
703-960-3000 x1001
www.browneacademy.org

Steve Salvo, Director of Admission
ssalvo@browneacademy.org

Coed: N–8th
Wheelchair accessible

Governance: Nonprofit
Accredited by: VAIS
Memberships: AISGW, ESP, LSF, NAIS, VAIS
Religious affiliation: Nonsectarian

PROFILE
Total enrollment: 300
Graduating class size: 25
Average class size: 12
Number of faculty: 50
Boarding option: No
School day: 8:15–3:15
Extended day hours: 7:00–6:00
Schools three or more graduates have attended over the past five years: Bishop Ireton, Bishop O'Connell, Episcopal High, Flint Hill, Georgetown Day, Madeira, Maret, Potomac, St. Stephen's and St. Agnes, Thomas Jefferson

APPLICATION PROCESS
Grades with openings (approximate): Varies
Birthday cutoff: September 30
Deadline: February 1
Fee: $60
Testing required: WPPSI-III/WISC-IV (N–8th) or SSAT or ISEE (6th–8th)
Steps: Application, open house/tour, student visit

COSTS
Tuition: $20,240 (K–8th)
Average additional fees: $1,200
Financial aid budget: $500,000
Average grant size: N/A
% of students receiving aid: 24%
Endowment: No

NOTE: This data applies to the 2009–2010 school year.

PRESCHOOL PROGRAM

Age	Days	Hours	Tuition	Openings	Class size	Teachers per class	Food provided
3	5	8:15–12:15	$12,210	36	18	3	Snack
3	5	8:15–3:15	$16,765	36	18	3	Snack
4	5	8:15–12:15	$12,210	10	18	2	Snack
4	5	8:15–3:15	$16,765	10	18	2	Snack

CURRICULUM

Languages and grades offered: French (N–8th), Spanish (3rd–8th)
AP classes/IB program: N/A
Tutors/learning specialists: Yes
Other resource specialists: Full-time nurse
Art programs: Art, band, choir, drawing, flute, handbells, jazz, painting, percussion, piano
Sports: Basketball, gymnastics, lacrosse, soccer, softball, tae kwon do
Special features and activities:
Summer programs: Academic, arts, athletics, CIT, extended day, swimming, technology

CAMPUS LIFE

Transportation available: Limited
Lunch options: Hot lunch with salad and sandwich bar available for all students
Food allergy policy: Coordinated with full-time school nurse
Uniform: Dress code (K–8th)

CAMPUS

Facilities: Three classroom buildings including library, computer lab, science labs, music and art departments set on 11 acres with stream, playing fields, swimming pool, basketball court, and outdoor amphitheater
Long-range plans: N/A

HISTORY AND MISSION STATEMENT

Browne Academy is a coeducational, independent day school for children in Preschool through eighth grade. We are committed to developing independent, passionate, lifelong learners who will actively participate as responsible, caring citizens in a global community. We are passionate about Excellence, Diversity, Character, and Community. Browne offers a challenging academic environment with an interdisciplinary curriculum fostering critical thinking skills as well as leadership and social responsibility.

NOTE: This data applies to the 2009–2010 school year.

BULLIS SCHOOL   est. 1930

Thomas B. Farquhar, Head of School
10601 Falls Road
Potomac, MD 20854
301-983-5724
www.bullis.org

Timothy Simpson, Director of Admission and Financial Aid
tim_simpson@bullis.org

Coed: 3rd–12th
Limited wheelchair access

Governance: Nonprofit
Accredited by: MSA, MSDE
Memberships: AIMS, AISGW, BSF, NAIS, SSATB
Religious affiliation: Nonsectarian

PROFILE
Total enrollment: 657
Graduating class size: 103
Average class size: 15
Number of faculty: 90
Boarding option: No
School day: 8:00–3:30 (3rd–8th),
8:00–2:45 (9th–12th)
Extended day hours: 8:00–6:00
**Schools three or more graduates
have attended over the past five
years:** Brown, Dickinson College,
George Washington, Gettysburg
College, Harvard, Johns Hopkins,
Northwestern, University of
Colorado–Boulder, University of
Maryland, University of Wisconsin

APPLICATION PROCESS
Grades with openings (approximate):
3rd (24), 4th (6), 6th (15–20), 7th
(15–20), 9th (35–40), 10th (10),
plus attrition
Birthday cutoff: September 1
Deadline: February 1
Fee: $60 (online), $75 (paper)
Testing required: WISC-IV (3rd), ERB
(4th–5th), SSAT or ISEE (6th–12th)
Steps: Tour, application, interview,
shadow day

COSTS
Tuition: $25,370 (3rd–5th), $27,320
(6th–8th), $28,430 (9th–12th)
Average additional fees: $700
Financial aid budget: $2.2M
Average grant size: $18,000
% of students receiving aid: 19%
Endowment: Yes

NOTE: This data applies to the 2009–2010 school year.

CURRICULUM
Languages and grades offered: Chinese (9th–12th), French (6th–12th), Latin (6th–12th), Spanish (6th–12th)
AP classes/IB program: 18 AP classes
Tutors/learning specialists: 2
Other resource specialists: School counselors
Art programs: Ceramics, choir, computer music, dance team, digital video, drama production, drawing, musical, painting, stagecraft, strings
Sports: Baseball, basketball, cross-country, dance, field hockey, football, golf, ice hockey, lacrosse, soccer, softball, swimming, tennis, track & field, wrestling
Special features and activities: Admissions Ambassadors, Bullis Global Studies and Service Program, extended day program, "It's Academic," Multicultural Student Union, peer mentors, Students Against Destructive Decisions (SADD)
Summer programs: 6-week academic summer school; baseball, basketball, field hockey, lacrosse, soccer and tennis camps; Bulldog Day Camp

CAMPUS LIFE
Transportation available: Bus service
Lunch options: Included in tuition
Food allergy policy: Peanut-free table, trans fat–free school
Uniform: Yes

CAMPUS
Facilities: Arts center, athletic center, library, stadium; North and South Halls housing Lower/Middle School and Upper School
Long-range plans: N/A

HISTORY AND MISSION STATEMENT
Bullis School is an independent, coeducational college preparatory day school offering boys and girls in grades 3 through 12 an educational program of excellence in a community that values integrity, respect, responsibility, diversity and service. A caring and supportive faculty fosters a positive attitude about learning and challenges our students to achieve their highest potential in academics, the arts and athletics.

NOTE: This data applies to the 2009–2010 school year.

BURGUNDY FARM COUNTRY DAY SCHOOL   est. 1946

Jeff Sindler, Head of School
3700 Burgundy Road
Alexandria, VA 22303
703-329-6968
www.burgundyfarm.org

Kathryn Robinson, Director of Admission & Multicultural Affairs
kathyr@burgundyfarm.org

Coed: JK–8th
Limited wheelchair access

Governance: Nonprofit
Accredited by: N/A
Memberships: N/A
Religious affiliation: Nonsectarian

PROFILE
Total enrollment: 284
Graduating class size: 32
Average class size: 16–28 (with two teachers)
Number of faculty: 25
Boarding option: No
School day: 8:30–3:15
Extended day hours: 8:30–6:00
Schools three or more graduates have attended over the past five years: N/A

APPLICATION PROCESS
Grades with openings (approximate): K (16), plus attrition
Birthday cutoff: September 30
Deadline: February 2
Fee: $60
Testing required: WPPSI-III/WISC-IV (JK–8th)
Steps: Application, classroom visit, parent meeting with Admission Director

COSTS
Tuition: $20,575 (K), $21,520 (1st–5th), $22,675 (6th–8th)
Average additional fees: $750
Financial aid budget: N/A
Average grant size: N/A
% of students receiving aid: N/A
Endowment: N/A

NOTE: This data applies to the 2009–2010 school year.

PRESCHOOL PROGRAM

Age	Days	Hours	Tuition	Openings	Class size	Teachers per class	Food provided
4	5	8:30–3:15	$20,575	16	16	2	Milk (low fat, no fat, whole)

CURRICULUM

Languages and grades offered: French, Spanish (K–8th)
AP classes/IB program: N/A
Tutors/learning specialists: 4
Other resource specialists: On-campus testing can be arranged
Art programs: Art, drama, music
Sports: Basketball, soccer, softball, track & field
Special features and activities: Progressive education model; Alexandria campus: 25 acres including a stocked barn; unique opportunities in environmental and wildlife studies
Summer programs: Day camp featuring arts, crafts, computers, performing and visual arts, science, sports, swimming; residential West Virginia natural science camp

CAMPUS LIFE
Transportation available: Limited bus service
Lunch options: Students bring lunch
Food allergy policy: Nut free
Uniform: No

CAMPUS
Facilities: Amphitheater, art studios, auditorium, barn (with chickens, goats, sheep), new Middle School with full-size gymnasium, media center/library, photography and science labs, pond, pool, woods; 500-acre West Virginia campus
Long-range plans: Build upon strong diversity/cultural training and curriculum; expand arts program

HISTORY AND MISSION STATEMENT

Founded as a parent cooperative; racially integrated in 1950; first school in Virginia to integrate. Philosophically, the school is in the Progressive tradition. The school's stated vision is, "Preparing the Whole Child for the Whole World" in a school community that has as its core values: citizenship, collaboration, cooperation, human diversity, learning by doing, responsibility for oneself, others, the natural world.

NOTE: This data applies to the 2009–2010 school year.

BUTLER SCHOOL   est. 1971

Becki Hardie, Head of School
15951 Germantown Road
Darnestown, MD 20874
301-977-6600
www.butlerschool.org

Diana Jellett
diana@butlerschool.org

Coed: N–8th
No wheelchair access

Governance: Nonprofit
Accredited by: AMI, MSDE
Memberships: AISGW, AMI, NAMTA
Religious affiliation: Nonsectarian

PROFILE

Total enrollment: 165
Graduating class size: 10
Average class size: Mixed age range
Number of faculty: 30
Boarding option: No
School day: 8:45–3:15
Extended day hours: 7:45–5:30
Schools three or more graduates have attended over the past five years: Bullis, Montgomery County Public Schools, Sandy Spring Friends

APPLICATION PROCESS

Grades with openings (approximate): All
Birthday cutoff: September 1
Deadline: N/A
Fee: $25
Testing required: None
Steps: Parent visit, application, child visit (K–8th)

COSTS

Tuition: $11,900
Average additional fees: None
Financial aid budget: N/A
Average grant size: $4,000
% of students receiving aid: 15%
Endowment: Yes

NOTE: This data applies to the 2009–2010 school year.

PRESCHOOL PROGRAM

Age	Days	Hours	Tuition	Openings	Class size	Teachers per class	Food provided
3	5	9:00–12:00	$7,900				None
3	5	9:00–3:00	$11,900				None
4	5	9:00–3:00	$11,900				None
5	5	9:00–3:00	$11,900				None

CURRICULUM

Languages and grades offered: Spanish (K–8th)
AP classes/IB program: N/A
Tutors/learning specialists: 2 part time
Other resource specialists: Speech
Art programs: Art, music, vocal
Sports: Equestrian
Special features and activities: Montessori curriculum
Summer programs: Yes

CAMPUS LIFE

Transportation available: Buses
Lunch options: Pizza Fridays
Food allergy policy: Classroom based, as needed
Uniform: Yes (1st–6th)

CAMPUS

Facilities: Library, tennis courts
Long-range plans: Cultural arts center

HISTORY AND MISSION STATEMENT

Butler School's mission is to educate young people to their fullest potential by implementing the educational philosophy of Dr. Maria Montessori as maintained by Association Montessori Internationale. Our commitment is to instill social responsibility, personal independence and the knowledge that education is a life-long process based on a solid academic foundation.

NOTE: This data applies to the 2009–2010 school year.

CAPITOL HILL DAY SCHOOL · est. 1968

Michael Eanes, Interim Head of School
210 South Carolina Avenue, SE
Washington, DC 20003
202-547-2244 x120
www.chds.org

Priscilla Lund, Director of Admissions
priscillal@chds.org

Coed: PK–8th
No wheelchair access

Governance: Nonprofit
Accredited by: AIMS
Memberships: AIMS, AISGW, BSF, ERB, NAIS
Religious affiliation: Nonsectarian

PROFILE
Total enrollment: 230
Graduating class size: 22
Average class size: 24
Number of faculty: 40
Boarding option: No
School day: 8:10–3:10, 8:10–2:10 (W)
Extended day hours: 8:10–6:00
Schools three or more graduates have attended over the past five years: Edmund Burke, Field, Georgetown Day, Georgetown Visitation, Gonzaga, Maret, National Cathedral, St. Andrew's Episcopal, Sidwell Friends, Stone Ridge

APPLICATION PROCESS
Grades with openings (approximate): See table, plus attrition
Birthday cutoff: October 1
Deadline: January 15
Fee: $50
Testing required: WPPSI-III/WISC-IV (PK–8th)
Steps: Application, tour, assessment, child visit

COSTS
Tuition: $22,220 (PK–5th), $23,350 (6th–8th)
Average additional fees: $1,000 (one-time fee)
Financial aid budget: $450,000
Average grant size: $6,800
% of students receiving aid: 20%
Endowment: Yes

NOTE: This data applies to the 2009–2010 school year.

PRESCHOOL PROGRAM

Age	Days	Hours	Tuition	Openings	Class size	Teachers per class	Food provided
4	5	8:10–3:10	$22,220	24			

CURRICULUM

Languages and grades offered: French, Spanish (PK–8th)
AP classes/IB program: N/A
Tutors/learning specialists: Tutors for math, languages, reading, writing
Other resource specialists: Child development, music
Art programs: Art, drama, music, poetry emphasized throughout the curriculum
Sports: Baseball, basketball, soccer, squash, track & field
Special features and activities: Weekly field education trips for every class. After school: chess club, Chinese language lessons, instrumental lessons, jazz choir, jazz ensemble, knitting club, yoga
Summer programs: History camp, summer camp

CAMPUS LIFE

Transportation available: Bus service
Lunch options: Box lunch available
Food allergy policy: Individual class restrictions
Uniform: No

CAMPUS

Facilities: 4-story building and neighboring townhouse
Long-range plans: Expansion planned for facilities, same enrollment

HISTORY AND MISSION STATEMENT

Located in a historic District of Columbia school building, Capitol Hill Day School offers a strong academic program in a creative environment. Children focus on patterns and relationships in studies of science, mathematics, literature, language, history, and culture. Self-expression is stressed through art and writing, and children are taught to respect each other's ideas and differences. To help children understand that learning occurs beyond the classroom walls, extensive use is made of resources of the Washington area, as children regularly visit sites related to their studies. Community participation is stressed through cooperative activities. Parents participate actively in school life.

NOTE: This data applies to the 2009–2010 school year.

CHARLES E. SMITH JEWISH DAY SCHOOL — est. 1965

Jonathan Cannon, Head of School
1901 East Jefferson Street
Rockville, MD 20852
301-881-1400 x4870
www.cesjds.org

Susan Cohen, Director of Admissions
scohen@cesjds.org

Coed: K–12th
Wheelchair accessible
7th–12th: 11710 Hunters Lane, Rockville, MD

Governance: Nonprofit
Accredited by: N/A
Memberships: N/A
Religious affiliation: Jewish

PROFILE
Total enrollment: 1,406
Graduating class size: 122
Average class size: 18
Number of faculty: 221
Boarding option: No
School day: 8:00–3:45
Extended day hours: None
Schools three or more graduates have attended over the past five years: Cornell, Tufts, University of Maryland, University of Michigan, University of Pennsylvania

APPLICATION PROCESS
Grades with openings (approximate): K–10th
Birthday cutoff: September 1
Deadline: January 18
Fee: $75
Testing required: None
Steps: Parent tour, application, student visit/screening

COSTS
Tuition: $17,830 (K–6th), $22,880 (7th–12th)
Average additional fees: Minimal
Financial aid budget: N/A
Average grant size: N/A
% of students receiving aid: 30%
Endowment: Yes

NOTE: This data applies to the 2009–2010 school year.

CURRICULUM
Languages and grades offered: Arabic (9th–12th), French (7th–12th),
Hebrew (K–12th), Spanish (7th–12th)
AP classes/IB program: None
Tutors/learning specialists: N/A
Other resource specialists: N/A
Art programs: Art, ceramics, photography
Sports: Baseball, basketball, cross-country, golf, ice hockey, soccer, softball,
tennis, track & field, volleyball, wrestling
Special features and activities: Dual curriculum, extensive co-curriculars
Summer programs: Sports camp

CAMPUS LIFE	**CAMPUS**
Transportation available: Bus service	**Facilities:** 2 campuses
	Long-range plans: N/A
Lunch options: Available for an additional fee	
Food allergy policy: Flexible	
Uniform: No	

HISTORY AND MISSION STATEMENT
The Charles E. Smith Jewish Day School is a coeducational, college preparatory, community day school enrolling over 1,500 students in kindergarten–
grade 12 with two beautiful campuses located in Rockville, MD. The school
is dedicated to creating an environment in which students can grow to their
fullest potential as responsible and dedicated members of the Jewish people
and of American society. JDS is widely recognized for excellence in both secular and Judaic studies. This challenging dual curriculum program and
wide variety of co-curricular activities develop intellectual abilities, religious
awareness, social conscience and personal integrity.

NOTE: This data applies to the 2009–2010 school year.

CHELSEA SCHOOL   est. 1976

Tony Messina, Head of School
711 Pershing Drive
Silver Spring, MD 20910
301-585-1430 x303
www.chelseaschool.edu

Deborah Lourie, Director of Admissions
dlourie@chelseaschool.edu

Coed: 5th–12th
Limited wheelchair access

Governance: Nonprofit
Accredited by: MSDE
Memberships: AISGW, NAIS
Religious affiliation: Nonsectarian

PROFILE

Total enrollment: 85
Graduating class size: 20
Average class size: 8
Number of faculty: 25
Boarding option: No
School day: 8:30–3:30,
8:30–1:00 (F)
Extended day hours: N/A
Schools three or more graduates have attended over the past five years: Davis and Elkins College, DeVry, Florida A&M, Hampton College, McDaniel College, Marshall, Muskingham College, Stevenson College, University of Maryland–Eastern Shore, Virginia Intermont College

APPLICATION PROCESS

Grades with openings (approximate): Varies
Birthday cutoff: N/A
Deadline: Rolling
Fee: $50
Testing required: Full battery of psychological testing (WISC-IV or Stanford-Binet) and of normed and standardized educational testing
Steps: Application, two-day school visit

COSTS

Tuition: $35,610
Average additional fees: For related services, if private pay
Financial aid budget: $50,000
Average grant size: $10,000–$15,000
% of students receiving aid: 1%
Endowment: Yes

NOTE: This data applies to the 2009–2010 school year.

CURRICULUM

Languages and grades offered: Spanish (9th–12th)

AP classes/IB program: None

Tutors/learning specialists: N/A

Other resource specialists: Counselors, nurse, occupational therapist, speech and language pathologists, reading specialists

Art programs: Traditional fine arts

Sports: Basketball, flag football, soccer, softball, track & field

Special features and activities: Literacy remediation and writing remediation; Completer Pathways in music & media productions, information systems management and computer graphics; clubs include photography, drama, movie, and chess clubs

Summer programs: Extended School Year Services—A five-week program focusing on remediation in reading, writing, and math skills

CAMPUS LIFE

Transportation available: Located 5 blocks from Silver Spring Metro station. Transportation provided for funded students.

Lunch options: Various menus offered daily

Food allergy policy: N/A

Uniform: No

CAMPUS

Facilities: N/A

Long-range plans: The school has a capital campaign that consists of four pillars: enhancing professional growth and development of faculty and staff, establishing a scholarship endowment fund for students in need, committing to learning technologies, and designing and building an innovative facility and campus for learning.

HISTORY AND MISSION STATEMENT

Betty Nehemias and Eleanor Blewitt Worthy, parents of children with dyslexia, founded Chelsea School. Their dream was to establish a school that could teach and improve the lives of students with language-based learning disabilities. The mission is to prepare students with language-based learning disabilities for higher education by providing a world-class school which embeds literacy remediation and technology into all aspects of the curriculum.

NOTE: This data applies to the 2009–2010 school year.

THE CHILDREN'S LEARNING CENTER   est. 1978

Rena Goldman Popkin, Director
4511 Bestor Drive
Rockville, MD 20853
301-871-6600
www.clcmd.org

Dottie Harris
dottieclc@gmail.com

Coed: N–5th
Limited wheelchair access

Governance: Nonprofit
Accredited by: MSDE
Memberships: N/A
Religious affiliation: Jewish

PROFILE
Total enrollment: 160
Graduating class size: N/A
Average class size: N/A
Number of faculty: 45
Boarding option: No
School day: 9:00–3:30
Extended day hours: 7:00–6:00
Schools three or more graduates have attended over the past five years: N/A

APPLICATION PROCESS
Grades with openings (approximate): All
Birthday cutoff: September 1
Deadline: N/A
Fee: N/A
Testing required: None
Steps: N/A

COSTS
Tuition: Varies depending on program
Average additional fees: N/A
Financial aid budget: Financial aid available
Average grant size: N/A
% of students receiving aid: N/A
Endowment: N/A

NOTE: This data applies to the 2009–2010 school year.

PRESCHOOL PROGRAM							
Age	Days	Hours	Tuition	Openings	Class size	Teachers per class	Food provided
Infant	5	9:30–1:00			6	2	Snacks
Infant	5	9:30–3:30			6	2	Snacks
Toddler	5	9:30–1:00			9	3	Snacks
Toddler	5	9:30–3:30			9	3	Snacks
2	5	9:30–1:00			12	2	Snacks
2	5	9:30–3:30			12	2	Snacks
3	5	9:30–1:00			18	3	Snacks
3	5	9:30–3:30			18	3	Snacks
4	5	9:30–1:00			18	3	Snacks
4	5	9:30–3:30			18	3	Snacks

CURRICULUM
Languages and grades offered: N/A
AP classes/IB program: N/A
Tutors/learning specialists: Occupational therapist, speech pathologist
Other resource specialists: Art, library, physical education, science
Art programs: N/A
Sports: N/A
Special features and activities: Optional enrichment classes, including cooking, dance/music, karate, soccer
Summer programs: CLC Camp, ages 2–6

CAMPUS LIFE
Transportation available: CLC van transportation
Lunch options: Vegetarian hot lunch program
Food allergy policy: Peanut- and nut-free school
Uniform: No

CAMPUS
Facilities: Computers
Long-range plans: N/A

HISTORY AND MISSION STATEMENT
The Children's Learning Center, Inc. (CLC) is dedicated to educating children by stimulating their imaginations, instilling confidence in themselves and promoting the child's self-esteem through exposure to a warm and nurturing learning environment.

NOTE: This data applies to the 2009–2010 school year.

CHRIST EPISCOPAL SCHOOL   est. 1966

Carol R. Shabe, Head of School
109 South Washington Street
Rockville, MD 20850
301-424-8702
www.ces-rockville.org

Carole K. Varghese, Director of Admissions
cvarghese@cesstaff.org

Coed: N–8th
Limited wheelchair access

Governance: Nonprofit
Accredited by: AIMS
Memberships: AISGW, MAESA, NAES, NAIS
Religious affiliation: Episcopal

PROFILE
Total enrollment: 204
Graduating class size: 13
Average class size: 13
Number of faculty: 56
Boarding option: No
School day: 8:00–3:00
Extended day hours: 7:20–6:00
Schools three or more graduates have attended over the past five years: Bullis, Georgetown Prep, Georgetown Visitation, Good Counsel, Holy Cross, Maret, Mercersburg, St. Albans, St. Andrew's Episcopal, Stone Ridge

APPLICATION PROCESS
Grades with openings (approximate): All
Birthday cutoff: September 1
Deadline: February 1
Fee: $50
Testing required: WPPSI-III/WISC-IV (K–5th), SSAT or ISEE (6th–8th)
Steps: Parent tour/open house, application, student visit

COSTS
Tuition: $12,615 (K–8th)
Average additional fees: $100 (N), $500 (K–8th)
Financial aid budget: $100,000
Average grant size: $4,970
% of students receiving aid: 12%
Endowment: No

NOTE: This data applies to the 2009–2010 school year.

PRESCHOOL PROGRAM

Age	Days	Hours	Tuition	Openings	Class size	Teachers per class	Food provided
2	3/5	8:30–11:45	TBD	TBD	TBD	TBD	Snack
3	2	8:30–11:45	$3,015	6	12	2	Snack
3	3	8:30–11:45	$4,520	6	12	2	Snack
3	5	8:30–11:45	$7,535	6	12	2	Snack
3	5	8:30–3:00	$11,130	12	12	2	Snack
4	5	8:30–11:45	$7,535	15	17	2	Snack
4	5	8:30–3:00	$11,130	15	17	2	Snack

CURRICULUM

Languages and grades offered: Spanish (K–8th)
AP classes/IB program: N/A
Tutors/learning specialists: 2
Other resource specialists: N/A
Art programs: Drama, music, studio art, technology
Sports: Basketball, soccer, softball, swimming, track & field
Special features and activities: Green School Certification, service learning, Shakespeare study, field trips, environmental studies, daily chapel, science fair, ballroom dance program
Summer programs: Camp Cardinal (day camp)

CAMPUS LIFE

Transportation available: Metro accessible
Lunch options: Lunch service available
Food allergy policy: N/A
Uniform: Yes (K–8th)

CAMPUS

Facilities: Preschool, Lower School and Middle School buildings; art studio, cafeteria, library, outdoor student garden, newly renovated playgrounds, sports court, computer and science labs
Long-range plans: Expand enrollment to two sections per grade, further renovations to buildings

HISTORY AND MISSION STATEMENT

Christ Episcopal School prepares talented boys and girls for the rigors of secondary education. Our students are members of a Christian community of learners, one that teaches them to use their minds well. A CES education instills a work ethic, a commitment to service, and an appreciation for the differences in others. We build confidence, integrity, and create an enduring sense of belonging.

NOTE: This data applies to the 2009–2010 school year.

COMMONWEALTH ACADEMY   est. 1997

Dr. Susan J. Johnson, Head of School
1321 Leslie Avenue
Alexandria, VA 22301
703-548-6912
www.commonwealthacademy.org

Josh Gwilliam, Director of Admission
josh_gwilliam@commonwealthacademy.org

Coed: 6th–12th
Wheelchair accessible

Governance: Nonprofit
Accredited by: VAIS
Memberships: AISGW, CASE, CHADD, NAIS, PCW
Religious affiliation: Nonsectarian

PROFILE
Total enrollment: 110
Graduating class size: 24
Average class size: 10 or fewer
Number of faculty: 25
Boarding option: No
School day: 7:30–2:55 (6th–8th), 8:20–3:40 (9th–12th)
Extended day hours: 7:30–5:00 (6th–8th), 8:20–5:30 (9th–12th)
Schools three or more graduates have attended over the past five years: N/A

APPLICATION PROCESS
Grades with openings (approximate): All
Birthday cutoff: N/A
Deadline: March 1, with mid-year rolling admissions
Fee: $100
Testing required: None
Steps: Test, interview, application, optional shadow day

COSTS
Tuition: $28,336
Average additional fees: $1,000
Financial aid budget: Need based
Average grant size: $14,000
% of students receiving aid: 15%
Endowment: Yes

NOTE: This data applies to the 2009–2010 school year.

CURRICULUM

Languages and grades offered: Spanish (9th–12th)

AP classes/IB program: AP classes, individual by student need

Tutors/learning specialists: Yes

Other resource specialists: Full-time LCSW, full-time RN; speech therapy available for an additional fee

Art programs: Computer graphics, fine arts, music/instrumental, theater, web design

Sports: Basketball, physical education

Special features and activities: After-school directed study halls, indoor and outdoor clubs meeting every Wednesday, Middle School and High School student governments, yearbook. Licensed by the State of Virginia to service Specific Learning Disabilities and ADHD.

Summer programs: Academic support, technology

CAMPUS LIFE

Transportation available: Metro accessible

Lunch options: Local restaurant delivery

Food allergy policy: RN on staff

Uniform: No

CAMPUS

Facilities: 21,000 square feet; chemistry, physics, and biology labs; 13 classrooms, 4 computer labs, 2 High School lounges, Middle School lunchroom

Long-range plans: N/A

HISTORY AND MISSION STATEMENT

Commonwealth Academy is a coeducational college preparatory day school for average to superior middle and high school students who benefit from small classes and instruction designed to address various learning styles, including those students who have organizational, attention, or learning differences.

We empower students to reach their highest achievement levels, reflective of their true potential, by teaching personal responsibility for learning and behavior in a comfortable community, conducive to academic risk-taking and social success. We offer a broad-based curriculum, compensatory strategies, and a focus on technology to prepare our students for the challenges of college, career and life pursuits.

NOTE: This data applies to the 2009–2010 school year.

CONCORD HILL SCHOOL est. 1965

Denise Gershowitz, Director
6050 Wisconsin Avenue
Chevy Chase, MD 20815
301-654-2626
www.concordhill.org

Susan Arzt, Director of Admissions
sarzt@concordhill.org

Coed: N–3rd
Limited wheelchair access

Governance: Nonprofit
Accredited by: AIMS, MSDE
Memberships: AIMS, AISGW, NAEYC
Religious affiliation: Nonsectarian

PROFILE
Total enrollment: 100
Graduating class size: 17
Average class size: 18
Number of faculty: 19
Boarding option: No
School day: 8:25–3:00
Extended day hours: 8:25–4:30
Schools three or more graduates have attended over the past five years: Holton-Arms, Landon, Maret, National Cathedral, Potomac, Sheridan, St. Albans, Washington Episcopal

APPLICATION PROCESS
Grades with openings (approximate): K (4–5), 1st (1–2), 2nd (1–2), 3rd (1–2)
Birthday cutoff: September 1
Deadline: January 31
Fee: $60
Testing required: None
Steps: Parent visit, application, child visit

COSTS
Tuition: $19,150 (K–3rd)
Average additional fees: N/A
Financial aid budget: N/A
Average grant size: Determined on an individual basis
% of students receiving aid: 7%
Endowment: Yes

NOTE: This data applies to the 2009–2010 school year.

PRESCHOOL PROGRAM

Age	Days	Hours	Tuition	Openings	Class size	Teachers per class	Food provided
3	5	8:25–12:15	$12,750	12–13	12–13	2	Snack
4	5	8:25–12:15	$12,750	7–8	19	2	Snack

CURRICULUM

Languages and grades offered: After-school enrichment—Chinese (2nd–3rd), Spanish (K–3rd)

AP classes/IB program: N/A

Tutors/learning specialists:

Other resource specialists: Art, language arts, library, math, music, physical education, science, technology

Art programs: Art, music

Sports: None

Special features and activities: Optional Lunch Bunch extended day for preschool students

Summer programs: Summer camp (3–5 year olds), art & technology camp (K–3rd)

CAMPUS LIFE

Transportation available: None

Lunch options: Children bring lunch; milk is provided

Food allergy policy: Peanut- and tree-nut-free school

Uniform: No

CAMPUS

Facilities: N/A

Long-range plans: No expansion plans

HISTORY AND MISSION STATEMENT

Concord Hill School emphasizes both the academic and the developmental growth of the young child. We strongly believe in educating the whole child by promoting intellectual, social, emotional, physical and character development. During these important and formative years, Concord Hill demonstrates that acquiring knowledge can be both challenging and fun. We celebrate each child's unique strengths and seek to build self-confidence through achievement. By maintaining small student-to-teacher ratios, we are able to respond to each student's ideas, needs and learning styles. Concord Hill instills a strong sense of caring and respect for others. Children experience the responsibilities and benefits of being positive, contributing members of their community and our diverse world.

NOTE: This data applies to the 2009–2010 school year.

THE CONGRESSIONAL SCHOOLS OF VIRGINIA   est. 1939

Seth W. Ahlborn, Head of School
3229 Sleepy Hollow Road
Falls Church, VA 22042
703-533-9711 x120
www.congressionalschools.org

Karen Weinberger, Admissions Director
kweinberger@bach.csov.org

Coed: N–8th
Wheelchair accessible

Governance: Nonprofit
Accredited by: SACS
Memberships: AISGW, NAIS
Religious affiliation: Nonsectarian

PROFILE

Total enrollment: 375
Graduating class size: 36
Average class size: 18
Number of faculty: 70
Boarding option: No
School day: 8:15–3:10
Extended day hours: 7:00–6:00
Schools three or more graduates have attended over the past five years: Bishop O'Connell, Flint Hill, Georgetown Day, Georgetown Prep, Gonzaga, Madeira, Potomac, Sidwell Friends, St. Stephen's and St. Agnes, Thomas Jefferson

APPLICATION PROCESS

Grades with openings (approximate):
Birthday cutoff: October 31
Deadline: Rolling
Fee: $75
Testing required: WPPSI-III/WISC-IV (JK–8th) or SSAT or ISEE (5th–8th)
Steps: Application, school visit

COSTS

Tuition: $17,500–$20,300, includes books and all fees
Average additional fees: Parent organization—$50 per family
Financial aid budget: Yes
Average grant size: N/A
% of students receiving aid: N/A
Endowment: N/A

NOTE: This data applies to the 2009–2010 school year.

PRESCHOOL PROGRAM

Age	Days	Hours	Tuition	Openings	Class size	Teachers per class	Food provided
3	5	8:15–3:30		32	16	2	Snacks, lunch
4	5	8:15–3:30		Varies	18	2	Snacks, lunch

CURRICULUM
Languages and grades offered: French (K–8th), Latin (7th–8th), Spanish (K–8th)
AP classes/IB program: N/A
Tutors/learning specialists: Reading, study skills
Other resource specialists: Full-time nurse, guidance counselor
Art programs: Art and music integrated into curriculum; also band, choir, winter & spring concerts, spring musical
Sports: Baseball, basketball, cross-country, health & fitness, soccer, softball; hiking, ski/snowboarding and sailing, kayaking & white water rafting trips (5th–8th)
Special features and activities: N/A
Summer programs: Day camp, pony camp, specialty camps, sports camps, travel camps

CAMPUS LIFE
Transportation available: Bus service
Lunch options: Provided for an additional fee
Food allergy policy: Yes; full-time school nurse
Uniform: Yes (K–8th)

CAMPUS
Facilities: 40 acres, including 2 libraries, stables, 2 swimming pools, 3 technology centers
Long-range plans: N/A

HISTORY AND MISSION STATEMENT
The mission of The Congressional Schools of Virginia is to prepare children, through an innovative and accelerated curriculum, to embrace the opportunities and responsibilities they will face as global citizens.

NOTE: This data applies to the 2009–2010 school year.

CONNELLY SCHOOL OF THE HOLY CHILD   est. 1961

Maureen K. Appel, Headmistress
9029 Bradley Boulevard
Potomac, MD 20854
301-365-0955 x2103
www.holychild.org

Meg Mayo, Director of Admissions
mmayo@holychild.org

Girls: 6th–12th
Wheelchair accessible

Governance: Nonprofit
Accredited by: AIMS, MSA, MSDE
Memberships: AIMS, AISGW, BSF, College Board, NACAC, NAIS, NCEA
Religious affiliation: Catholic

PROFILE
Total enrollment: 320
Graduating class size: 60
Average class size: 15
Number of faculty: 51
Boarding option: No
School day: 8:10–3:20
Extended day hours: None
Schools three or more graduates have attended over the past five years: Catholic University, Elon, Georgetown, University of Maryland, Virginia Tech

APPLICATION PROCESS
Grades with openings (approximate): 6th–10th
Birthday cutoff: N/A
Deadline: December 15 (9th–12th), February 6 (6th–8th)
Fee: $50
Testing required: SSAT or ISEE (6th–8th, 10th–12th), HSPT (9th)
Steps: Shadow visit, application, family interview

COSTS
Tuition: $19,840 (6th–8th), $20,580 (9th–12th)
Average additional fees: $250–$500
Financial aid budget: $567,000
Average grant size: $10,000
% of students receiving aid: 55%
Endowment: Yes

NOTE: This data applies to the 2009–2010 school year.

CURRICULUM
Languages and grades offered: French (7th–12th), Latin (6th), Spanish (7th–12th)
AP classes/IB program: 13 AP classes
Tutors/learning specialists: 1 full time, 1 part time
Other resource specialists: Advisory program, college counselor, learning specialist, 2 guidance counselors
Art programs: Art, freshman fine arts rotation, instrumental & vocal jazz ensemble, music theory & history, theater production
Sports: Basketball, cross-country, dance, equestrian, field hockey, lacrosse, soccer, softball, swimming & diving, tennis, track, volleyball
Special features and activities: CYO Annual Girls Basketball Tournament; Penn State Track and Field Relays; Folger Theatre Shakespeare Festival; 17 community-service oriented clubs, including Operation Smile and Cancer Awareness; membership in a consortium of schools offering year-long seminar classes in addition to the school's standard curriculum
Summer programs: Academic enrichment in English and math for incoming freshmen, art, digital photography, lacrosse

CAMPUS LIFE
Transportation available: Ride-On Bus; limited central location pick-up offered
Lunch options: Hot lunch program offered
Food allergy policy: None
Uniform: Yes

CAMPUS
Facilities: 9-acre campus with two buildings
Long-range plans: Auditorium, turf field

HISTORY AND MISSION STATEMENT
Connelly School of the Holy Child is a Catholic, college preparatory school, committed to the intellectual, spiritual, artistic, physical and social development of young women in grades 6–12. The school emphasizes academic challenge, joy of learning, and the education of well-rounded women of faith and action. The Holy Child community welcomes students and families of different faiths and diverse backgrounds. In keeping with the traditions of our founder Cornelia Connelly, Holy Child values the uniqueness of each individual and fosters a life of service to others.

NOTE: This data applies to the 2009–2010 school year.

THE DIENER SCHOOL   est. 2007

Jillian Copeland, Director
11510 Falls Road
Potomac, MD 20854
301-299-4602
www.thedienerschool.org

Lois McCabe, Director of Admissions
admissions@thedienerschool.org

Coed: K–5th
Limited wheelchair access

Governance: Nonprofit
Accredited by: NAPSEC
Memberships: MANSEF
Religious affiliation: Nonsectarian

PROFILE
Total enrollment: 25
Graduating class size: N/A
Average class size: 8 or fewer
Number of faculty: 19
Boarding option: No
School day: 8:30–2:45
Extended day hours: 8:30–4:00
Schools three or more graduates have attended over the past five years: N/A

APPLICATION PROCESS
Grades with openings (approximate): All
Birthday cutoff: September
Deadline: End of January
Fee: $100
Testing required: Extensive battery of testing
Steps: Application, school visit

COSTS
Tuition: $34,000
Average additional fees: For after-school care and after-school activities
Financial aid budget: Varies
Average grant size: Partial scholarship available
% of students receiving aid: N/A
Endowment: N/A

NOTE: This data applies to the 2009–2010 school year.

CURRICULUM

Languages and grades offered: None
AP classes/IB program: N/A
Tutors/learning specialists: 1
Other resource specialists: Behaviorist, occupational therapist, speech therapist
Art programs: Art, drama, music
Sports: Fitness program, yoga
Special features and activities: All therapies, including speech therapy, occupational therapy, and academic tutoring, included in tuition
Summer programs: N/A

CAMPUS LIFE

Transportation available: None
Lunch options: None
Food allergy policy: No nuts
Uniform: No

CAMPUS

Facilities: N/A
Long-range plans: Adding 5th grade in fall 2009; possibly add 6th in 2010

HISTORY AND MISSION STATEMENT

The Diener School provides a developmental, educational, and therapeutic environment for students requiring smaller class sizes and individualized attention. Students learn experientially, with much repetition, through a variety of multi-sensory, collaborative approaches. The cornerstone of the Diener School, the "Diener Pyramid of Learning for the Whole Child," provides our students with a holistic approach that promotes academics; cognitive functions; constructive social, language, and sensory experiences; and real-life organizational skills. The faculty, in concert with experts in all disciplines, works collaboratively to create a nurturing yet challenging environment empowering children to think independently and have a strong sense of self and spirit.

NOTE: This data applies to the 2009–2010 school year.

EDLIN SCHOOL   est. 1989

Linda Schreibstein, Director
10742 Sunset Hills Road
Reston, VA 20190
703-438-3990
www.edlinschool.com

Linda Schreibstein
director@edlinschool.com

Coed: PK–8th
Wheelchair accessible

Governance: Proprietary
Accredited by: N/A
Memberships: N/A
Religious affiliation: Nonsectarian

PROFILE
Total enrollment: 200
Graduating class size: 15
Average class size: 15
Number of faculty: 30
Boarding option: No
School day: 8:45–3:15
Extended day hours: 7:30–6:00
Schools three or more graduates have attended over the past five years: Bishop O'Connell, Flint Hill, Foxcroft, Gonzaga, Madeira, Paul VI, public school IB programs, Thomas Jefferson

APPLICATION PROCESS
Grades with openings (approximate): K, plus limited openings in other grades
Birthday cutoff: Case by case
Deadline: Rolling
Fee: $75
Testing required: WISC-IV (1st–8th)
Steps: Applicant visit, application

COSTS
Tuition: $15,000
Average additional fees: $300
Financial aid budget: N/A
Average grant size: Case-by-case basis
% of students receiving aid: 5%
Endowment: No

NOTE: This data applies to the 2009–2010 school year.

PRESCHOOL PROGRAM

Age	Days	Hours	Tuition	Openings	Class size	Teachers per class	Food provided
4	5	8:45–3:15	$15,000				

CURRICULUM

Languages and grades offered: French, Latin, Spanish (PK–8th)
AP classes/IB program: N/A
Tutors/learning specialists: As required for children who are academically advanced
Other resource specialists: Computer science
Art programs: Art, computer animation, digital photography, drama, music, studio art
Sports: Basketball, field hockey, lacrosse, soccer
Special features and activities: AMC-8 (Math Olympiad), aviation technology, MathCounts, Science Olympiad
Summer programs: Yes—see website

CAMPUS LIFE

Transportation available: Yes
Lunch options: Purchased lunches available daily
Food allergy policy: As required
Uniform: Yes

CAMPUS

Facilities: 5-acre sylvan campus convenient to Dulles Toll Road; computer labs, gym, playground, science labs, sports field
Long-range plans: Sports field expansion

HISTORY AND MISSION STATEMENT

Edlin School provides a gifted education for bright children who are eager to learn. Edlin is a school that defies the tradition-expected idea of student-teacher relationships. It engenders laughter and excitement for learning. Bright students can explore new ideas and challenge old ideas. We offer the opportunity to excel in a small, non-pressured, friendly and respectful community. Children are placed at their learning levels within each grade. We have no ceiling on how high children can be placed.

NOTE: This data applies to the 2009–2010 school year.

EDMUND BURKE SCHOOL   est. 1968

David Shapiro, Head of School
4101 Connecticut Avenue, NW
Washington, DC 20008
202-362-8882 x670
www.eburke.org

Kai-Anasa George, Director of Admissions
kai_george@eburke.org

Coed: 6th–12th
Limited wheelchair access

Governance: Nonprofit
Accredited by: MSA
Memberships: AIMS, AISGW, NAIS, PEN
Religious affiliation: Nonsectarian

PROFILE

Total enrollment: 310
Graduating class size: 65
Average class size: 15
Number of faculty: 70
Boarding option: No
School day: 8:00–2:50 (6th–8th), 8:15–3:30 (9th–12th)
Extended day hours: 8:00–6:00 (6th–8th)
Schools three or more graduates have attended over the past five years: Brown, Colby, Dartmouth, George Washington, Georgetown, Kenyon, New York University, Oberlin

APPLICATION PROCESS

Grades with openings (approximate): 6th (15), 7th (15), 9th (25)
Birthday cutoff: September 1
Deadline: January 15
Fee: $60
Testing required: SSAT or ISEE (6th–12th)
Steps: Tour, online inquiry, application, shadow visit, interview

COSTS

Tuition: $28,110
Average additional fees: $115–$250
Financial aid budget: $1.1M
Average grant size: $15,000
% of students receiving aid: 22%
Endowment: Yes

NOTE: This data applies to the 2009–2010 school year.

CURRICULUM

Languages and grades offered: French, Latin, Spanish (6th–12th)

AP classes/IB program: 12 AP classes

Tutors/learning specialists: 2

Other resource specialists: N/A

Art programs: Acting, ceramics, drama, drawing, instrumental & vocal music, mixed media, painting, photography, playwriting, sculpture, theater production, video production

Sports: Basketball, cross-country, dance team, golf, polar bear running, soccer, softball, swimming, track & field, volleyball, wrestling

Special features and activities: N/A

Summer programs: Yes, various

CAMPUS LIFE

Transportation available: Two blocks from Van Ness metro station

Lunch options: Bring from home or purchase at school

Food allergy policy: None

Uniform: No

CAMPUS

Facilities: Art room, ceramics studio, 2 computer labs, digital media suite, gym, library, 5 science labs, theater

Long-range plans: N/A

HISTORY AND MISSION STATEMENT

Edmund Burke School is a challenging and empowering school that offers rigorous academic and arts curricula. Burke consciously brings together students who are different from one another in many ways, affords students respect for who they are, places them at the center of their education and gives them power and responsibility. Our students grow into young women and men who have the skill and determination to make positive contributions to the worlds in which they live.

NOTE: This data applies to the 2009–2010 school year.

EMERSON PREPARATORY SCHOOL   est. 1852

John Morris Glick, Head of School
1324 18th Street, NW
Washington, DC 20036
202-785-2877
www.emersonprep.net

John Morris Glick
john.glick@emersonprep.net

Coed: 9th–12th
No wheelchair access

Governance: Nonprofit
Accredited by: DC Board of Education
Memberships: N/A
Religious affiliation: Nonsectarian

PROFILE
Total enrollment: 75
Graduating class size: 20
Average class size: 8
Number of faculty: 9
Boarding option: No
School day: 8:15–3:30
Extended day hours: 7:30–5:00
Schools three or more graduates have attended over the past five years: American University, Eugene Lang College, George Washington, Goucher College, St. John's College (MD), University of Maryland, Wheaton College

APPLICATION PROCESS
Grades with openings (approximate): All
Birthday cutoff: N/A
Deadline: Rolling
Fee: $75
Testing required: None
Steps: Interview and tour, shadow visit, application

COSTS
Tuition: $20,000
Average additional fees: $300–$1,500
Financial aid budget: N/A
Average grant size: N/A
% of students receiving aid: N/A
Endowment: N/A

NOTE: This data applies to the 2009–2010 school year.

CURRICULUM

Languages and grades offered: Arabic, French, Italian, Japanese, Spanish (9th–12th)

AP classes/IB program: AP classes vary by need

Tutors/learning specialists: Varies according to need

Other resource specialists: N/A

Art programs: N/A

Sports: N/A

Special features and activities: Purely academic curriculum, unusually flexible scheduling, maximum of four 90-minute classes per day; inspiring field trips and after-school clubs; unique opportunity to complete high school within three school years

Summer programs: Six-week academic program for high school credit

CAMPUS LIFE

Transportation available: Easily accessible by Metro Red Line and Metro Bus

Lunch options: 1-hour open lunch period; numerous restaurants and carry-outs in the area

Food allergy policy: N/A

Uniform: No

CAMPUS

Facilities: Vibrant Dupont Circle location; 9 classrooms, computer lab, conference room, courtyard, reading room, science laboratory

Long-range plans: Expansion of enrollment to 170 over the next five years; development of an integrated internship program for students of all four grades; participation in IB program beginning in 2010

HISTORY AND MISSION STATEMENT

Emerson Preparatory School was founded in 1852. In 1946, the school adopted its purely academic program. At Emerson, classes begin and are completed in a single four-and-one-half-month term, allowing students to satisfy the required number of credits for graduation within three school years. Following graduation, 95% of students attend a four-year college, and 5% attend a two-year college or take a gap year before entering college.

Emerson offers a challenging and intellectually stimulating curriculum in an informal atmosphere. We value the uniqueness of each individual student and welcome the diversity that they create.

NOTE: This data applies to the 2009–2010 school year.

EPISCOPAL HIGH SCHOOL   est. 1839

F. Robertson Hershey, Headmaster
1200 North Quaker Lane
Alexandria, VA 22301
703-933-4062
www.episcopalhighschool.org

Emily M. Atkinson, Director of Admissions
admissions@episcopalhighschool.org

Coed: 9th–12th
Limited wheelchair access

Governance: Nonprofit
Accredited by: SACS, VAIS
Memberships: AISGW, NAES, NAIS, TABS
Religious affiliation: Episcopal

PROFILE
Total enrollment: 435
Graduating class size: 120
Average class size: 12
Number of faculty: 85
Boarding option: Yes, 100%
School day: N/A
Extended day hours: N/A
Schools three or more graduates have attended over the past five years: Boston College, Brown, Davidson, Duke, Harvard, Princeton, University of North Carolina, University of Virginia, Vanderbilt, William and Mary

APPLICATION PROCESS
Grades with openings (approximate): 9th (80–90), 10th (25–30), 11th (5–10)
Birthday cutoff: N/A
Deadline: January 31
Fee: $50 (domestic), $100 (international)
Testing required: SSAT, ISEE, or PSAT
Steps: Application, on-campus interview

COSTS
Tuition: $40,875
Average additional fees: $600
Financial aid budget: $3.6M
Average grant size: $24,937
% of students receiving aid: 30%
Endowment: Yes

NOTE: This data applies to the 2009–2010 school year.

CURRICULUM

Languages and grades offered: Chinese, French, German (9th–12th); Greek (2 years); Latin, Spanish (9th–12th)

AP classes/IB program: 24 AP classes

Tutors/learning specialists: Yes, learning specialists

Other resource specialists: N/A

Art programs: Ceramics, choir, dance, drama, music theory, orchestra, photography, visual arts

Sports: Aerobics, baseball, basketball, crew, cross-country, field hockey, football, golf, lacrosse, soccer, softball, tennis, track, volleyball, wrestling

Special features and activities: N/A

Summer programs: Academic and athletic camps

CAMPUS LIFE

Transportation available: None

Lunch options: Full food service

Food allergy policy: None

Uniform: Dress code

CAMPUS

Facilities: 130 acres; 30 buildings, 45 classrooms, 8 dormitories, athletics fields, chapel, 2 gymnasiums, indoor field house, library, outdoor pool, 5 squash courts, 12 tennis courts; new arts and science centers

Long-range plans: Classroom and library renovations, new athletic complex

HISTORY AND MISSION STATEMENT

Episcopal High School fosters empathy and responsibility for self and others through a commitment to spiritual inquiry and growth in a fully residential community. Students are encouraged to think creatively, work collaboratively, develop individual passions, and celebrate the talents of others.

Sharing diverse life experiences, ideas, and values, students learn humility, resilience, and mutual respect. Through access to the educational and cultural resources of the nation's capital, students are inspired to understand and embrace a changing world.

Episcopal strives to prepare young people to become discerning individuals with the intellectual and moral courage to lead principled lives of leadership and service.

NOTE: This data applies to the 2009–2010 school year.

EVERGREEN SCHOOL   est. 1964

Marcia Jacques
10700 Georgia Avenue
Wheaton, MD 20902
301-942-5979
www.evergreenschool.com

Lorie Allion
admissions@evergreenschool.com

Coed: N–6th
No wheelchair access

Governance: Nonprofit
Accredited by: AIMS
Memberships: N/A
Religious affiliation: Nonsectarian

PROFILE
Total enrollment: 73
Graduating class size: N/A
Average class size: 17
Number of faculty: 11
Boarding option: No
School day: 8:30–3:00
Extended day hours: 7:30–6:00
Schools three or more graduates have attended over the past five years: N/A

APPLICATION PROCESS
Grades with openings (approximate): All
Birthday cutoff: Must be 2.5 to attend
Deadline: Rolling
Fee: $75
Testing required: None
Steps: Application, interview/visit

COSTS
Tuition: $13,600 (K–6th)
Average additional fees: N/A
Financial aid budget: N/A
Average grant size: N/A
% of students receiving aid: N/A
Endowment: No

NOTE: This data applies to the 2009–2010 school year.

PRESCHOOL PROGRAM

Age	Days	Hours	Tuition	Openings	Class size	Teachers per class	Food provided
2.5–6	5	8:30–12:00	$8,800		17	2	None
2.5–6	5	8:30–3:00	$13,050		17	2	None

CURRICULUM

Languages and grades offered: Spanish
AP classes/IB program: N/A
Tutors/learning specialists: None
Other resource specialists: Music, PE, Spanish
Art programs: N/A
Sports: N/A
Special features and activities: Small group and individual instruction, Montessori program
Summer programs: Camp, Montessori enrichment

CAMPUS LIFE

Transportation available: None
Lunch options: Students bring their own lunches
Food allergy policy: N/A
Uniform: No

CAMPUS

Facilities: Computer lab, library, playground
Long-range plans: N/A

HISTORY AND MISSION STATEMENT

N/A

NOTE: This data applies to the 2009–2010 school year.

THE FIELD SCHOOL   est. 1972

Dale Johnson, Head of School
2301 Foxhall Road, NW
Washington, DC 20007
202-295-5839
www.fieldschool.org

Will Layman, Director of Admissions
willl@fieldschool.org

Coed: 7th–12th
Wheelchair accessible

Governance: Nonprofit
Accredited by: MSA
Memberships: AISGW, NAIS, NCISR
Religious affiliation: Nonsectarian

PROFILE

Total enrollment: 320
Graduating class size: 61
Average class size: 11
Number of faculty: 53
Boarding option: No
School day: 8:00–2:45 (7th–8th), 8:50–2:45 (9th–12th)
Extended day hours: 8:00–6:15
Schools three or more graduates have attended over the past five years: Barnard, Colorado College, Columbia, Guilford College, Kenyon, New York University, Pitzer College, Reed, University of Pennsylvania, Wesleyan

APPLICATION PROCESS

Grades with openings (approximate): 7th (30), 9th (35), plus attrition
Birthday cutoff: N/A
Deadline: January 15
Fee: $80
Testing required: SSAT or WISC-IV (7th–12th)
Steps: Parent tour or open house, online application, student visit and interview

COSTS

Tuition: $30,150
Average additional fees: $300
Financial aid budget: $1.2M
Average grant size: $20,000
% of students receiving aid: 18%
Endowment: No

NOTE: This data applies to the 2009–2010 school year.

CURRICULUM

Languages and grades offered: French, Latin, Spanish (7th–12th)

AP classes/IB program: None

Tutors/learning specialists: N/A

Other resource specialists: School psychologist

Art programs: Acting, ceramics/sculpture, digital arts, drawing/painting/printmaking, music, musical theater, photography, publication arts (journalism/yearbook)

Sports: Baseball, basketball, cross-country, dance, golf, lacrosse, soccer, softball, swimming, tennis, track & field, volleyball, ultimate Frisbee

Special features and activities: Two-week winter internship program, daily instruction in the arts for every student at every grade, no-cut athletics for every student at every grade, small class size, exceptional range of activities

Summer programs: Arts, remedial tutoring

CAMPUS LIFE

Transportation available: Shuttle buses to and from Metro

Lunch options: Two menus provided daily

Food allergy policy: None

Uniform: No

CAMPUS

Facilities: New campus as of 2002, including 5 science labs, darkroom, pottery studio with full-sized kiln, music room and recording studio, media center, 2 computer labs, gymnasium, turf playing field (new in 2007), locker rooms, all built around a 1930s Art Moderne mansion on 10.5 acres in northwest DC.

Long-range plans: N/A

HISTORY AND MISSION STATEMENT

Founded in 1972 around the animating principle of small class size (average: 11) and individual attention to students, The Field School makes school a joyful experience. Informal instruction combines with traditional curriculum to create students who are exceptional writers, thinkers, problem-solvers, and citizens.

Our Mission:
Self-Discovery
Skills of Mind
Generosity of Heart

NOTE: This data applies to the 2009–2010 school year.

FLINT HILL SCHOOL   est. 1956

John M. Thomas, Headmaster
3320 Jermantown Road
Oakton, VA 22124
703-584-2300
www.flinthill.org

Stacey Ahner, Director of Admission
sahner@flinthill.org

Coed: JK–12th
Limited wheelchair access
JK–8th: 10409 Academic Drive, Oakton, VA

Governance: Nonprofit
Accredited by: VAIS
Memberships: CASE, VAIS
Religious affiliation: Nonsectarian

PROFILE

Total enrollment: 1,100
Graduating class size: 130
Average class size: 18
Number of faculty: 142
Boarding option: No
School day: 8:10–3:00 (1st–4th), 7:50–3:30 (5th–8th); 8:00–3:00 (9th–12th)
Extended day hours: 7:50–6:00
Schools three or more graduates have attended over the past five years: Christopher Newport, George Mason, George Washington, James Madison, Penn State, Radford, Syracuse, University of Virginia, Virginia Tech, William and Mary

APPLICATION PROCESS

Grades with openings (approximate): K (34), 4th (11), 7th (14), 9th (32), 10th (6), 11th (2), 12th (5)
Birthday cutoff: None
Deadline: January 30; rolling
Application fee: $75
Testing required: WPPSI-III/WISC-IV (K–5th), SSAT (6th–12th)
Steps: Open house, online application, parent interview, student visit and evaluation

COSTS

Tuition: $24,050–$27,510
Average additional fees: N/A
Financial aid budget: $2.5M
Average grant size: $15,725
% of students receiving aid: 14%
Endowment: Yes

NOTE: This data applies to the 2009–2010 school year.

PRESCHOOL PROGRAM

Age	Days	Hours	Tuition	Openings	Class size	Teachers per class	Food provided
4	5	8:10–3:00	$21,370	18	18	2	Snack; lunch can be purchased

CURRICULUM

Languages and grades offered: Chinese (7th–12th), French (8th–12th), Spanish (PK–12th)

AP classes/IB program: 22 AP classes

Tutors/learning specialists: 11

Other resource specialists: Counselors, differentiated specialists, full-time nurse practitioner and RN, technology

Art programs: Art, band, dance, drama, digital art, music, orchestra

Sports: Baseball, basketball, cross-country, dance, football, golf, lacrosse, soccer, softball, swimming, tennis, track & field, volleyball

Special features and activities: Senior project and presentation, experiential education

Summer programs: Academics, creative arts, day camps, enrichment, sports, trips

CAMPUS LIFE

Transportation available: 7 bus routes, at additional fee

Lunch options: Included in tuition (9th–12th)

Food allergy policy: Parents submit Allergy Action Plan; faculty and staff trained in use of EpiPen

Uniform: Yes (JK–8th), strict dress code (9th–12th)

CAMPUS

Facilities: 2 campuses on 45 acres; art, dance & music studios; athletic fields, 2 gyms, 8 tennis courts, track; fully networked classrooms; computer, language & science labs; libraries, learning & media centers, theater

Long-range plans: Refurbish Lower & Middle School

HISTORY AND MISSION STATEMENT

Flint Hill School welcomes and values individuals from all backgrounds. Our personalized, innovative, stimulating learning environment challenges students to achieve their unique potential. We focus on our students—one child at a time. Academic instruction is integrated with character education; wide-ranging choices in arts and athletics allow students to find and develop potential lifelong passions.

NOTE: This data applies to the 2009–2010 school year.

THE FOURTH PRESBYTERIAN SCHOOL   est. 1999

John A. Murray, Headmaster
10701 South Glen Road
Potomac, MD 20854
301-765-8132
www.fourthschool.org

Ani Law, Director of Admissions
alaw@fourthschool.org

Coed: PK–7th
Limited wheelchair access

Governance: Nonprofit
Accredited by: N/A
Memberships: AIMS
Religious affiliation: Presbyterian

PROFILE
Total enrollment: 111
Graduating class size: 7
Average class size: 13
Number of faculty: 18
Boarding option: No
School day: 8:00–3:00
Extended day hours: 8:00–6:00
**Schools three or more graduates
have attended over the past five
years:** Bullis, Landon, Montgomery
County Public Schools, Potomac,
St. Andrew's Episcopal, Stone
Ridge, Washington Christian
Academy

APPLICATION PROCESS
Grades with openings (approximate):
K (2), 1st (4), 2nd (5), 3rd (3), 4th
(6), 5th (1), 7th (12)
Birthday cutoff: September 1
Deadline: Mid-February
Fee: $100 (PK–K), $300 (1st–7th)
Testing required: In-house (PK–K),
WJ-III (1st–7th, included in applica-
tion fee), TOWL-3 (6th–7th)
Steps: Open house, classroom obser-
vation, application, interview

COSTS
Tuition: $12,500 (K–7th)
Average additional fees: N/A
Financial aid budget: $300,000
Average grant size: $6,380
% of students receiving aid: 30%
Endowment: Yes

NOTE: This data applies to the 2009–2010 school year.

PRESCHOOL PROGRAM

Age	Days	Hours	Tuition	Openings	Class size	Teachers per class	Food provided
4	5	8:00–11:30	$5,950	13	16	2	Snack

CURRICULUM
Languages and grades offered: Latin (4th–7th), Spanish (K–7th)
AP classes/IB program: N/A
Tutors/learning specialists: 1
Other resource specialists: N/A
Art programs: Visual arts
Sports: Basketball, cross-country, soccer
Special features and activities: Morning assemblies, "Friday Finales" (themed monthly community-building events), PK "Lunch Bunch" extended day option, Honor Code Service, Math Night, Young Authors Teas, Operation Christmas Child Dedication Assembly, The Fourth School Run, Scripps Spelling Bee, National Geography Bee, book clubs, recycling team
Summer programs: N/A

CAMPUS LIFE
Transportation available: N/A
Lunch options: Hot lunch option 3 days per week
Food allergy policy: None
Uniform: Yes

CAMPUS
Facilities: 32 wooded acres; media center, Weather Bug, wireless networked campus
Long-range plans: Add 8th grade in 2010; AISGW and NAIS application to begin 2009–10, AIMS accreditation in process; currently in development: football & lacrosse programs, new facility and playing fields, transportation plan

HISTORY AND MISSION STATEMENT
Founded in 1999, The Fourth School is an independent coeducational day school dedicated to providing students with an excellent college preparatory education within a safe, nurturing environment. As a Christ-centered, academically challenging school, we are committed to preparing young men and women for college and life by providing opportunities to excel in the vital areas of faith, virtue and knowledge.

NOTE: This data applies to the 2009–2010 school year.

FOXCROFT SCHOOL   est. 1914

Mary Louise Leipheimer, Head of School
22407 Foxhound Lane
Middleburg, VA 20117
540-687-4340
www.foxcroft.org

Erica L. Ohanesian, Director of Admission & Financial Aid
eohanesian@foxcroft.org

Girls: 9th–12th
No wheelchair access

Governance: Nonprofit
Accredited by: VAIS
Memberships: AISGW, NAIS, NCGS, SBSA, SSATB, TABS, VAIS
Religious affiliation: Nonsectarian

PROFILE
Total enrollment: 185
Graduating class size: 44
Average class size: 10
Number of faculty: 48
Boarding option: Yes, 79%
School day: 8:00–3:15
Extended day hours: Athletics meet after school Monday–Friday
Schools three or more graduates have attended over the past five years: College of Charleston, Davidson College, Duke, Elon, James Madison, Johns Hopkins, Rhodes College, George Washington, University of Virginia, William and Mary

APPLICATION PROCESS
Grades with openings (approximate):
9th (45), 10th (15), 11th (5)
Birthday cutoff: N/A
Deadline: February 15
Fee: $50 (domestic), $150 (international)
Testing required: SSAT (9th–12th), TOEFL if applicable
Steps: Interview/campus tour, application

COSTS
Tuition: $40,950 (boarding), $30,712 (day)
Average additional fees: $300–$600
Financial aid budget: $1.3M
Average grant size: $27,855
% of students receiving aid: 24%
Endowment: Yes

NOTE: This data applies to the 2009–2010 school year.

CURRICULUM

Languages and grades offered: French, Latin, Spanish

AP classes/IB program: 16 AP classes

Tutors/learning specialists: 13

Other resource specialists: N/A

Art programs: Art studio, "Bach, Beethoven and The Boyz," basic acting, ceramics, chorale, digital graphic design & publishing, drawing & design, history of rock music, Intro to the Arts, music ensemble, music theory, painting, photography, public speaking, technical theater, theater audition workshop, theater production, vocal/instrumental lessons

Sports: Basketball, core conditioning, cross-country, dance/cheer, field hockey, golf, lacrosse, riding, soccer, softball, swimming, tennis, total fitness, volleyball, yoga

Special features and activities: 2-week Interim program built around a social/cultural theme; lectures/seminars from artists, performers, scientists, public figures; students from 22 states and 8 countries

Summer programs: Day and residential camp for children 5–14; soccer; equine rescue training program; Science Research Institute, offering the opportunity to do groundbreaking research in molecular biology

CAMPUS LIFE

Transportation available: To and from airports/train station at school vacations at a per-trip rate; no daily transportation for day students

Lunch options: Hot and cold options included in tuition

Food allergy policy: Case-by-case basis

Uniform: Dress code

CAMPUS

Facilities: 500-acre campus; gym/activities center, indoor and outdoor riding facilities, 50,000-volume library, observatory, pool, 5 athletic fields, 8 tennis courts

Long-range plans: By 2014: new residence hall, Activities Center; renovated Athletics Center, dormitories; Visual & Performing Arts Center

HISTORY AND MISSION STATEMENT

Foxcroft was founded in 1914 by Charlotte Haxall Noland. Miss Charlotte, as she was called by the students, valued determination, courage, and character. She sought to establish a school that would instill in its graduates high purpose, leadership, integrity, and understanding—at the same time as it provided a community and experience that the students would love. The motto Miss Charlotte chose for Foxcroft—*mens sana in corpore sano* ("a sound mind in a healthy body"), her values and her spirit continue to influence the school today.

NOTE: This data applies to the 2009–2010 school year.

FRENCH INTERNATIONAL SCHOOL (LYCEE ROCHAMBEAU)   est. 1955

Gilles Joseph, Headmaster
9600 Forest Road
Bethesda, MD 20814
301-530-8260
www.rochambeau.org

Agnes Finucan
finucana@rochambeau.org

Coed: N–12th
Limited wheelchair access
N–K: 7108 Bradley Blvd., Bethesda, MD, 301-767-1683
1st–4th: 3200 Woodbine Street, Chevy Chase, MD, 301-907-3265

Governance: Nonprofit
Accredited by: French Ministry of Education, MSDE
Memberships: N/A
Religious affiliation: Nonsectarian

PROFILE
Total enrollment: 1,100
Graduating class size: 110
Average class size: 20
Number of faculty: 200
Boarding option: No
School day: 8:30–3:15 (1st–5th), 8:30–5:30 (6th–12th)
Extended day hours: 8:30–5:30
Schools three or more graduates have attended over the past five years: North American and European universities

APPLICATION PROCESS
Grades with openings (approximate): All
Birthday cutoff: December 31
Deadline: Rolling
Fee: $800
Testing required: None
Steps: Informal assessment

COSTS
Tuition: $11,717 (1st–5th), $13,270 (6th–9th), $15,190 (10th–12th)
Average additional fees: $400
Financial aid budget: $100,000
Average grant size: N/A
% of students receiving aid: N/A
Endowment: No

NOTE: This data applies to the 2009–2010 school year.

PRESCHOOL PROGRAM

Age	Days	Hours	Tuition	Openings	Class size	Teachers per class	Food provided
3	5	9:00–3:00	$13,150		20	1+	None
4	5	9:00–3:00	$13,150		20	1+	None

CURRICULUM

Languages and grades offered: German, Italian, Latin, Spanish (8th–12th)
AP classes/IB program: IB program
Tutors/learning specialists: Yes
Other resource specialists: N/A
Art programs: N/A
Sports: Basketball, soccer, swimming, volleyball
Special features and activities: Students educated in the French system are admitted as space permits. All classes are taught in French except English and U.S. History.
Summer programs: None

CAMPUS LIFE

Transportation available: Yes
Lunch options: None
Food allergy policy: N/A
Uniform: No

CAMPUS

Facilities: 3 campuses
Long-range plans: N/A

HISTORY AND MISSION STATEMENT

Offers French educational curriculum with French Baccalauréat exam, and qualifies students for high school diplomas and entrance to North American universities.

NOTE: This data applies to the 2009–2010 school year.

GEORGETOWN DAY SCHOOL   est. 1945

Peter Branch, Head of School
4200 Davenport Street, NW
Washington, DC 20016
202-274-3210
www.gds.org

Vince Rowe, Director of Enrollment Management and Financial Aid
vrowe@gds.org

Coed: PK–12th
Wheelchair accessible
PK–8th: 4530 MacArthur Boulevard NW, Washington, DC, 202-295-1078

Governance: Nonprofit
Accredited by: AIMS, NAIS
Memberships: AIMS, AISGW, NAIS
Religious affiliation: Nonsectarian

PROFILE
Total enrollment: 1,040
Graduating class size: 115
Average class size: N/A
Number of faculty: 205
Boarding option: No
School day: 8:00–3:00 (K–8th),
8:15–3:15 (9th–12th)
Extended day hours: 8:00–6:00
Schools three or more graduates
have attended over the past five
years: Brown, Duke, Emory,
Harvard, Stanford, Tufts,
University of Michigan, University
of Pennsylvania, University of
Virginia, Yale

APPLICATION PROCESS
Grades with openings (approximate):
K (20), 1st (8–10), 3rd (8–12), 4th
(8–12), 6th (8–12), 7th (8–12), 9th
(35–40)
Birthday cutoff: June 1 (guideline)
Deadline: January 15
Fee: $65
Testing required: WPPSI-III/WISC-IV
(PK–5th), SSAT or ISEE (6th–12th)
Application steps: N/A

COSTS
Tuition: $26,185–$29,895
Average additional fees: $500
Financial aid budget: $3.3M
Average grant size: $14,000
% of students receiving aid: 18%
Endowment: Yes

NOTE: This data applies to the 2009–2010 school year.

PRESCHOOL PROGRAM

Age	Days	Hours	Tuition	Openings	Class size	Teachers per class	Food provided
4 (PK)	5	8:00–3:00	$26,185	20			None

CURRICULUM

Languages and grades offered: Arabic (7th–12th), Chinese (9th–12th), French (3rd–12th), Latin (6th–12th), Spanish (3rd–12th)

AP classes/IB program: 20 AP classes

Tutors/learning specialists: 5

Other resource specialists: N/A

Art programs: Performing and studio arts

Sports: Baseball, basketball, crew, cross-country, golf, lacrosse, soccer, softball, tennis, track, volleyball, wrestling

Special features and activities: N/A

Summer programs: See www.gds.org/programs

CAMPUS LIFE

Transportation available: School buses for sports and special trips

Lunch options: Parents provide lunch

Food allergy policy: N/A

Uniform: No

CAMPUS

Facilities: Two 5-acre campuses with athletic fields and black box theaters

Long-range plans: N/A

HISTORY AND MISSION STATEMENT

Georgetown Day School honors the integrity and worth of each individual within a diverse school community. GDS is dedicated to providing a supportive educational atmosphere in which teachers challenge the intellectual, creative, and physical abilities of our students and foster strength of character and concern for others. From the earliest grades, we encourage our students to wonder, to inquire, to be self-reliant, laying the foundation for a lifelong love of learning.

NOTE: This data applies to the 2009–2010 school year.

GEORGETOWN PREPARATORY SCHOOL   est. 1789

Reverend William L. George, President
10900 Rockville Pike
North Bethesda, MD 20852
301-214-1215
www.gprep.org

Brian J. Gilbert, Dean of Admissions
bgilbert@gprep.org

Boys: 9th–12th
Limited wheelchair access

Governance: Nonprofit
Accredited by: MSA
Memberships: AIMS, AISGW, CBSA, IBSC, JSEA, NAIS, TABS
Religious affiliation: Roman Catholic, Jesuit

PROFILE
Total enrollment: 466
Graduating class size: 115
Average class size: 16
Number of faculty: 52
Boarding option: Yes
School day: 8:15–2:50
Extended day hours: N/A
Schools three or more graduates have attended over the past five years: Boston College, Cornell, Georgetown, Harvard, Notre Dame, Princeton, Stanford, University of California–Berkeley, University of Pennsylvania, University of Virginia

APPLICATION PROCESS
Grades with openings (approximate):
9th (91 day, 24 boarding),
10th–11th (5 boarding)
Birthday cutoff: 12th grade: 19 after August 31 to play sports
Deadline: January 15
Fee: $50 (domestic);
$100 (international)
Testing required: SSAT, TOEFL if applicable
Steps: Online application, interview

COSTS
Tuition: $24,200 (day), $42,150 (boarding)
Average additional fees: $5,000
Financial aid budget: $2M
Average grant size: $19,000
% of students receiving aid: 25%
Endowment: Yes

NOTE: This data applies to the 2009–2010 school year.

CURRICULUM
Languages and grades offered: French, German, Greek, Latin, Mandarin Chinese, Spanish (9th–12th)
AP classes/IB program: 24 AP classes
Tutors/learning specialists: 3
Other resource specialists: N/A
Art programs: A cappella group, art, choir, digital photography, drama, drum line, jazz band, orchestra, stained glass studio, string ensemble, visual art
Sports: Baseball, basketball, cross-country, fencing, football, golf, hockey, lacrosse, rugby, soccer, swimming & diving, tennis, track (indoor and outdoor), wrestling
Special features and activities: N/A
Summer programs: Academic courses: ESL, geometry, Greek, Latin, pre-calculus. Athletic camps: baseball, basketball, football, golf, tennis. Cultural exchanges: France, Germany, Japan, Spain. Service trips: Alaska, Appalachia, Argentina (for academic credit), Dominican Republic, New Orleans

CAMPUS LIFE
Transportation available: Grosvenor Metro station ¼ mile from campus; bus from Metro in the morning
Lunch options: Included in tuition: hot lunch, sandwich and salad bars, soup, dessert
Food allergy policy: We accommodate allergies as best we can
Uniform: Dress code

CAMPUS
Facilities: 92-acre campus; athletic center: pool, weight room, wrestling room, indoor track, basketball courts, film room; baseball field, golf course, tennis courts, stadium, chapel, theater, art studio
Long-range plans: Increase endowment, refurbish dorms; learning center with new library, classrooms, student commons and recording studio opening in 2010

HISTORY AND MISSION STATEMENT
Georgetown Preparatory School enjoys the unique distinction of being the oldest of the Catholic preparatory schools in the United States. The first Archbishop of Baltimore, John Carroll, established the "Academy on the Potomack" in 1789, continuing a tradition of Jesuit education in Maryland that dates back to the founding of the colony more than three hundred fifty years ago. As an independent Jesuit day and boarding college preparatory school for young men in grades 9–12, Georgetown Prep's mission is to form men of competence, conscience, courage, and compassion; Men of Faith, Men for Others.

NOTE: This data applies to the 2009–2010 school year.

GEORGETOWN VISITATION PREPARATORY SCHOOL

est. 1799

Daniel M. Kerns, Jr., Head of School
1524 35th Street, NW
Washington, DC 20007
202-337-3350 x2241
www.visi.org

Janet Donnelly Keller, Director of Admissions
jkeller@visi.org

Girls: 9th–12th
Wheelchair accessible

Governance: Nonprofit
Accredited by: MSA
Memberships: AISGW, NAIS, NCEA
Religious affiliation: Roman Catholic

PROFILE

Total enrollment: 480
Graduating class size: 120
Average class size: 15–18
Number of faculty: 47
Boarding option: No
School day: 8:00–3:00
Extended day hours: Campus open for students on weekends and evenings
Schools three or more graduates have attended over the past five years: Boston College, Georgetown, Notre Dame, University of Maryland, University of Virginia

APPLICATION PROCESS

Grades with openings (approximate): 9th (115), plus attrition
Birthday cutoff: N/A
Deadline: December 4, then rolling
Fee: $50
Testing required: HSPT (9th)
Steps: Application, interview

COSTS

Tuition: $20,600
Average additional fees: $700
Financial aid budget: $1.3M
Average grant size: $10,800
% of students receiving aid: 25%
Endowment: Yes

NOTE: This data applies to the 2009–2010 school year.

CURRICULUM

Languages and grades offered: French (9th–12th), Latin (11th–12th), Spanish (9th–12th)

AP classes/IB program: 18 AP classes

Tutors/learning specialists: Director of Learning Support and teacher tutors

Other resource specialists: N/A

Art programs: Art club; chamber, dance, instrumental & orchestra ensembles; chorus; creative writing; fall drama & spring musical; madrigals; guitar, piano, string & vocal studios; studio art

Sports: Basketball, cross-country, diving, field hockey, lacrosse, soccer, softball, swimming, tennis, track & field, volleyball

Special features and activities: Christian service (minimum of 80 hours over 4 years); clubs: Amnesty International, Black Women's Society, Booster Club, Buddies Against Drunk Driving, Christian Action Service Society, French, great books, instrumental music, Kaleidoscope multicultural, math, Model UN, Salesian spirituality, science, ski, Stand Up for Justice, Think Pink, Visitation for Life

Summer programs: Math & English for incoming freshmen, U.S. history

CAMPUS LIFE

Transportation available: Metro

Lunch options: Pre-paid hot lunch, cafeteria

Food allergy policy: None

Uniform: Yes

CAMPUS

Facilities: 23-acre campus in Georgetown with gymnasium and performing arts center

Long-range plans: N/A

HISTORY AND MISSION STATEMENT

Georgetown Visitation, founded in 1799, is a college preparatory school rooted in the Roman Catholic faith and Salesian tradition, committed to educating young women from diverse backgrounds. We are a faith-centered community dedicated to educational excellence enriched by co-curricular and service programs.

Our mission is to empower our students to meet the demands and challenges of today's rapidly changing and morally complex world. We guide our students to become self-reliant, intellectually mature, and morally responsible women of faith, vision, and purpose.

NOTE: This data applies to the 2009–2010 school year.

GERMAN SCHOOL WASHINGTON, DC   est. 1961

Waldemar Grice, Principal
8617 Chateau Drive
Potomac, MD 20854
301-767-3807
www.dswashington.org

Julia Merck-Rocha, Admissions Coordinator
jmerck@dswash.org

Coed: N–12th
Limited wheelchair access

Governance: Nonprofit
Accredited by: German Conference of Ministers of Education
Memberships: AISGW, NAIS
Religious affiliation: Nonsectarian

PROFILE
Total enrollment: 634
Graduating class size: 23
Average class size: 20
Number of faculty: 77
Boarding option: No
School day: 8:10–3:10
Extended day hours: 8:10–5:00
Schools three or more graduates have attended over the past five years: American University, Brown, Duke, Georgetown, Harvard, Johns Hopkins, Stanford, University of Virginia, Yale

APPLICATION PROCESS
Grades with openings (approximate): All
Birthday cutoff: September 1
Deadline: Rolling
Fee: Enrollment fee $600 (N), $2,000 (1st–12th)
Testing required: None
Steps: Open house (N), application, tour/appointment

COSTS
Tuition: $6,540–$11,670
Average additional fees: $3,500
Financial aid budget: N/A
Average grant size: N/A
% of students receiving aid: 6.6%
Endowment: Yes

NOTE: This data applies to the 2009–2010 school year.

CURRICULUM

Languages and grades offered: English (N–12th), French (6th–12th), German (N–12th), Latin (8th–10th), Spanish (6th–12th)

AP classes/IB program: 8 AP classes

Tutors/learning specialists: N/A

Other resource specialists: Counselor, social education worker, special education worker, 2 librarians

Art programs: Art program encompasses a variety of art education classes

Sports: Badminton, basketball, beach volleyball, field hockey, gymnastics, handball, soccer, table tennis, track & field, volleyball

Special features and activities: Some subjects taught bilingual, mandatory swimming classes, lecture series with experts from various fields introducing their professions

Summer programs: None

CAMPUS LIFE

Transportation available: 8 school buses

Lunch options: Home-cooked, nutritious meals served daily in cafeteria. Vegetarian options available.

Food allergy policy: Nut-free policy (N)

Uniform: No

CAMPUS

Facilities: 3 gyms, indoor swimming pool, 2 outdoor soccer fields, beach volleyball field, 2 playgrounds, 2 libraries, computer lab

Long-range plans: N/A

HISTORY AND MISSION STATEMENT

The German School Washington, DC, offers its students a challenging, multi-lingual and cross-cultural learning environment, as well as a strong community committed to social and personal responsibility, integrity, diversity, respect and autonomy. Our teaching philosophy incorporates technological, scientific, cultural, social and pedagogical developments to help our students meet high expectations, reach their fullest potential and become mature global citizens.

NOTE: This data applies to the 2009–2010 school year.

GONZAGA COLLEGE HIGH SCHOOL   est. 1821

Rev. Vince Conti, SJ, Headmaster
19 Eye Street, NW
Washington, DC 20001
202-336-7101
www.gonzaga.org

Andrew C. Battaile, Director of Admission
abattaile@gonzaga.org

Boys: 9th–12th
No wheelchair access

Governance: Nonprofit
Accredited by: MSA
Memberships: AISGW, JSEA, NCEA
Religious affiliation: Roman Catholic

PROFILE
Total enrollment: 945
Graduating class size: 235
Average class size: 24
Number of faculty: 75
Boarding option: No
School day: 8:10–2:45
Extended day hours: N/A
Schools three or more graduates have attended over the past five years: Boston College, College of the Holy Cross, Fordham, Georgetown, Harvard, James Madison, Princeton, U.S. Naval Academy, University of Maryland, University of Virginia

APPLICATION PROCESS
Grades with openings (approximate):
9th (240), 10th (2–7), 11th (2–7)
Birthday cutoff: N/A
Deadline: December 10
Fee: $35
Testing required: HSPT
Steps: Open house, campus visit, application

COSTS
Tuition: $14,850
Average additional fees: $500
Financial aid budget: $1,785,000
Average grant size: $5,500
% of students receiving aid: 33%
Endowment: Yes

NOTE: This data applies to the 2009–2010 school year.

CURRICULUM

Languages and grades offered: Chinese, French, German (9th–12th); Greek (10th–12th); Latin, Spanish (9th–12th)

AP classes/IB program: 27 AP classes

Tutors/learning specialists: N/A

Other resource specialists: Full library staff

Art programs: Band, choral arts, drama (club), television communications, visual & photographic arts

Sports: Baseball, basketball, crew, cross-country, football, golf, ice hockey, indoor track, lacrosse, rugby, soccer, squash, swimming & diving, tennis, track & field, water polo, wrestling

Special features and activities: Local, national and international community service programs; retreat program; over fifty academic and extracurricular clubs

Summer programs: Freshman transition workshop; summer enrichment classes; basketball, football, lacrosse, rugby, and soccer camps

CAMPUS LIFE

Transportation available: Metro and Metro Bus

Lunch options: Full-service cafeteria

Food allergy policy: N/A

Uniform: No

CAMPUS

Facilities: 6 blocks from our nation's Capitol building in the heart of Washington; campus comprised of 8 buildings on one square city block; St. Aloysius Church, state-of-the-art science and computer labs, classrooms, lecture hall, gymnasium, synthetic turf athletic field, assigned parking for faculty and students

Long-range plans: N/A

HISTORY AND MISSION STATEMENT

Founded in 1821, Gonzaga is a Catholic college preparatory school for boys founded by the Society of Jesus (Jesuits). Gonzaga offers a values-oriented and academically challenging curriculum to young men of diverse backgrounds from all over the Washington metropolitan area. The urban setting allows its students to interact with the larger Washington community and to learn leadership skills and civic responsibility as part of their overall development. The school strives to create a dynamic and caring learning environment which it unites with its academic, extra-curricular and athletic programs to help form Men for Others, that is, graduates who are open to growth, intellectually competent, religious, loving, and committed to doing justice.

NOTE: This data applies to the 2009–2010 school year.

GRACE EPISCOPAL DAY SCHOOL — est. 1960

Carol Franek, Head of School
9115 Georgia Avenue
Silver Spring, MD 20910
301-585-3513 x18
www.geds.org

Courtney Hundley, Director of Admission & Financial Aid
chundley@geds.org

Coed: N–8th
Wheelchair accessible
1st–8th: 9411 Connecticut Avenue, Kensington, MD

Governance: Nonprofit
Accredited by: AIMS, NAEYC
Memberships: AIMS, AISGW, BSF, LSF, NAES, NAEYC
Religious affiliation: Episcopal

PROFILE
Total enrollment: 240
Graduating class size: 24
Average class size: 15
Number of faculty: 39
Boarding option: No
School day: 8:30–3:15 (K–5th), 8:00–3:45 (6th–8th)
Extended day hours: 7:35–6:00
Schools three or more graduates have attended over the past five years: Bullis, Connelly School of the Holy Child, Edmund Burke, Field, Holy Cross, National Cathedral, Sidwell Friends, St. Albans, St. Andrew's Episcopal, Stone Ridge

APPLICATION PROCESS
Grades with openings (approximate):
K (8), 1st (13), 2nd (14), 3rd (10), 4th (10), 5th (4), 6th (8), 7th (10), 8th (10)
Birthday cutoff: Varies
Deadline: January 15; rolling
Fee: $75
Testing required: WPPSI-III/WISC-IV, SSAT
Steps: Application, tour, student visit, parent interview

COSTS
Tuition: $17,693–$17,918
Average additional fees: $165
Financial aid budget: $391,000
Average grant size: $9,000
% of students receiving aid: 43%
Endowment: No

NOTE: This data applies to the 2009–2010 school year.

PRESCHOOL PROGRAM

Age	Days	Hours	Tuition	Openings	Class size	Teachers per class	Food provided
3	3	9:00–12:00	$6,366	10	10	2	Snack
3	5	9:00–12:00	$10,617	12	12	2	Snack
3	5	9:00–3:00	$17,693	12	12	2	Snack
4	5	9:00–12:00	$10,617	4	16	2	Snack
4	5	9:00–3:00	$17,693	4	16	2	Snack

CURRICULUM

Languages and grades offered: Latin (5th–6th), Spanish (K–8th)
AP classes/IB program: N/A
Tutors/learning specialists: 2
Other resource specialists: Computer teacher, librarian
Art programs: Drama, drawing, music, painting, printmaking, sculpture
Sports: Basketball, cross-country, lacrosse, soccer, softball
Special features and activities: After-school enrichment classes: Art Café, clay class, Global Actions Club, martial arts, Tech Time, Total Golf Adventure, yoga
Summer programs: Academic enrichment, baseball, cultural arts & dance, Excite Soccer, Outdoor Adventure, Spanish immersion, Techno Kids

CAMPUS LIFE

Transportation available: None
Lunch options: PTO provides pizza on Thursdays for a fee
Food allergy policy: Classes are peanut free as needed
Uniform: Yes (K–8th)

CAMPUS

Facilities: 11-acre Kensington campus, multi-purpose rooms, 20-Mac computer lab
Long-range plans: Soon to break ground on a Middle School-sized gymnasium with locker rooms and multi-purpose space for community gatherings, chapel, performances and lunch

HISTORY AND MISSION STATEMENT

Grace Episcopal Day School will provide every student the opportunity for academic excellence in a caring, nurturing, moral environment that embraces diversity and promotes creativity, self-confidence, and service to others.

NOTE: This data applies to the 2009–2010 school year.

GRACE EPISCOPAL SCHOOL   est. 1959

Chris Stegmaier Byrnes, Head of School
3601 Russell Road
Alexandria, VA 22305
703-549-5067 x115
www.graceschoolalex.org

Debra J. Busker, Director of Admissions and Financial Aid
admissions@graceschoolalex.org

Coed: N–5th
Wheelchair accessible (playground has limited access)

Governance: Nonprofit
Accredited by: Commonwealth of Virginia, VAIS
Memberships: AISGW, MAESA, NAES, NAIS, VAIS, VCPE
Religious affiliation: Episcopal

PROFILE
Total enrollment: 116
Graduating class size: 12
Average class size: 12–14
Number of faculty: 20
Boarding option: No
School day: 8:30–3:15 (K–8th)
Extended day hours: 7:30–6:00
Schools three or more graduates have attended over the past five years: Alexandria Country Day, Browne, National Cathedral, St. Stephen's and St. Agnes

APPLICATION PROCESS
Grades with openings (approximate): See table, plus attrition
Birthday cutoff: June 30 (N–JK), September 30 (K)
Deadline: February 1
Fee: $75
Testing required: In-house (N), WPPSI-III/WISC-IV (JK–5th)
Steps: Parent tour (optional), application, play date (N–JK), group Play Day (K–1st), classroom visit (2nd–5th)

COSTS
Tuition: $14,470
Average additional fees: $815 (N–JK), $990 (K–5th)
Financial aid budget: N/A
Average grant size: Varies
% of students receiving aid: 10–15%
Endowment: Yes

NOTE: This data applies to the 2009–2010 school year.

PRESCHOOL PROGRAM

Age	Days	Hours	Tuition	Openings	Class size	Teachers per class	Food provided
3–4 (N)	5	8:30–12:00	$7,235	22	22	5	Snack
3–4 (N)	5	8:30–3:15	$12,485	22	22	5	Snack, lunch
4–5 (JK)	5	8:30–12:00	$7,235		22	6	Snack
4–5 (JK)	5	8:30–3:15	$12,485		22	6	Snack, lunch

CURRICULUM

Languages and grades offered: Spanish (JK–5th)
AP classes/IB program: N/A
Tutors/learning specialists: 1 language arts resource teacher
Other resource specialists: Psychologist
Art programs: Drama, Orff music, studio art
Sports: Physical education, running clubs, soccer, yoga
Special features and activities: Experienced teachers (50% have 20+ years, 81% have 10+ years); integrated technology—wireless, mobile computer lab, laptop and desktop computers, interactive SMARTBoard; after-school clubs and activities include arts, cooking, science, scouting, soccer, yoga
Summer programs: 4-week "June Jamboree" summer camp

CAMPUS LIFE

Transportation available: None
Lunch options: Bring lunch; milk available for purchase
Food allergy policy: Compliant with ADA; adults trained in EpiPen use.
Uniform: Yes

CAMPUS

Facilities: 5-acre campus, 2 playgrounds, 2 playing fields (including a new artificial turf soccer field), outdoor basketball court
Long-range plans: New Sports Court, playground additions/improvements

HISTORY AND MISSION STATEMENT

Founded in 1959, Grace Episcopal provides an academically challenging and developmentally appropriate education for children in preschool through fifth grade. Our academic program emphasizes the basic tools of learning: reading, writing, and mathematics. Students receive personal attention in small classes, and learn to be critical thinkers and successful problem-solvers. The curriculum is rich in music, literature, art, history, science, physical education, and spiritual development.

NOTE: This data applies to the 2009–2010 school year.

GREEN ACRES SCHOOL   est. 1934

Dr. Neal M. Brown, Head of School
11701 Danville Drive
Rockville, MD 20852
301-881-4100 x189
www.greenacres.org

Nina Chibber, Director of Admission for grades PK–1
Susan Friend, Director of Admission for grades 2–8
ninac@greenacres.org, susanf@greenacres.org

Coed: PK–8th
Wheelchair accessible

Governance: Nonprofit
Accredited by: AIMS
Memberships: AIMS, AISGW, NAIS, NCISR
Religious affiliation: Nonsectarian

PROFILE
Total enrollment: 320
Graduating class size: 30
Average class size: 12
Number of faculty: 50
Boarding option: No
School day: 8:20–3:05; 8:20–2:20 (W)
Extended day hours: 8:20–6:00
Schools three or more graduates have attended over the past five years: Edmund Burke, Georgetown Day, St. Andrew's Episcopal, Sandy Spring Friends, Walter Johnson High

APPLICATION PROCESS
Grades with openings (approximate): K (15), plus attrition
Birthday cutoff: September 1
Deadline: January 19
Fee: $75
Testing required: None
Steps: Tour/open house, application, parent interview, student visit, student assessment (2nd–8th)

COSTS
Tuition: $24,790
Average additional fees: $75–$900
Financial aid budget: $770,969
Average grant size: $15,418
% of students receiving aid: 16%
Endowment: Yes

NOTE: This data applies to the 2009–2010 school year.

PRESCHOOL PROGRAM

Age	Days	Hours	Tuition	Openings	Class size	Teachers per class	Food provided
4–5	5	8:20–3:05	$24,790	21	21	3	Snack

CURRICULUM

Languages and grades offered: Spanish (3rd–8th)
AP classes/IB program: N/A
Tutors/learning specialists: 1 part time
Other resource specialists: 2 part-time counselors
Art programs: Art, ceramics, chorus, creative movement, drama, handbells, music, musical theater, photography
Sports: Basketball, lacrosse, soccer, softball, track
Special features and activities: 15-acre wooded campus with sports & play areas, stream, pond; integrated teaching with infusion of technology and the arts; computer labs, laptops available (4th–8th); 30+ minutes of recess per day, PE 3–4 times a week, "no-cut" sports program; cooking/teaching kitchen; community service, field trips; turtle ranch; after-school enrichment programs; students and staff working together to increase environmental awareness
Summer programs: 6-week camp

CAMPUS LIFE

Transportation available: Bus and carpool
Lunch options: Optional catered lunch, milk/juice provided
Food allergy policy: On an individual basis
Uniform: No

CAMPUS

Facilities: Multiple classroom buildings, with gathering spaces, natural light, access to the outdoors; newly renovated classrooms, state-of-the-art science labs and art studios
Long-range plans: Spanish language to begin in 1st grade

HISTORY AND MISSION STATEMENT

Green Acres School is an intentional model of progressive education. We carefully consider research and experience to develop an academically challenging, age-appropriate program that is based on child development and fosters the cognitive, social/emotional, physical and creative growth of children. In small groups, students learn to think critically and solve problems through hands-on experiences. We value a broad view of diversity within an environment of trust, cooperation, and mutual respect.

NOTE: This data applies to the 2009–2010 school year.

GREEN HEDGES SCHOOL   est. 1942

Robert Gregg, Head of School
415 Windover Avenue NW
Vienna, VA 22180
703-938-8323 x228
www.greenhedges.org

Leslie H. Dixon, Director of Admission
ldixon@greenhedges.org

Coed: N–8th
Limited wheelchair access

Governance: Nonprofit
Accredited by: VAIS
Memberships: AISGW, AMS, NAIS, NMSA, WSSA
Religious affiliation: Nonsectarian

PROFILE
Total enrollment: 190
Graduating class size: 17
Average class size: 18
Number of faculty: 44
Boarding option: No
School day: 8:10–3:30
Extended day hours: 7:45–6:00
Schools three or more graduates have attended over the past five years: Episcopal High, Flint Hill, Georgetown Day, Georgetown Visitation, Madeira, Potomac, Thomas Jefferson High

APPLICATION PROCESS
Grades with openings (approximate): 1st (8), plus attrition
Birthday cutoff: September 30
Deadline: February 15
Fee: $65
Testing required: WISC-IV (1st–8th)
Steps: Application, assessment and visit

COSTS
Tuition: $20,400–$21,000
Average additional fees: $400
Financial aid budget: 10% of tuition revenue
Average grant size: $11,000
% of students receiving aid: 20%
Endowment: Yes

NOTE: This data applies to the 2009–2010 school year.

PRESCHOOL PROGRAM

Age	Days	Hours	Tuition	Openings	Class size	Teachers per class	Food provided
3	5	8:00–12:00	$11,900	14	14		
4	5	8:00–12:00	$11,900	2–4	14		

CURRICULUM

Languages and grades offered: French (N–8th), Latin (5th–8th), Spanish (N–8th)

AP classes/IB program: N/A

Tutors/learning specialists: None

Other resource specialists: N/A

Art programs: Part of comprehensive curriculum

Sports: Basketball, cross-country, soccer, softball

Special features and activities: Band, music, drama, art, and foreign language are all requirements

Summer programs: Camp for ages 3–6

CAMPUS LIFE

Transportation available: None

Lunch options: Options provided by PTO

Food allergy policy: None

Uniform: Yes (3rd–8th for special occasions)

CAMPUS

Facilities: Village-like setting with four buildings and two playing fields situated on 4 acres

Long-range plans: Campus Master Plan to include renovation, restoration, and enhancement of student learning spaces and overall facilities

HISTORY AND MISSION STATEMENT

We inspire young people of talent and promise to develop clear values, a desire for wisdom, and an appreciation for all endeavors that broaden the mind and enlighten the spirit for children age 3 years through grade 8. We are a small school by design, with a dedicated and talented teaching staff who demonstrate excellence in teaching. Music, art, drama, French, Spanish, Latin, and technology as well as character development and values are important parts of the Green Hedges program.

NOTE: This data applies to the 2009–2010 school year.

THE GW COMMUNITY SCHOOL   est. 1999

Alexa Warden, Director
9001 Braddock Road, Suite 111
Springfield, VA 22151
703-978-7208
www.gwcommunityschool.com

Cassie Sinichko, Administrative Director
sinichkocm@gwcommunityschool.com

Coed: 9th–12th
Wheelchair accessible

Governance: Proprietary
Accredited by: SACS, SAIS
Memberships: N/A
Religious affiliation: Nonsectarian

PROFILE
Total enrollment: 60
Graduating class size: 20
Average class size: 10
Number of faculty: 13
Boarding option: No
School day: 8:30–3:30
Extended day hours: 6:30–4:30
Schools three or more graduates have attended over the past five years: George Mason, McDaniel, University of Mary Washington, Virginia Commonwealth University

APPLICATION PROCESS
Grades with openings (approximate): 9th (10), 10th (10), 11th (9)
Birthday cutoff: N/A
Deadline: Rolling
Fee: $85
Testing required: None
Steps: Appointment/student interview with director, application

COSTS
Tuition: $21,600
Average additional fees: None
Financial aid budget: None
Average grant size: N/A
% of students receiving aid: N/A
Endowment: No

NOTE: This data applies to the 2009–2010 school year.

CURRICULUM

Languages and grades offered: French, Latin, Spanish (9th–12th)
AP classes/IB program: 5 AP classes
Tutors/learning specialists: None
Other resource specialists: College counselor, dean of students, faculty advisor
Art programs: Film, graphic design, improv, sound recording, theater
Sports: Basketball (varsity), conditioning, soccer (intramural)
Special features and activities: Experiential learning; laptop computers provided; annual ski trip, class trips, international travel, senior beach trip, senior essay-writing retreat; coffee house, community service, internships, robotics club, student government, yearbook
Summer programs: Summer school

CAMPUS LIFE

Transportation available: None
Lunch options: Refrigerator, microwave, and water cooler available for students who bring their lunches; school store with snacks, drinks; students can buy lunch at local restaurants
Food allergy policy: None
Uniform: No

CAMPUS

Facilities: N/A
Long-range plans: Continued excellence in education

HISTORY AND MISSION STATEMENT

Founded in the summer of 1999, the GW Community School embraces as its mission the development and implementation of a holistic educational program that will develop and optimize the giftedness and intelligence of each student in an in-depth, enriched, and technically advanced college preparatory environment that emphasizes authentic application of knowledge, not merely assimilation of information.

Students will experience academic success and the development of social awareness and responsibility in an atmosphere where all are treated with respect and courtesy.

The GW Community School recognizes the unique contribution of parents, students and community members striving for unity of purpose.

NOTE: This data applies to the 2009–2010 school year.

THE HARBOR SCHOOL   est. 1972

Valaida Wise, Head of School
7701 Bradley Boulevard
Bethesda, MD 20817
301-365-1100
www.theharborschool.org

Steven Greisdorf, Director of Admission
steven_greisdorf@theharborschool.org

Coed: N–2nd
Limited wheelchair access

Governance: Nonprofit
Accredited by: AIMS
Memberships: AIMS, AISGW, CASE, NAIS, WSSA
Religious affiliation: Nonsectarian

PROFILE
Total enrollment: 105
Graduating class size: 10
Average class size: 12
Number of faculty: 23
Boarding option: No
School day (hours): 8:45–3:00,
8:45–12:00 (F)
Extended day hours: 8:00–5:30
**Schools three or more graduates
have attended over the past five
years:** Bullis, Green Acres, Holton-
Arms, Landon, McLean, Norwood

APPLICATION PROCESS
Grades with openings (approximate):
See table, plus attrition
Birthday cutoff: December 31 (3s),
September 1 (4s–2nd)
Deadline: February 1
Fee: $60
Testing required: None
Steps: Open house or parent visit,
application, student visit

COSTS
Tuition: $16,500 (K–2nd)
Average additional fees: $1,000
Financial aid budget: 1.3% of budget
Average grant size: Maximum of
50% of tuition
% of students receiving aid: 4%
Endowment: No

NOTE: This data applies to the 2009–2010 school year.

PRESCHOOL PROGRAM

Age	Days	Hours	Tuition	Openings	Class size	Teachers per class	Food provided
3	5	9:00–12:00	$8,950	28	28	2	Snack
4	5	9:00–3:00	$15,500	Attrition	28	2	Snack
JK	5	8:45–3:00	$16,500	Attrition	14	2	Snack

CURRICULUM

Languages and grades offered: Spanish (N–2nd)
AP classes/IB program: N/A
Tutors/learning specialists: Reading/learning specialist
Other resource specialists: Art, librarian, music, PE/movement, Spanish, speech & language pathologist
Art programs: Art, dance, music, storyteller
Sports: After-school sports programs
Special features and activities: Inquiry-based social and academic program; small class size; Spanish beginning in nursery; international student body
Summer programs: Summer camp for 3–8-year-olds

CAMPUS LIFE

Transportation available: None
Lunch options: Hot lunch offered each Wednesday
Food allergy policy: Peanut-free school; teachers receive records of allergies and allergy training
Uniform: No

CAMPUS

Facilities: Two-story building with 9 classrooms, library, art room, large gymnasium, playground
Long-range plans: Add an 18-month and two-year-old program

HISTORY AND MISSION STATEMENT

The Harbor School prepares children for life's journey. Our community of families and the school's entire professional staff work to provide a positive school environment where children feel safe, nurtured and respected.

We believe that children are diverse learners and achieve success by working in a setting that promotes learning, self-expression and creativity. Children are encouraged to question, experiment, explore, take risks and assume responsibility in the world around them. In this way, The Harbor School fosters the child's continuing love of learning and a respect for the uniqueness of each individual.

NOTE: This data applies to the 2009–2010 school year.

THE HEIGHTS SCHOOL   est. 1969

Alvaro de Vicente, Headmaster
10400 Seven Locks Road
Potomac, MD 20854
301-765-2093
www.heights.edu

Colin Gleason, Director of Admissions
cgleason@heights.edu

Boys: 3rd–12th
Wheelchair accessible

Governance: Nonprofit
Accredited by: MSA
Memberships: AISGW, NAIS
Religious affiliation: Roman Catholic

PROFILE
Total enrollment: 460
Graduating class size: 50
Average class size: 15
Number of faculty: 58
Boarding option: No
School day: 8:20–3:05
Extended day hours: N/A
Schools three or more graduates have attended over the past five years: N/A

APPLICATION PROCESS
Grades with openings (approximate): 3rd (26), 6th (20), 9th (10), plus attrition
Birthday cutoff: N/A
Deadline: January 29
Fee: $50
Testing required: SSAT (9th–12th)
Steps: Application, student visit, family interview

COSTS
Tuition: $13,960 (3rd–5th), $16,320 (6th–8th), $18,075 (9th–12th)
Average additional fees: $350–$600
Financial aid budget: N/A
Average grant size: N/A
% of students receiving aid: N/A
Endowment: No

NOTE: This data applies to the 2009–2010 school year.

CURRICULUM
Languages and grades offered: Greek, Latin, Spanish (6th–12th)
AP classes/IB program: 20 AP classes
Tutors/learning specialists: None
Other resource specialists: School counselor
Art programs: A cappella group, band, boys' and men's choir, jazz, music (vocal and instrumental)
Sports: Baseball, basketball, cross-country, golf, lacrosse, soccer, squash, swimming, tennis, track & field, wrestling
Special features and activities: Skateboarding
Summer programs: 8 weeks, end of June to early August

CAMPUS LIFE
Transportation available: Bus and van
Lunch options: Options
Food allergy policy: None
Uniform: Dress code

CAMPUS
Facilities: 20 acres, basketball and tennis courts, baseball field
Long-range plans: New Upper School building and chapel

HISTORY AND MISSION STATEMENT
The Heights, founded by a group of laymen, offers a rigorous and traditional liberal arts academic program as a means of working with parents to help form young men ready to succeed in college and professional work. Spiritual direction of the school is entrusted to Opus Dei, a prelature of the Catholic Church, which seeks to promote the pursuit of holiness through one's ordinary work and daily life.

NOTE: This data applies to the 2009–2010 school year.

HIGHLAND SCHOOL   est. 1928

Henry D. Berg, Head of School
597 Broadview Avenue
Warrenton, VA 20186
540-878-2740
www.highlandschool.org

Chris Pryor, Director of Admission and Financial Aid
cpryor@highlandschool.org

Coed: PK–12th
Limited wheelchair access

Governance: Nonprofit
Accredited by: VAIS
Memberships: College Board, ESP, LSF, NACAC, NAIS, SSATB, VAIS
Religious affiliation: Nonsectarian

PROFILE
Total enrollment: 540
Graduating class size: 60
Average class size: 11 (9th–12th)
Number of faculty: 75
Boarding option: No
School day: 8:00–3:30
Extended day hours: 7:45–5:45
Schools three or more graduates have attended over the past five years: Clemson University, Denison College, High Point University, James Madison, Roanoke College, University of Georgia, University of Mary Washington, University of Richmond, University of Virginia, William and Mary

APPLICATION PROCESS
Grades with openings (approximate): K (12), 3rd (2), 8th (10), 9th (25), 10th (10)
Birthday cutoff: September 30
Deadline: January 30, then rolling
Fee: $50
Testing required: SSAT (6th–12th)
Steps: Open house, school visit/interviews, application

COSTS
Tuition: $15,400–$19,100
Average additional fees: $500 (9th–12th)
Financial aid budget: $750,000
Average grant size: $7,700
% of students receiving aid: 18%
Endowment: Yes

NOTE: This data applies to the 2009–2010 school year.

PRESCHOOL PROGRAM

Age	Days	Hours	Tuition	Openings	Class size	Teachers per class	Food provided
3/4	5	9:00–12:00	$5,900	12	12	2	None
4/5	5	9:00–1:00	$9,360	6	18	2	None

CURRICULUM

Languages and grades offered: French (PK–12th), Latin (7th–12th), Spanish (PK–12th)

AP classes/IB program: 19 AP classes

Tutors/learning specialists: 5

Other resource specialists: Differentiated learning specialist, 2 guidance counselors, nurse, speech-language pathologist

Art programs: Ceramics, chorus, digital filmmaking, guitar, handbells, jazz ensemble, photography, strings, theater, visual arts, yearbook

Sports: Baseball, basketball, cheerleading, cross-country, dance, field hockey, golf, lacrosse, outdoor adventures, soccer, softball, swimming, tennis, volleyball

Special features and activities: Chess, class plays, forensics, field studies, international trips, Junior Class Internship, Leadership Certificate Program, service learning, senior project, wilderness trips

Summer programs: Academic enrichment, art, athletics

CAMPUS LIFE

Transportation available: Yes

Lunch options: Yes

Food allergy policy: Yes—see school handbook online

Uniform: Dress code

CAMPUS

Facilities: 42-acre campus, modern school complex, 2 gymnasiums, 355-seat theater, black box theater, art gallery

Long-range plans: Turf field, new Lower School for 2010, renovations to Upper and Middle Schools

HISTORY AND MISSION STATEMENT

Founded in 1928, Highland is a coed, college preparatory, day school environment. Students matriculate from both independent and public schools and come from ten countries. The mission of Highland School is to provide a demanding academic program to develop the skills and character essential for students to meet the challenges of college and leadership in the twenty-first century.

NOTE: This data applies to the 2009–2010 school year.

THE HILL SCHOOL   est. 1926

Thomas A. Northrup, Headmaster
130 South Madison Street
Middleburg, VA 20117
540-687-5897
www.thehillschool.org

Treavor Lord, Associate Headmaster
tlord@thehillschool.org

Coed: K–8th
Wheelchair accessible

Governance: Nonprofit
Accredited by: VAIS
Memberships: AISGW, NAIS, VAIS
Religious affiliation: Nonsectarian

PROFILE
Total enrollment: 240
Graduating class size: 30
Average class size: 12
Number of faculty: 60 (faculty and staff)
Boarding option: No
School day: 8:30–4:00
Extended day hours: 7:45–6:00
Schools three or more graduates have attended over the past five years: Episcopal High, Foxcroft, Highland, Madeira, Mercersburg, Notre Dame Academy, St. Andrew's (DE), Woodberry Forest

APPLICATION PROCESS
Grades with openings (approximate): K (24), plus attrition
Birthday cutoff: N/A
Deadline: February 1, then rolling
Fee: $25; $40 per family
Testing required: In-house
Steps: Application, parent orientation (K), classroom visit (K) or daylong visit (1st–8th), in-house testing

COSTS
Tuition: $14,250 (K), $18,800 (1st–8th)
Average additional fees: $200
Financial aid budget: $550,000
Average grant size: $9,700
% of students receiving aid: 26%
Endowment: Yes

NOTE: This data applies to the 2009–2010 school year.

CURRICULUM
Languages and grades offered: Language fundamentals (4th–5th), Latin (6th–8th), Spanish (1st–3rd)
AP classes/IB program: N/A
Tutors/learning specialists: 3
Other resource specialists: N/A
Art programs: Art workshop, drama, music
Sports: Basketball, cross-country, field hockey, gymnastics, lacrosse, soccer, track
Special features and activities: Strong academic and co-curricular programs
Summer programs: Enrichment—art, cooking, crafts, drama, sports

CAMPUS LIFE
Transportation available: None
Lunch options: Through local vendors only
Food allergy policy: On a case-by-case basis
Uniform: No

CAMPUS
Facilities: 136-acre campus; art building, athletic center, 3 classroom buildings, lunchroom & kitchen, music room, outdoor nature center, performing arts center, 5 sports fields; school owns 13 houses for faculty and staff
Long-range plans: N/A

HISTORY AND MISSION STATEMENT
Hill School was founded in 1926 as an independent coeducational day school. It is located on a 136-acre campus overlooking the town of Middleburg, Virginia.

The goal of a Hill School education is to build character, self-confidence, and scholarship through academic and co-curricular excellence, individualized attention, and a strong sense of community.

NOTE: This data applies to the 2009–2010 school year.

HOLTON-ARMS SCHOOL   est. 1901

Susanna A. Jones, Head of School
7303 River Road
Bethesda, MD 20817
301-365-5300
www.holton-arms.edu

Sharron Rodgers, Director of Enrollment and Marketing
sharron.rodgers@holton-arms.edu

Girls: 3rd–12th
Wheelchair accessible

Governance: Nonprofit
Accredited by: AIMS, MSA, MSDE
Memberships: AIMS, AISGW, College Board, CRIS, ERB, HMAE,
NACAC, NAIS, NAPSG, NCGS, PCW, SSATB
Religious affiliation: Nonsectarian

PROFILE

Total enrollment: 644
Graduating class size: 89
Average class size: 15
Number of faculty: 97
Boarding option: No
School day: 8:30–3:30
Extended day hours: 8:30–6:00
Schools three or more graduates have attended over the past five years: Cornell, Duke, Georgetown, Princeton, Trinity (CT), University of Maryland, University of Pennsylvania, University of Virginia, Vanderbilt, Yale

APPLICATION PROCESS

Grades with openings (approximate):
3rd (30), 6th (15), 7th (15), 9th (15)
Birthday cutoff: N/A
Deadline: January 1
Fee: $60 (domestic), $100 (international)
Testing required: WISC-IV and CTP (ERB) (3rd–5th), SSAT or ISEE (6th–12th)
Steps: Tour/interview, application

COSTS

Tuition: $27,200 (3rd–6th), $28,500 (7th–12th)
Average additional fees: $700–$1,600
Financial aid budget: $2.2M
Average grant size: $17,288
% of students receiving aid: 20%
Endowment: Yes

NOTE: This data applies to the 2009–2010 school year.

CURRICULUM

Languages and grades offered: Chinese, French, Latin, Spanish
AP classes/IB program: 15 AP classes
Tutors/learning specialists: 3 (one per division)
Other resource specialists: Math, reading
Art programs: Acting workshop, ceramics, chorus & music theory, dance composition & choreography, dance technique, drawing & painting, life drawing & painting, music history, music technology, orchesis, performance production & technology, photography, string orchestra, wind ensemble
Sports: Basketball, crew, cross-country, field hockey, ice hockey, lacrosse, soccer, softball, swimming & diving, tennis, track & field, volleyball
Special features and activities: Design Technology, a pre-engineering program for elementary students developed by three Holton-Arms faculty members; engineering and robotics classes available in the Upper School
Summer programs: Creative Summer, a coeducational day camp focusing on the fine and performing arts, sports, and academic enrichment

CAMPUS LIFE

Transportation available: Limited bus service
Lunch options: Included in tuition
Food allergy policy: N/A
Uniform: Yes

CAMPUS

Facilities: 2 academic buildings, 3 art studios, 3 athletic fields, black box theater, child-care facility, 3 dance studios, double gymnasium, field house, lecture hall, 2 libraries, photograph lab/darkroom, pool, 7 tennis courts, 400-seat theater, track, weight/training room
Long-range plans: Continued development of Global Education Program and Sustainability Program

HISTORY AND MISSION STATEMENT

The mission of the Holton-Arms School is to cultivate the unique potential of young women through the "education not only of the mind, but of the soul and spirit." Founded in 1901, Holton remains true to the vision of its founders, to prepare confident, competent young women to lead and to serve their community.

NOTE: This data applies to the 2009–2010 school year.

HOLY TRINITY SCHOOL   est. 1818

Mary Shannon, Principal
1325 36th Street, NW
Washington, DC 20007
202-337-2339 x203
www.htsdc.org

Kim Calnan Crismali, Director of Admissions
kcrismali@htsdc.org

Coed: N–8th
Limited wheelchair access

Governance: Nonprofit
Accredited by: MSA
Memberships: ASCD, MSA, NCEA
Religious affiliation: Catholic, Jesuit

PROFILE
Total enrollment: 330
Graduating class size: 45
Average class size: 20
Number of faculty: 60
Boarding option: No
School day: 8:10–3:00
Extended day hours: 7:30–6:00
Extended day hours: N/A
Schools three or more graduates have attended over the past five years: Georgetown Prep, Georgetown Visitation, Gonzaga, Madeira, Maret, National Cathedral, St. Albans, St. Anselm's, St. John's College High, Stone Ridge

APPLICATION PROCESS
Grades with openings (approximate): K (10), 6th (12–15), 7th (5–7), plus attrition
Birthday cutoff: September 1
Deadline: February 1 for priority status
Fee: $60
Testing required: In-house (2nd–8th)
Steps: Application, visit

COSTS
Tuition: $13,000–$17,000 (K), $10,000–$15,000 (1st–8th)
Average additional fees: $100
Financial aid budget: $350,000
Average grant size: $5,200
% of students receiving aid: 13%
Endowment: Yes

NOTE: This data applies to the 2009–2010 school year.

PRESCHOOL PROGRAM

Age	Days	Hours	Tuition	Openings	Class size	Teachers per class	Food provided
3 (N)			$13,000–$17,000		16	16	
4 (PK)			$13,000–$17,000				

CURRICULUM

Languages and grades offered: Spanish (K–8th)
AP classes/IB program: N/A
Tutors/learning specialists: Reading, speech & language specialists
Other resource specialists: Math and science resource teachers
Art programs: Yes
Sports: Basketball, track
Special features and activities: Afterschool, Irish dance, musical theater &
Shakespeare theater workshop
Summer programs: None

CAMPUS LIFE

Transportation available: None
Lunch options: Hot lunch may be
purchased
Food allergy policy: Individual plan
for student
Uniform: Yes

CAMPUS

Facilities: 2 large Federal style buildings spanning a full city block in the
heart of Georgetown. Lower School
(1st–4th) cafeteria, health room,
library, media center, resource
rooms; Upper School (5th–8th)
administrative offices, art room,
cafeteria, science lab, Spanish room,
theater
Long-range plans: N/A

HISTORY AND MISSION STATEMENT

Holy Trinity School is a Catholic School founded in the Jesuit tradition as an
integral part of the mission of Holy Trinity Catholic Church. Holy Trinity
School continues a 200-year-old tradition of education and service. We work
toward the development of skills, knowledge, character, and attitudes that
reflect Christian responsibility.

NOTE: This data applies to the 2009–2010 school year.

THE HOWARD GARDNER SCHOOL · est. 2004

Katherine Keith, Director
4913 Franconia Road
Alexandria, VA 22310
703-822-9300
www.thehowardgardnerschool.org

Katherine Keith
katherine@thehowardgardnerschool.org

Coed: 9th–12th
Wheelchair accessible

Governance: Nonprofit
Accredited by: N/A
Memberships: N/A
Religious affiliation: Nonsectarian

PROFILE
Total enrollment: 48
Graduating class size: 14
Average class size: 8
Number of faculty: 8
Boarding option: No
School day: 9:15–3:25
Extended day hours: N/A
Schools three or more graduates have attended over the past five years: Earlham College, Elon, Guilford College, Hampshire College, McDaniel College, Virginia Commonwealth University, Washington College

APPLICATION PROCESS
Grades with openings (approximate): 9th (9), 10th (3), 11th (2). Does not accept seniors
Birthday cutoff: N/A
Deadline: Rolling
Fee: $50
Testing required: Varies
Steps: Open house, visit, application

COSTS
Tuition: $19,450
Average additional fees: $1,500
Financial aid budget: $120,000
Average grant size: $10,000
% of students receiving aid: 25%
Endowment: No

NOTE: This data applies to the 2009–2010 school year.

CURRICULUM

Languages and grades offered: French, Latin, Spanish
AP classes/IB program: N/A
Tutors/learning specialists: 1
Other resource specialists: N/A
Art programs: Animation & graphic arts, music & music recording, studio arts
Sports: Basketball, golf, rock climbing
Special features and activities: Tuesday field studies, Friday internships
Summer programs: N/A

CAMPUS LIFE

Transportation available: Accessible by Metro and bus
Lunch options: Open lunch—students may leave campus or bring lunch
Food allergy policy: Accommodate student needs
Uniform: No

CAMPUS

Facilities: Administration building, classrooms, Environmental Science cottage, Outdoor Learning Center
Long-range plans: New classroom building will be available for the 2009–10 school year

HISTORY AND MISSION STATEMENT

The Howard Gardner School is a small, independent progressive high school that values community, mutual respect, group work as well as individual differences, and sense of place. Based on Howard Gardner's theory of multiple intelligences, the school strives to encourage students to develop their strengths in all areas. For this reason, we attract many bright, creative young people who are musicians, artists, and naturalists, as well as students whose strengths are primarily verbal or mathematical. It is our goal to help these students truly thrive—intellectually and emotionally—and develop into the adults they are meant to be.

NOTE: This data applies to the 2009–2010 school year.

IDEAL SCHOOLS HIGH SCHOOL   est. 2007

Dr. Deep Sran, Principal
44675 Cape Court, Unit 105
Beaumeade Technology Campus
Ashburn, VA 20147
703-956-5020
www.idealschools.org

Deep Sran
admissions@idealschools.org

Coed: 9th–12th
Wheelchair accessible

Governance: Proprietary
Accredited by: N/A
Memberships: CES
Religious affiliation: Nonsectarian

PROFILE
Total enrollment: 10
Graduating class size: N/A
Average class size: 5
Number of faculty: 4
Boarding option: No
School day: 8:30–3:30
Extended day hours: 8:00–5:30
Schools three or more graduates have attended over the past five years: N/A

APPLICATION PROCESS
Grades with openings (approximate): 9th (5), 10th (5), 11th (5)
Birthday cutoff: N/A
Deadline: Rolling
Fee: None
Testing required: None
Steps: Application, student/parent interviews

COSTS
Tuition: $18,000
Average additional fees: $400
Financial aid budget: N/A
Average grant size: N/A
% of students receiving aid: N/A
Endowment: No

NOTE: This data applies to the 2009–2010 school year.

CURRICULUM
Languages and grades offered: Chinese, French, German, Japanese, Russian, Spanish (9th–12th)
AP classes/IB program:
Tutors/learning specialists: N/A
Other resource specialists: N/A
Art programs: Architecture, art
Sports: Twice-weekly physical education activities include sports selected by students (cross-country, cycling, football, soccer, etc.)
Special features and activities: Small classrooms with students working around a large conference table; high-tech learning environment, including laptops for all students, Advanced Technology coursework and Activboards; computer-based foreign language instruction using Rosetta Stone software used by Department of State; $750 tuition discount for students with Apple laptops
Summer programs: N/A

CAMPUS LIFE
Transportation available: None
Lunch options: Students provide lunch or travel off-campus as a group for lunch
Food allergy policy: Food not prepared on site
Uniform: No

CAMPUS
Facilities:
Long-range plans: The school will grow to 60 students in grades 9–12 in its current location. Introduction of AP classes in the 2009–10 school year.

HISTORY AND MISSION STATEMENT
Our objective at Ideal Schools is to prepare students for college in a small school setting where we can balance a rigorous academic program with personalized instruction and guidance in a supportive social climate. Our school is ideal for students who are not sufficiently challenged or engaged in larger, more traditional private and public schools.

NOTE: This data applies to the 2009–2010 school year.

THE IVYMOUNT SCHOOL   est. 1961

Janet Wintrol, Executive Director
11614 Seven Locks Road
Potomac, MD 20854
301-469-0223
www.ivymount.org

Lennie Gladstone
lgladstone@ivymount.org

Coed: 4–21 years (ungraded)
Wheelchair accessible

Governance: Nonprofit
Accredited by: MSDE
Memberships: MANSEF, NAPSEC
Religious affiliation: Nonsectarian

PROFILE
Total enrollment: 205
Graduating class size: 16
Average class size: 6–12
Number of faculty: 230
Boarding option: No
School day: 6 (half-day Wednesdays for conferences and teacher development)
Extended day hours: N/A
Schools three or more graduates have attended over the past five years: Most of Ivymount's programs are non-degree-granting. The Model Asperger Program will have its first graduating class in 2012.

APPLICATION PROCESS
Grades with openings (approximate): Varies
Birthday cutoff: N/A
Deadline: Rolling
Fee: $30
Testing required: Ivymount is a special education school
Steps: Parent informational session, application packets, student intake assessment, final meeting with parents/guardians & child

COSTS
Tuition: $40,000+, includes therapy and related services
Average additional fees: None
Financial aid budget: N/A
Average grant size: N/A
% of students receiving aid: 95% funded by their local school districts
Endowment: N/A

NOTE: This data applies to the 2009–2010 school year.

CURRICULUM

Languages and grades offered: None
AP classes/IB program: N/A
Tutors/learning specialists: Yes
Other resource specialists: More than 25 certified trained special educators, 26 speech and occupational therapists, 6 social workers, 4 vocational specialists, trained nurses. Each class also has teaching assistants and one-on-one student aides where necessary.
Art programs: The arts are an integrated part of every Ivymount Program. Students take part in traditional art classes as well as creative movement, music and expression classes.
Sports: Every student participates in physical education classes with teachers specially trained to provide support and physical training to special needs students. After-school physical fitness and recreational classes available.
Special features and activities: Model Asperger Program (1st–8th); Ivymount Outreach Services program helps individuals throughout the DC area identify specific developmental and learning issues and provides strategies and consultation on dealing with the needs of these young people.
Summer programs: Autism and Multiple Learning Need programs run on an 11-month calendar

CAMPUS LIFE

Transportation available: N/A
Lunch options: Students bring their lunches
Food allergy policy: Nut-free classroom and hallway environment
Uniform: No

CAMPUS

Facilities: Assistive technology resources, computer labs, gymnasium/exercise room, library; physical, occupational, and speech therapy facilities and staff; vocational and life skills training facilities
Long-range plans: Expand Model Asperger Program to go all the way through high school by 2012

HISTORY AND MISSION STATEMENT

Named twice by the U.S. Department of Education as a Blue Ribbon School of Excellence, Ivymount is a nonsectarian, non-public special education day school. Ivymount's integrated approach to learning includes educational programs and therapeutic services for over 200 students annually, ages 4–21, from throughout the Washington metropolitan area with serious developmental delays, learning disabilities, communication disorders, autism, and/or multiple handicaps.

NOTE: This data applies to the 2009–2010 school year.

THE JEWISH PRIMARY DAY SCHOOL   est. 1987
OF THE NATION'S CAPITAL

Naomi Reem, Head of School
6045 16th Street, NW
Washington, DC 20011
202-291-5737 x103
www.jpds.org

Sindy Udell, Director of Admission
sindy.udell@jpds.org

Coed: PK–6th
Limited wheelchair access

Governance: Nonprofit
Accredited by: AIMS
Memberships: AISGW
Religious affiliation: Jewish

PROFILE
Total enrollment: 245
Graduating class size: 18
Average class size: 16
Number of faculty: 64
Boarding option: No
School day: 8:30–3:30,
8:30–2:15 (F)
Extended day hours: 8:30–6:30,
8:30–6:00 (F)
**Schools three or more graduates
have attended over the past five
years:** Charles E. Smith Jewish Day,
City Collegiate Charter, Edmund
Burke, Field, Maret, McLean,
Melvin J. Berman Hebrew
Academy, Montgomery County
Public Schools, National
Cathedral, St. Andrew's Episcopal

APPLICATION PROCESS
Grades with openings (approximate):
K (30), plus attrition
Birthday cutoff: September 1
Deadline: January 8
Fee: $150
Testing required: None
Steps: Open house/tour, application,
playdate and screening (PK–K),
interview/tour (1st–6th)

COSTS
Tuition: $17,515
Average additional fees: None
Financial aid budget: N/A
Average grant size: N/A
% of students receiving aid: 31%
Endowment: No

NOTE: This data applies to the 2009–2010 school year.

PRESCHOOL PROGRAM							
Age	Days	Hours	Tuition	Openings	Class size	Teachers per class	Food provided
PK	5		$17,515	18			

CURRICULUM
Languages and grades offered: Hebrew (PK–6th)
AP classes/IB program: N/A
Tutors/learning specialists: 1
Other resource specialists: Guidance counselor, contracted occupational therapists, speech and language therapists, child development specialists on an as-needed basis
Art programs: Art history, choir, cooking, drama, Israeli dancing, musical theater, podcasting, singing
Sports: Baseball, basketball, cross-country, football, karate, kickball, soccer, softball, track, yoga
Special features and activities: After-school clubs; field trips, including a 4-day trip in 5th grade to the Teva Learning Center in Western Maryland and a 3-day trip to New York in 6th grade
Summer programs: N/A

CAMPUS LIFE
Transportation available: Bus service
Lunch options: 2 days a week, for an additional fee
Food allergy policy: All common areas nut free; classrooms have restrictions based on student needs
Uniform: No

CAMPUS
Facilities: Computer lab, science lab, indoor gym, think tank; promethium board in 6th-grade classrooms
Long-range plans: N/A

HISTORY AND MISSION STATEMENT
The mission of the Jewish Primary Day School of the Nation's Capital is to provide a strong foundation in Jewish and secular learning, laying the groundwork for our students to become knowledgeable, responsible Jews and citizens, deeply committed to the community at large, to Jewish living and values, and to the people and state of Israel. Our school strives to create an environment filled with warmth, joy, and intellectual excitement that celebrates the unique qualities of each student, respects varied approaches to Judaism, fosters a strong sense of ethics and of self, embraces diversity, and builds a community of lifelong learners.

NOTE: This data applies to the 2009–2010 school year.

THE JULIA BROWN MONTESSORI SCHOOLS   est. 1967

Julia Brown, Founder
Theresa Brown Leonhart, Director
Ellen Brown Komesarook, General Manager
3400 Queen Mary Drive
Olney, MD 20832
301-774-5700
www.juliabrownmontessorischools.com

mpjbms@aol.com

Coed: N–3rd
9450 Madison Avenue, Laurel, MD, 301-498-0604
1300 Milestone Drive, Silver Spring, MD, 301-622-7808

Governance: Proprietary
Accredited by: MSDE Office of Child Care
Memberships: AIMS
Religious affiliation: Nonsectarian

PROFILE
Total enrollment: Approximately 150 (varies by location)
Graduating class size: 15–20
Average class size: 29
Number of faculty: 15–18 per location
Boarding option: No
School day: 8:30–3:00
Extended day hours: 7:00–6:00
Schools three or more graduates have attended over the past five years: N/A

APPLICATION PROCESS
Grades with openings (approximate): Varies
Birthday cutoff: December 31
Deadline: Rolling
Fee: $90–$120
Testing required: None
Steps: Contact school, tour, application

COSTS
Tuition: $450–$950/month (varies by location)
Average additional fees: None
Financial aid budget: None
Average grant size: N/A
% of students receiving aid: N/A
Endowment: No

NOTE: This data applies to the 2009–2010 school year.

PRESCHOOL PROGRAM

Age	Days	Hours	Tuition	Openings	Class size	Teachers per class	Food provided
2.5–5	5	8:30–11:15			30	2–3	Snack
2.5–5	5	12:15–3:00			30	2–3	Snack
2.5–5	5	8:30–3:00			30	2–3	Snack, lunch

CURRICULUM

Languages and grades offered: N/A
AP classes/IB program: N/A
Tutors/learning specialists: N/A
Other resource specialists: Music and Spanish instruction
Art programs: Art offered daily
Sports: Daily outdoor play
Special features and activities: N/A
Summer programs: Yes, from the end of one school year to the beginning of the next, for current and incoming students.

CAMPUS LIFE

Transportation available: None
Lunch options: Included in tuition. Milk and water are provided at all snacks and meals.
Food allergy policy: Peanut- and nut-free environment
Uniform: Yes

CAMPUS

Facilities: 4 campuses—Columbia, Laurel, Olney, and Silver Spring—each on at least one acre of land.
Long-range plans: N/A

HISTORY AND MISSION STATEMENT

The Julia Brown Montessori School was one of the first Montessori schools in Maryland. Julia Brown received her Montessori teaching degree in 1965 and wanted to bring this method of teaching small children to the Laurel area; she and her husband, Charles, started their "children's house" in a rented apartment with only 20 students. The Browns felt it was important for parents to know who was ultimately responsible for the program—hence the name.

At The Julia Brown Montessori Schools, we work with nature, not against it, in helping your child achieve their goal. Our program accepts the endless energies, the creative impulses, and insatiable curiosities of the child and gradually directs their efforts into rewarding channels.

NOTE: This data applies to the 2009–2010 school year.

THE KATHERINE THOMAS SCHOOL   est. 1995

Thomas Sweet, Lower/Middle School Director
Rhona Schwartz, High School Director
9975 Medical Center Drive
Rockville, MD 20850
301-738-9691 x193
www.ttlc.org

Melanie Roberts, Admissions Coordinator
meroberts@ttlc.org

Coed: PK–12th
Wheelchair accessible

Governance: Nonprofit
Accredited by: MSDE
Memberships: CHADD, IDA, MANSEF
Religious affiliation: Nonsectarian

PROFILE
Total enrollment: 185
Graduating class size: 30
Average class size: 10
Number of faculty: 100
Boarding option: No
School day: 8:50–3:30 (K–8th),
8:00–2:45 (9th–12th)
Extended day hours: 8:00–5:30
**Schools three or more graduates
have attended over the past five
years:** Accotink Academy, Chelsea,
High Road Academy, Kingsbury,
Lab, Siena, public schools

APPLICATION PROCESS
Grades with openings (approximate):
K–5th (15), 6th–8th (20), 9th–12th
(30)
Birthday cutoff: September 1
Deadline: Rolling
Fee: $100
Testing required: Psychological, educational; as needed—speech-language,
occupational therapy testing
Steps: Open house/tour, application,
school visit

COSTS
Tuition: $21,500
Average additional fees: $4,000
Financial aid budget: $300,000
Average grant size: $17,500
% of students receiving aid: 9%
Endowment: No

NOTE: This data applies to the 2009–2010 school year.

PRESCHOOL PROGRAM

Age	Days	Hours	Tuition	Openings	Class size	Teachers per class	Food provided
4–5	5	12:30–3:30	$15,000	8	8	5	

CURRICULUM

Languages and grades offered: Spanish (9th–12th)

AP classes/IB program: None

Tutors/learning specialists: 25

Other resource specialists: Counseling, occupational therapy, physical therapy, reading, speech-language

Art programs: Art, drama, music

Sports: Basketball, physical education, soccer, Special Olympics

Special features: Independent day school for students with language/learning disabilities and/or high-functioning autism. Preschool program model: DIR/Floortime

Summer programs: Yes—6-week program

CAMPUS LIFE

Transportation available: Funded (DCPS/VA/MCPS public transportation), private (carpool)

Lunch provided: No

Food allergy policy: None

Uniform: No

CAMPUS

Facilities: 2-story building, 3 OT gyms, 3 playground areas

Long-range plans: Continue to expand extracurricular after-school program, sports, and technology programs

HISTORY AND MISSION STATEMENT

To improve the lives of and expand possibilities for individuals with special needs.

THE KINGSBURY DAY SCHOOL   est. 1938

Dr. Eric M. Isselhardt, CEO/Head of School
5000 14th Street, NW
Washington, DC 20011
202-722-5555
www.kingsbury.org

Thaddisa Fulwood, Director of Admissions
admissions@kingsbury.org

Coed: K–12th
Wheelchair accessible

Governance: Nonprofit
Accredited by: MSA
Memberships: AISGW, CHADD, IDA
Religious affiliation: Nonsectarian

PROFILE
Total enrollment: 230
Graduating class size: 15
Average class size: 8–10 with 2 teachers
Number of faculty: 128
Boarding option: No
School day: 8:30–3:05 (K–8th), 8:00–3:05 (9th–12th)
Extended day hours: None
Schools three or more graduates have attended over the past five years: N/A

APPLICATION PROCESS
Grades with openings (approximate): All
Birthday cutoff: N/A
Deadline: February 2
Fee: $100
Testing required: Psycho-educational or neuro-psychological evaluation; speech/language, occupational therapy or physical therapy evaluations, if applicable
Steps: N/A

COSTS
Tuition: $29,640 (K–8th), $33,140 (9th–12th)
Average additional fees: Varies by number of related services
Financial aid budget: $150,000
Average grant size: Varies
% of students receiving aid: 8%
Endowment: No

NOTE: This data applies to the 2009–2010 school year.

CURRICULUM
Languages and grades offered: Spanish
AP classes/IB program: N/A
Tutors/learning specialists: 80
Other resource specialists: Reading specialist
Art programs: Drama, Intro to Art, Intro to Music, music, painting & drawing, percussion, portfolio art, studio art, theater
Sports: Basketball, cheerleading, crew, dance, flag football, kickball, soccer, squad, track
Special features and activities: After-school enrichment program, aftercare, transcendental meditation
Summer programs: Extended school year, tutoring summer camp

CAMPUS LIFE
Transportation available: None
Lunch options: Yes
Food allergy policy: Yes
Uniform: No

CAMPUS
Facilities: N/A
Long-range plans: N/A

HISTORY AND MISSION STATEMENT

Kingsbury is a Tutoring Center, Diagnostic and Psychological Service Center and the oldest Day School in Washington, DC, designed to meet the needs of students with language-based learning disabilities. Kingsbury is a coeducational, independent, special education day school serving students ranging from 5 to 18 years of age. Learning goals are met through multi-sensory, individualized and experiential learning approaches. Social and emotional growth is facilitated through collaboration among a team of special education professionals, including an occupational therapist, a physical therapist, psychologists, a speech and language pathologist and a reading specialist.

NOTE: This data applies to the 2009–2010 school year.

THE LAB SCHOOL OF WASHINGTON   est. 1967

Katherine Schantz, Head of School
4759 Reservoir Road, NW
Washington, DC 20007
202-965-6600
www.labschool.org

Susan Feeley, Director of Admissions
alexandra.freeman@labschool.org

Coed: 1st–12th
Wheelchair accessible
1st–4th: 1550 Foxhall Road NW, Washington, DC

Governance: Nonprofit
Accredited by: MSA
Memberships: AISGW
Religious affiliation: Nonsectarian

PROFILE
Total enrollment: 340
Graduating class size: 30
Average class size: Student-to-teacher ratios of 12: 2/3 (1st–4th), 7/8: 1 (5th–12th)
Number of faculty: 190
Boarding option: No
School day: 8:30–3:15
Extended day hours: 8:30–5:30
Schools three or more graduates have attended over the past five years: Boarding schools, Edmund Burke, Field, Georgetown Day, Georgetown Prep, McLean, public schools

APPLICATION PROCESS
Grades with openings (approximate): All, varies
Birthday cutoff: December 31
Deadline: February 1
Fee: $100 (re-application is $25)
Testing required: WPPSI-III/WISC-IV/WAIS, WJ-III
Steps: Application, school visit

COSTS
Tuition: Varies according to services provided
Average additional fees: N/A
Financial aid budget: N/A
Average grant size: N/A
% of students receiving aid: N/A
Endowment: Yes

NOTE: This data applies to the 2009–2010 school year.

CURRICULUM
Languages and grades offered: Latin, Spanish (9th–12th)
AP classes/IB program: N/A
Tutors/learning specialists: 100
Other resource specialists: Yes
Art programs: Yes—the arts employed at the Lab School enhance the process of neural maturation, increase attention, and build organizational skills and competencies leading to scholarly pursuits and a strong sense of self-worth.
Sports: Basketball, cross-country, golf, soccer, swimming, volleyball, etc.
Special features and activities: Validated by the Department of Education's National Diffusion Network recognizing Exemplary Educational Programs; selected as a National Blue Ribbon School of Excellence from the Department of Education
Summer programs: 5-week Summer Session

CAMPUS LIFE
Transportation available: Shuttle bus to 3 Metro stations for students in 5th–12th
Lunch options: Brown bag lunch, school store, optional "Healthy Lunch" delivery
Food allergy policy: N/A
Uniform: No

CAMPUS
Facilities: Washington, DC (2 campuses), Baltimore
Long-range plans: N/A

HISTORY AND MISSION STATEMENT
Founded in 1967 by Sally L. Smith, The Lab School of Washington is internationally recognized for its innovative programs for children and adults with learning disabilities. The Lab School Day School offers individualized instruction to students in 1st through 12th grade.

The Lab School of Washington Day School exists to educate intelligent, often gifted, children with moderate to severe learning disabilities, so they can return to the mainstream as soon as possible and become productive citizens.

NOTE: This data applies to the 2009–2010 school year.

LANDON SCHOOL   est. 1929

David M. Armstrong, Headmaster
6101 Wilson Lane
Bethesda, MD 20817
301-320-1067
www.landon.net

George Mulligan, Director of Admissions
george_mulligan@landon.net

Boys: 3rd–12th
Wheelchair accessible

Governance: Nonprofit
Accredited by: AIMS, MSA, MSDE
Memberships: AIMS, AISGW, NAIS
Religious affiliation: Nonsectarian

PROFILE
Total enrollment: 678
Graduating class size: 83
Average class size: 16
Number of faculty: 81
Boarding option: No
School day: 8:05–3:45
Extended day hours: 8:05–6:00
Schools three or more graduates have attended over the past five years: Brown, Cornell, Duke, Georgetown, Princeton, University of Maryland, University of Pennsylvania, University of Virginia, Vanderbilt, Yale

APPLICATION PROCESS
Grades with openings (approximate): 3rd (30), 4th (15), 6th (15), 7th (15), 8th (3–5), 9th (20)
Birthday cutoff: N/A
Deadline: January 30
Fee: $75
Testing required: In-house (3rd–4th), SSAT or ISEE (5th–12th)
Steps: Open house, appointment, application, student visit

COSTS
Tuition: $27,810 (3rd–5th), $28,836 (6th–12th)
Average additional fees: $800–$1,000
Financial aid budget: $2.1M
Average grant size: $18,000
% of students receiving aid: 11%
Endowment: Yes

NOTE: This data applies to the 2009–2010 school year.

CURRICULUM

Languages and grades offered: Chinese, French, Latin, Spanish
AP classes/IB program: 18 AP classes
Tutors/learning specialists: 2
Other resource specialists: Counselors, nurse
Art programs: Art history, ceramics, digital art & photography, drawing, painting, printmaking, sculpture
Sports: Baseball, basketball, cross-country, fencing, football, golf, hockey, lacrosse, riflery, rugby, soccer, squash, swimming, tennis, track & field, ultimate Frisbee, water polo, winter soccer, winter track, wrestling
Special features and activities: Landon is the only all-boys, non-denominational day school between Baltimore and Richmond. All Lower and Middle School boys are required to be part of a performing group, take art classes, and compulsory athletics. Upper School boys have a two-year art requirement (either music, art, or drama classes) as well as compulsory athletics.
Summer programs: Coed offerings for enrichment and academic classes, studio arts, music programs, day camps, sports camps

CAMPUS LIFE

Transportation available: Bus service
Lunch options: Yes
Food allergy policy: Peanut-free tables during lunch
Uniform: Yes

CAMPUS

Facilities: 75-acre campus with separate Lower, Middle, and Upper School academic buildings. New Center for Athletic Achievement, learning center, performing arts center, sports center, 6 athletic fields
Long-range plans: N/A

HISTORY AND MISSION STATEMENT

Landon School prepares talented boys for productive lives as accomplished, responsible and caring men, whose actions are guided by the principles of perseverance, teamwork, honor and fair play.

NOTE: This data applies to the 2009–2010 school year.

THE LANGLEY SCHOOL   est. 1942

Doris E. Cottam, Head of School
1411 Balls Hill Road
McLean, VA 22101
703-848-2782
www.langleyschool.org

Kerry Moody, Director of Admission and Financial Aid
kmoody@langleyschool.org

Coed: N–8th
Limited wheelchair access

Governance: Nonprofit
Accredited by: VAIS
Memberships: AISGW, BSF, CASE, ERB, LSF, NAIS, SSATB
Religious affiliation: Nonsectarian

PROFILE
Total enrollment: 478
Graduating class size: 41
Average class size: 7:1 student/teacher ratio
Number of faculty: 67
Boarding option: No
School day: 8:00–3:00 (K–8th)
Extended day hours: 8:00–6:00 (K–8th)
Schools three or more graduates have attended over the past five years: Bullis, Flint Hill, Georgetown Day, Landon, Madeira, Maret, National Cathedral, Potomac, Sidwell Friends, Thomas Jefferson

APPLICATION PROCESS
Grades with openings (approximate): K (18), plus attrition
Birthday cutoff: September 1 (N), September 30 (JK–K)
Deadline: January 14
Fee: $75
Testing required: WPPSI-III/WISC-IV (JK–5th), SSAT (6th–8th)
Steps: Parent interview/tour, application, student visit

COSTS
Tuition: $24,140–$25,410
Average additional fees: None
Financial aid budget: $733,000
Average grant size: $16,615
% of students receiving aid: 8%
Endowment: Yes

NOTE: This data applies to the 2009–2010 school year.

PRESCHOOL PROGRAM

Age	Days	Hours	Tuition	Openings	Class size	Teachers per class	Food provided
3 (N)	5	8:00–11:00	$12,600	24	12	2	
3 (N)	5	12:00–3:00	$12,600	24	12	2	
4 (JK)	5	8:00–11:00	$12,600	12	15	2	
4 (JK)	5	12:00–3:00	$12,600	12	15	2	

CURRICULUM
Languages and grades offered: French, Spanish (K–8th)
AP classes/IB program: N/A
Tutors/learning specialists: N/A
Other resource specialists: Counselor, math specialists, nurse, reading specialists
Art programs: Band, drama, music, studio art
Sports: Basketball, cross-country, lacrosse, soccer, softball, track & field
Special features and activities: Modern languages begin in K, science labs in 1st grade, band in 4th; wide variety of electives, frequent field trips, leadership opportunities, community service projects at all ages; 3 computer labs, media studio with green screen technology, interactive whiteboards in each classroom
Summer programs: Langley Summer Studio

CAMPUS LIFE
Transportation available: Bus service
Lunch options: Yes
Food allergy policy: Peanut controlled (N–2nd)
Uniform: No

CAMPUS
Facilities: 9.2 acres; arts & science building; arts center with auditorium, band & art rooms; library; athletic center, gyms, climbing wall, turf field
Long-range plans: Recently completed new strategic plan

HISTORY AND MISSION STATEMENT
The Langley School first opened its doors as a cooperative nursery school in 1942, and is now a preschool–8th grade day school. We believe that each child's potential is boundless and every child can act with integrity, generosity, and consideration for others. We reach across multiple disciplines to discover, amplify, and embrace the talents of every child, every day. By nurturing, supporting and challenging our students, our inclusive community builds quietly confident independent thinkers who flourish as learners and individuals.

NOTE: This data applies to the 2009–2010 school year.

LITTLE FLOWER SCHOOL   est. 1953

Sister Rosemaron Rynn, Principal
5601 Massachusetts Avenue
Bethesda, MD 20816
301-320-3273
www.littleflowerschool.org

Sister Rosemaron Rynn
office@lfschool.org

Coed: PK–8th
Limited wheelchair access

Governance: Nonprofit
Accredited by: MSA
Memberships: ASCD, NCEA, TACSC
Religious affiliation: Roman Catholic

PROFILE
Total enrollment: 258
Graduating class size: 24
Average class size: 26
Number of faculty: 28
Boarding option: No
School day: 8:15–2:50
Extended day hours: 8:15–6:00
Schools three or more graduates have attended over the past five years: Bethesda Chevy Chase, Connelly School of the Holy Child, Georgetown Prep, Georgetown Visitation, Gonzaga, Holy Cross, St. John's College High, Stone Ridge, Walt Whitman

APPLICATION PROCESS
Grades with openings (approximate): PK–7th
Birthday cutoff: September 1
Deadline: February 4
Fee: $25
Testing required: Varies
Steps: Open house, meeting with principal, application

COSTS
Tuition: $6,400 (Parishioner families)
Average additional fees: None
Financial aid budget: Minimal
Average grant size: Varies
% of students receiving aid: 4%
Endowment: No

NOTE: This data applies to the 2009–2010 school year.

PRESCHOOL PROGRAM

Age	Days	Hours	Tuition	Openings	Class size	Teachers per class	Food provided
4	5	8:15–12:00	$5,800 (Parishioners)	22	22	2	None

CURRICULUM

Languages and grades offered: French, Spanish (1st–8th)
AP classes/IB program: N/A
Tutors/learning specialists: 1
Other resource specialists: Reading specialist
Art programs: General art (PK–8th)
Sports: CYO sports program
Special features and activities: Strong academic program, Blue Ribbon School (one of 50 non-public schools recognized for academic excellence in 2008), after-school programs
Summer programs: None

CAMPUS LIFE

Transportation available: Provided by families
Lunch options: Hot lunch Tuesday and Thursday
Food allergy policy: Peanut free
Uniform: Yes

CAMPUS

Facilities: N/A
Long-range plans: N/A

HISTORY AND MISSION STATEMENT

The mission of Little Flower School is to proclaim the Good News of Jesus Christ. Our aim is to help children enrich their lives by embracing and implementing the values and attitudes of the Catholic faith community.

By providing a loving, supportive environment we strive to help our students realize their own self-worth as well as a genuine concern and respect for others. We endeavor to provide a curriculum that is both flexible and sensitive to the uniqueness of each child in order to facilitate the development of the individual's spiritual, academic and social potential.

NOTE: This data applies to the 2009–2010 school year.

LOUDOUN COUNTRY DAY SCHOOL   est. 1953

Randall Hollister, Headmaster
20600 Red Cedar Drive
Leesburg, VA 20175
703-777-3841
www.lcds.org

Pam Larimer, Admissions Coordinator
pam.larimer@lcds.org

Coed: PK–8th
Wheelchair accessible

Governance: Nonprofit
Accredited by: VAIS
Memberships: AISGW, NAIS, VAIS
Religious affiliation: Nonsectarian

PROFILE
Total enrollment: 283
Graduating class size: 22
Average class size: 16
Number of faculty: 55
Boarding option: No
School day: 8:30–3:20
Extended day hours: 7:15–6:00
Schools three or more graduates have attended over the past five years: Flint Hill, Foxcroft, Georgetown Prep, Highland, Loudoun County Academy of Science, Madeira, Notre Dame Academy, Thomas Jefferson, Wakefield

APPLICATION PROCESS
Grades with openings (approximate): All
Birthday cutoff: September 1
Deadline: March 1
Fee: $75
Testing required: DIAL2, WPPSI-III/WISC-IV
Steps: Application, informal assessment, school visit

COSTS
Tuition: $10,000–$17,000
Average additional fees: $150
Financial aid budget: N/A
Average grant size: N/A
% of students receiving aid: N/A
Endowment: N/A

NOTE: This data applies to the 2009–2010 school year.

PRESCHOOL PROGRAM

Age	Days	Hours	Tuition	Openings	Class size	Teachers per class	Food provided
4	5	8:30–12:00	$9,900	24	12	2	None
4–5	5	8:30–3:20	$13,750	12	12	2	None

CURRICULUM

Languages and grades offered: French, Spanish (PK–8th)
AP classes/IB program: N/A
Tutors/learning specialists: 2
Other resource specialists: N/A
Art programs: Chorus, drama, instruments, music, visual arts
Sports: Basketball, cross-country, field hockey, lacrosse, soccer, tennis, track & field
Special features and activities: New campus allows for expansion of all grades
Summer programs: N/A

CAMPUS LIFE
Transportation available: Bus service
Lunch options: PA sponsored
Food allergy policy: Yes
Uniform: Yes

CAMPUS
Facilities: New campus, July 2009
Long-range plans: N/A

HISTORY AND MISSION STATEMENT
Loudoun Country Day School, an accredited, independent, coeducational school, educates students in pre-kindergarten through eighth grade. We cultivate the intellectual, social, emotional, and physical growth of each child. We pride ourselves on our rigorous core curriculum, nurturing environment, and extensive programs in foreign languages, arts, computers, and athletics. LCDS inspires excellence and builds character, preparing each child for the challenges ahead.

NOTE: This data applies to the 2009–2010 school year.

THE LOURIE CENTER SCHOOL   est. 1986

Tamieka Skinner-Thomasson, Director
12301 Academy Way
Rockville, MD 20852
301-984-4444 x109
www.louriecenter.org

Tamieka Skinner-Thomasson
tskinner@louriecenter.org

Coed: PK–5th
Wheelchair accessible

Governance: Nonprofit
Accredited by: DCPS, MSDE
Memberships: MANSEF
Religious affiliation: Nonsectarian

PROFILE
Total enrollment: 40
Graduating class size: Varies
Average class size: 8 at most
Number of faculty: N/A
Boarding option: No
School day: 9:00–3:00, 9:00–1:00 (W)
Extended day hours: N/A
Schools three or more graduates have attended over the past five years: Children's Guild, Katherine Thomas, Kennedy Kreiger, Kingsbury, Leary School

APPLICATION PROCESS
Grades with openings (approximate):
Birthday cutoff: None
Deadline: Open enrollment
Fee: None
Testing required: Psycho-ed, academic, clinical
Steps: Submit intake packet, tour

COSTS
Tuition: $53,988.80
Average additional fees: N/A
Financial aid budget: None
Average grant size: N/A
% of students receiving aid: N/A
Endowment: No

NOTE: This data applies to the 2009–2010 school year.

CURRICULUM
Languages and grades offered: N/A
AP classes/IB program: N/A
Tutors/learning specialists: N/A
Other resource specialists: N/A
Art programs: N/A
Sports: N/A
Special features and activities: N/A
Summer programs: 11-month programming

CAMPUS LIFE
Transportation available: Provided by county
Lunch options: Students bring lunch
Food allergy policy: Notification to staff by family
Uniform: No

CAMPUS
Facilities: N/A
Long-range plans: N/A

HISTORY AND MISSION STATEMENT

The Reginald S. Lourie Center for Infants and Young Children is a private, nonprofit agency dedicated to helping at-risk children and their families achieve a healthy emotional start in life through early intervention programs, consultation, research, and training.

The center was founded in 1983 by the late Dr. Reginald S. Lourie, a worldwide leader in the fields of pediatric child psychiatry and infant mental health, and his colleagues, including Dr. T. Berry Brazelton and Dr. Stanley Greenspan, as an outgrowth of their six-year clinical research project funded by the National Institute of Mental Health. In July 2006, the center affiliated with Adventist HealthCare, Inc.

Serving more than 4,200 children and families in the Washington metropolitan area, regardless of ability to pay, the center is a pioneer and leader in the field of infant and child mental health.

NOTE: This data applies to the 2009–2010 school year.

LOWELL SCHOOL   est. 1965

Debbie Gibbs, Head of School
1640 Kalmia Road, NW
Washington, DC 20012
202-577-2004
www.lowellschool.org

Michelle Belton, Director of Admissions
mbelton@lowellschool.org

Coed: N–6th
Wheelchair accessible

Governance: Nonprofit
Accredited by: AIMS
Memberships: AIMS, AISGW, NAIS, SSATB
Religious affiliation: Nonsectarian

PROFILE
Total enrollment: 312
Graduating class size: 33
Average class size: 18
Number of faculty: 51
Boarding option: No
School day: 8:15–3:15, 8:15–2:00 (W)
Extended day hours: 8:15–6:00
Schools three or more graduates have attended over the past five years: Barrie, Bullis, Edmund Burke, Field, Georgetown Day, Green Acres, Holton-Arms, Maret, National Cathedral, St. Anselm's Abbey, Sidwell Friends

APPLICATION PROCESS
Grades with openings (approximate): PK and K (50), plus attrition
Birthday cutoff: June 30, but will consider September 30 as well
Deadline: January 15
Fee: $65
Testing required: Informal assessment (N–2nd), WISC-IV (3rd–6th)
Steps: Tour, application, student visit, interview

COSTS
Tuition: $25,997
Average additional fees: $1,500–$3,800
Financial aid budget: $1M
Average grant size: $12,021
% of students receiving aid: 27%
Endowment: Yes

NOTE: This data applies to the 2009–2010 school year.

PRESCHOOL PROGRAM

Age	Days	Hours	Tuition	Openings	Class size	Teachers per class	Food provided
3–5	5	8:00–12:15	$14,990		18	2	Snack
3–5	5	8:00–12:15, 3 days, 8:00–3:15, 2 days	$19,500		18	2	Snack
3–5	5	8:00–3:15	$23,700		18	2	Snack
JK	5	8:00–3:15	$24,400		18	2	Snack

CURRICULUM

Languages and grades offered: Spanish (N–6th)

AP classes/IB program: N/A

Tutors/learning specialists: 5

Other resource specialists: N/A

Art programs: Art studio, creative movement, music, woodworking

Sports: Basketball, kickball, track

Special features and activities: N/A

Summer programs: Non-academic day camp

CAMPUS LIFE

Transportation available: None

Lunch options: Students bring their lunches

Food allergy policy: Nut-free school

Uniform: No

CAMPUS

Facilities: Art studios, computer lab, dining room, gymnasium, libraries, playgrounds, pool, stream, woodshop

Long-range plans: Expand to 8th grade

HISTORY AND MISSION STATEMENT

Our curriculum evolves from an understanding of the stages of cognitive, social/emotional, artistic and physical development. It promotes active, collaborative learning with an emphasis on building conceptual understanding; promoting creative, critical and analytical thinking; and encouraging problem solving. Lowell's mission is to create an inclusive community of lifelong learners in which each child is valued and respected. Our charge then is to strengthen minds, ensure equity and honor individuality.

NOTE: This data applies to the 2009–2010 school year.

THE MADEIRA SCHOOL   est. 1906

Dr. Elizabeth Griffith, Head of School
8328 Georgetown Pike
McLean, VA 22102
703-556-8325
www.madeira.org

Ann Miller, Director of Admission and Financial Aid
amiller@madeira.org

Girls: 9th–12th
Limited wheelchair access

Governance: Nonprofit
Accredited by: VAIS
Memberships: AISGW, NAIS, NCGS, TABS
Religious affiliation: Nonsectarian

PROFILE
Total enrollment: 320
Graduating class size: 75
Average class size: 14
Number of faculty: 46
Boarding option: Yes
School day: 7:50–3:15
Extended day hours: N/A
Schools three or more graduates have attended over the past five years: Connecticut College, Cornell, Dartmouth, Duke, Georgetown, New York University, University of Pennsylvania, University of Virginia, Wake Forest, William and Mary

APPLICATION PROCESS
Grades with openings (approximate):
9th (75), 10th (10–15), 11th (2–5)
Birthday cutoff: N/A
Deadline: January 31
Fee: $70
Testing required: SSAT (9th–11th)
Steps: Application, interview

COSTS
Tuition: $35,000 (day), $46,100 (boarding)
Average additional fees: N/A
Financial aid budget: $2.3M
Average grant size: $32,000
% of students receiving aid: 20%
Endowment: Yes

NOTE: This data applies to the 2009–2010 school year.

CURRICULUM
Languages and grades offered: Chinese, French, Latin, Spanish (9th–12th)
AP classes/IB program: 12 AP classes
Tutors/learning specialists: N/A
Other resource specialists: N/A
Art programs: Graphic design, photography
Sports: Basketball, cross-country, dance, field hockey, lacrosse, riding, soccer, softball, squash, swimming & diving, tennis, track & field, volleyball, winter soccer
Special features and activities: Co-curriculum program
Summer programs: Girls First girls' leadership camp

CAMPUS LIFE
Transportation available: None
Lunch options: Yes
Food allergy policy: Yes
Uniform: No

CAMPUS
Facilities: 376-acre campus, Performing Arts Center, indoor pool, stables
Long-range plans: Major dorm renovation, expand global curriculum

HISTORY AND MISSION STATEMENT
The mission of The Madeira School, as envisioned by Lucy Madeira in 1906, is that it is both our duty and our privilege to help young women to understand their changing world and to have the confidence to live lives that are of their own making, their own passions, their own dreams.

We believe that the most effective and ethical leaders for tomorrow, whether academic, artistic, athletic, political, social, or professional will be those possessing a clear sense of self, of community, and the world, as well as a strong commitment to lifelong learning and social service.

In our commitment to Lucy Madeira, we provide a rich and varied community that appreciates the distinctive social, emotional, and academic needs of young women.

NOTE: This data applies to the 2009–2010 school year.

MARET SCHOOL — est. 1911

Marjo Talbott, Head of School
3000 Cathedral Avenue, NW
Washington, DC 20008
202-939-8814
www.maret.org

Annie Farquhar, Director of Admission and Financial Aid
afarquhar@maret.org

Coed: K–12th
Wheelchair accessible

Governance: Nonprofit
Accredited by: AIMS, MSA
Memberships: AIMS, AISGW
Religious affiliation: Nonsectarian

PROFILE
Total enrollment: 600
Graduating class size: 75
Average class size: 12–14
Number of faculty: 106
Boarding option: No
School day: 8:00–3:00
Extended day hours: 8:00–6:00
Schools three or more graduates have attended over the past five years: Brown, Cornell, Harvard, Oberlin, Princeton, Stanford, University of Michigan, University of Pennsylvania, Washington University in St. Louis, Yale

APPLICATION PROCESS
Grades with openings (approximate): K (18–20), 1st (7–9), 4th (7–9), 6th (10–13), 7th (20), 9th (15–20)
Birthday cutoff: September 1
Deadline: December 28 (4th), January 8 (all other grades)
Fee: $65
Testing required: WPPSI-III/WISC-IV (K–5th), SSAT or ISEE (6th–11th) or PSAT (11th)
Steps: Tour/open house, application, interview (6th–11th), school visit (K–4th)

COSTS
Tuition: $24,695–$28,430
Average additional fees: $550
Financial aid budget: $2.2M
Average grant size: $19,500
% of students receiving aid: 18%
Endowment: Yes

NOTE: This data applies to the 2009–2010 school year.

CURRICULUM

Languages and grades offered: Chinese (9th–12th), French (5th–12th), Latin (6th–12th), Spanish (K–12th)

AP classes/IB program: 12 AP classes

Tutors/learning specialists: 2

Other resource specialists: Full-time nurse, school counselor

Art programs: Ceramics, computer graphics, mixed media, painting & drawing, photography, sculpture, woodworking

Sports: Baseball, basketball, cross-country, football, golf, lacrosse, soccer, softball, swimming, tennis, track, volleyball, wrestling

Special features and activities: Intensive Study Week in February allows students and faculty to explore in depth a subject of interest together in small groups; service learning incorporated throughout the curriculum for all grade levels; annual Lower, Middle, and Upper School drama productions

Summer programs: Basketball, soccer, volleyball camps; filmmaking camp; Horizons @Maret; trips to China, France, Honduras, Florida

CAMPUS LIFE

Transportation available: DC Metrobus stops in front of school; 2 Red Line Metro stops within a 10-minute walk

Lunch options: Included in tuition

Food allergy policy: We work with each family; peanut butter in sealed containers, nut-free table (Lower School), no nut products used in food preparation

Uniform: No

CAMPUS

Facilities: 1 all-turf field, 2 gyms, 2 libraries, 3 technology labs, 1 theater. Separate Lower, Middle, and Upper School buildings

Long-range plans: N/A

HISTORY AND MISSION STATEMENT

Maret's community supports and celebrates a number of dichotomies: We emphasize both faculty individuality and widespread collaboration. We value traditional academic rigor and innovative methods of teaching, such as cross-disciplinary approaches, independent study, and the incorporation of technology into many facets of our curriculum. We encourage a deep sense of accountability to the school community and an atmosphere unencumbered by elaborate rules. In all areas—academic, artistic, and athletic—we applaud high achievement while promoting a philosophy of nurtured risk taking.

NOTE: This data applies to the 2009–2010 school year.

MATER DEI SCHOOL   est. 1960

Edward N. Williams, Headmaster
9600 Seven Locks Road
Bethesda, MD 20817
301-365-2700
www.materdeischool.org

Edward N. Williams
nwilliams@materdeischool.org

Boys: 1st–8th
Wheelchair accessible

Governance: Nonprofit
Accredited by: AIMS
Memberships: AIMS, AISGW, NAIS
Religious affiliation: Catholic

PROFILE
Total enrollment: 225
Graduating class size: 40
Average class size: 20
Number of faculty: 24
Boarding option: No
School day: 8:20–3:00
Extended day hours: N/A
Schools three or more graduates have attended over the past five years: Georgetown Prep, Gonzaga, Landon, St. Albans, St. John's College High

APPLICATION PROCESS
Grades with openings (approximate): 1st (20), 6th (20)
Birthday cutoff: N/A
Deadline: December 15
Fee: $100
Testing required: In-house testing
Steps: Online application, in-house testing/informal assessment

COSTS
Tuition: $13,400
Average additional fees: $300
Financial aid budget: N/A
Average grant size: N/A
% of students receiving aid: N/A
Endowment: Yes

NOTE: This data applies to the 2009–2010 school year.

CURRICULUM

Languages and grades offered: Latin (8th)
AP classes/IB program: N/A
Tutors/learning specialists: N/A
Other resource specialists: N/A
Art programs: Music, studio art
Sports: Baseball, basketball, football, hockey, lacrosse, soccer, tennis, wrestling
Special features and activities: DC Week, Outdoor Week
Summer programs: Boys' summer sports camp

CAMPUS LIFE

Transportation available: None
Lunch options: N/A
Food allergy policy: N/A
Uniform: Yes

CAMPUS

Facilities: 2 gyms, turf field, 2 practice fields
Long-range plans: N/A

HISTORY AND MISSION STATEMENT

Based on the teachings of Christ and the Catholic Church, in partnership with the family and parish community, Mater Dei Catholic School will provide each child the opportunity to reach their potential and to develop the academic, technological, and social skills necessary to become lifelong learners who serve God in our community and the world.

MCLEAN SCHOOL OF MARYLAND   est. 1954

Darlene B. Pierro, Head of School
8224 Lochinver Lane
Potomac, MD 20854
240-395-0698
www.mcleanschool.org

Judy Jankowski, Director of Admission
jjankowski@mcleanschool.org

Coed: K–12th
Wheelchair accessible

Governance: Nonprofit
Accredited by: AIMS, Maryland State Department of Non-Public Education
Memberships: AIMS, BSF, CEC, NAIS, Parents of Gifted and Talented
Learning-Disabled Children, PCW
Religious affiliation: Nonsectarian

PROFILE
Total enrollment: 470
Graduating class size: 40
Average class size: 10
Number of faculty: 82
Boarding option: No
School day: 8:15–3:15
Extended day hours: 8:15–6:00
**Schools three or more graduates
have attended over the past five
years:** American University,
Cornell, George Mason, George
Washington, Howard, Indiana
University, University of Maryland,
Oberlin, University of
Pennsylvania, Smith

APPLICATION PROCESS
Grades with openings (approximate):
K (30), 3rd (15), 6th (12), 9th (48)
Birthday cutoff: N/A
Deadline: February 1
Fee: $100
Testing required: IQ (WISC-IV,
Stanford-Binet V), achievement
(WJ-III)
Steps: Application, parent interview,
student visit

COSTS
Tuition: $24,000–$29,000
Average additional fees: $1,200
Financial aid budget: $900,000
Average grant size: $17,085
% of students receiving aid: 12%
Endowment: Yes

NOTE: This data applies to the 2009–2010 school year.

CURRICULUM
Languages and grades offered: American Sign Language (7th–12th), Latin (5th–12th), Spanish (K–12th)
AP classes/IB program: 7 AP classes
Tutors/learning specialists: 6 on staff, plus outside providers
Other resource specialists: Academic coaches, counselors, nurses, occupational therapists, speech-language pathologists
Art programs: Beginning guitar, ceramics, choir, drama, jazz band, photography, portfolio art, studio art
Sports: Basketball, cross-country, lacrosse, soccer, track & field, volleyball, wrestling
Special features and activities: Activity committee, anime, chess club, drama/improv, environmental awareness, equity board, film club, jazz band, martial arts, outdoor education, photography, student government, yearbook
Summer programs: "Summer Edge"—academic and recreational programs for students in grades K–10

CAMPUS LIFE
Transportation available: Bus service
Lunch options: Catered lunch optional
Food allergy policy: Accommodations made as necessary
Uniform: Yes

CAMPUS
Facilities: Located on 9 acres; 67 classrooms, including 3 art rooms, 3 music rooms, 3 technology labs, 7 science labs, 1 all-purpose room, 1 gymnasium, 2 athletic fields and a weight room
Long-range plans: Acquisition of a separate Upper School campus located in Bethesda, slated to open in September 2010

HISTORY AND MISSION STATEMENT
McLean makes learning accessible, stimulating, and meaningful for a broad range of learners. Our students flourish because McLean responds to students' learning styles. McLean prepares students intellectually and socially by encouraging self-advocacy and building self-confidence. Our students succeed because they learn how to learn.

McLean School was founded by Lenore and Delbert Foster in 1954. Their mission: to provide a unique learning environment that would serve the needs and gifts of all kinds of students. After the Fosters retired in 1978, a group of parents, faculty and staff formed a nonprofit corporation for McLean School and relocated to the present location.

NOTE: This data applies to the 2009–2010 school year.

MELVIN J. BERMAN HEBREW ACADEMY　　est. 1944

Dr. Joshua Levisohn, Headmaster
13300 Arctic Avenue
Rockville, MD 20853
301-962-9400 x5630
www.mjbha.org

Sharon Butler, Admissions Director
butlers@mjbha.org

Coed: N–12th
Wheelchair accessible

Governance: Nonprofit
Accredited by: N/A
Memberships: N/A
Religious affiliation: Modern Orthodox Jewish

PROFILE
Total enrollment: 700
Graduating class size: 31
Average class size: 15–20
Number of faculty: 120
Boarding option: No
School day: 8:15–3:30 (K–5th), 8:15–4:30 (6th–8th), 8:15–5:30 (9th–12th)
Extended day hours: 8:15–5:30
Schools three or more graduates have attended over the past five years: Brandeis, Cornell, New York University, Stern College, University of Maryland, University of Michigan, Yeshiva University

APPLICATION PROCESS
Grades with openings (approximate): Most
Birthday cutoff: September 1
Deadline: Rolling
Fee: N/A
Testing required: None
Steps: Open house, parent visit, student visit, interviews

COSTS
Tuition: $12,515 (K–5th), $15,400 (6th–8th), $18,230 (9th–12th)
Average additional fees: $750
Financial aid budget: $2.1M
Average grant size: $8,000
% of students receiving aid: 25%
Endowment: Yes

NOTE: This data applies to the 2009–2010 school year.

PRESCHOOL PROGRAM

Age	Days	Hours	Tuition	Openings	Class size	Teachers per class	Food provided
2–4	3	8:15–12:00	$4,160	Yes	8–15	2–3	Snacks
2–4	5	8:15–12:00	$5,305	Yes	8–15	2–3	Snacks
2–4	5	8:15–2:15	$8,105	Yes	8–15	2–3	Snacks
2–4	5	8:15–3:30	$9,305	Yes	8–15	2–3	Snacks

CURRICULUM

Languages and grades offered: Arabic, Hebrew
AP classes/IB program: 7 AP classes
Tutors/learning specialists: 8
Other resource specialists: Music, science
Art programs: Ceramics, drama, photography, studio arts
Sports: Basketball, soccer, softball, tennis, track & field, volleyball
Special features and activities: N/A
Summer programs: N/A

CAMPUS LIFE

Transportation available: Yes
Lunch options: Hot lunch available daily for $5
Food allergy policy: Peanut free
Uniform: No

CAMPUS

Facilities: 20-acre campus; art studios, 1,200-seat auditorium, full-size gym, music room, full-size track, 2 playgrounds, softball field, tennis courts
Long-range plans: N/A

HISTORY AND MISSION STATEMENT

Melvin J. Berman Hebrew Academy is the only Modern Orthodox Preschool–12th grade day school in the Washington area.

About 700 students learn in our dual-curriculum college preparatory program in an atmosphere of reverence, good citizenship and love of the Jewish people and Israel.

NOTE: This data applies to the 2009–2010 school year.

NATIONAL CATHEDRAL SCHOOL   est. 1900

Kathleen O'Neill Jamieson, Head of School
Mount St. Alban
Washington, DC 20016
202-537-6374
www.ncs.cathedral.org

Susan A. Mantilla-Goin, Director of Admission and Financial Aid
smantilla-goin@cathedral.org

Girls: 4th–12th
Wheelchair accessible

Governance: Nonprofit
Accredited by: AIMS
Memberships: AISGW, NCGS
Religious affiliation: Episcopal

PROFILE
Total enrollment: 582
Graduating class size: 78
Average class size: 13
Number of faculty: 127
Boarding option: No
School day: 8:00–3:30
Extended day hours: None
Schools three or more graduates have attended over the past five years: Columbia, Cornell, Dartmouth, Duke, Princeton, Stanford, University of Pennsylvania, University of Virginia, Yale

APPLICATION PROCESS
Grades with openings (approximate): 4th (46), 6th (10), 7th (10–15), 9th (15), plus attrition
Birthday cutoff: N/A
Deadline: January 15
Fee: $75
Testing required: ERB (4th), WISC-IV (4th–6th), ISEE (5th), SSAT (6th–11th)
Steps: Application, tour/interview

COSTS
Tuition: $30,700
Average additional fees: Varies
Financial aid budget: $2M+
Average grant size: $19,901
% of students receiving aid: 17%
Endowment: Yes

NOTE: This data applies to the 2009–2010 school year.

CURRICULUM

Languages and grades offered: Chinese (9th–12th), French (4th–12th), Greek (9th–12th), Japanese (9th–12th), Latin (7th–12th), Spanish (4th–12th)

AP classes/IB program: 16 AP classes

Tutors/learning specialists: Yes

Other resource specialists: N/A

Art programs: Extensive offerings in all areas of performing and studio art

Sports: Basketball, climbing, crew, cross-country, dance team, field hockey, lacrosse, soccer, softball, swimming & diving, tennis, track & field, volleyball

Special features and activities: Coordinate program with St. Albans School for Boys

Summer programs: Academic, sports

CAMPUS LIFE

Transportation available: Morning pick-up service available from Woodley North Metro stop

Lunch options: Included in tuition; salad and sandwich bars, soup of the day, fresh fruit, 2 meat and vegetarian options daily

Food allergy policy: N/A

Uniform: Yes (4th–6th)

CAMPUS

Facilities: 57-acre close of Washington National Cathedral, 4 interconnected academic buildings, historic Hearst Hall with auditorium and dining room, athletic & fitness center

Long-range plans: N/A

HISTORY AND MISSION STATEMENT

For over a century, National Cathedral School has provided girls in grades 4–12 an exceptional college preparatory program which prepares them to be leaders in their fields and in their everyday lives. Among the brightest in the DC metropolitan area, our girls are diverse in their backgrounds and interests. They arrive to our campus, on the 57-acre Cathedral Close and adjacent to the Washington National Cathedral, eager to share their own talents and learn from others in turn. We foster a community that builds confidence, self-esteem and leadership skills. Continually challenging and supporting students to reach beyond themselves, our faculty stands ready to guide the girls in this remarkable experience. Our structured interdisciplinary curriculum and innovative teaching styles allow girls to grow as they encounter unfamiliar learning situations and learn to take risks.

NOTE: This data applies to the 2009–2010 school year.

NATIONAL PRESBYTERIAN SCHOOL   est. 1969

James T. Neill, Head of School
4121 Nebraska Avenue, NW
Washington, DC 20016
202-537-7508
www.nps-dc.org

Katy Harvey, Director of Admissions
kharvey@nps-dc.org

Coed: N–6th
Wheelchair accessible

Governance: Nonprofit
Accredited by: AIMS, MSA
Memberships: AIMS, AISGW
Religious affiliation: Presbyterian

PROFILE

Total enrollment: 250
Graduating class size: 15–30
Average class size: 13
Number of faculty: 40
Boarding option: No
School day: 8:30–3:15, 8:30–12:15 (F)
Extended day hours: 7:30–6:00
Schools three or more graduates have attended over the past five years: Bullis, Field, Holton-Arms, Landon, Maret, National Cathedral, Potomac, St. Albans, St. Andrew's Episcopal, Sidwell Friends

APPLICATION PROCESS

Grades with openings (approximate): K (10), plus attrition
Birthday cutoff: September 1
Deadline: January 22
Fee: $60; $15 if applying for tuition assistance
Testing required: WPPSI-III/WISC-IV (K–6th)
Steps: Open house, application, parent visit, student visit/play date

COSTS

Tuition: $20,960 (K–6th)
Average additional fees: $840 (Early Birds), $4,100 (After 3 Club)
Financial aid budget: $592,000
Average grant size: $15,000
% of students receiving aid: 15%
Endowment: No

NOTE: This data applies to the 2009–2010 school year.

PRESCHOOL PROGRAM

Age	Days	Hours	Tuition	Openings	Class size	Teachers per class	Food provided
3	5	8:30–12:00, + PM options	$13,500– $19,500	22	22	3	Snack
4	5	8:30–12:00, + minimum 2 afternoons	$18,130– $20,960	11	11–12	1	Snack

CURRICULUM
Languages and grades offered: Spanish (1st–6th)
AP classes/IB program: N/A
Tutors/learning specialists: 4
Other resource specialists: Counselor, math coordinator
Art programs: Art, chorus, drama, handbell choirs, music
Sports: Basketball, lacrosse, soccer, softball, track
Special features and activities: After-school classes in art, music, writing, geography, math, cooking, language, sports clinics, martial arts
Summer programs: Summer Horizons Camp

CAMPUS LIFE
Transportation available: None
Lunch options: Bring lunch
Food allergy policy: Allergy sensitive; teachers trained in use of EpiPen
Uniform: No

CAMPUS
Facilities: Gymnasium, media lab, science lab
Long-range plans: N/A

HISTORY AND MISSION STATEMENT
Founded in 1969 as an educational mission of The National Presbyterian Church, National Presbyterian School (NPS) is a traditional, coeducational elementary school dedicated to educational excellence in an ecumenical Christian environment. A loving and inclusive community, NPS strives to help children develop intellectual, spiritual, and personal foundations that will serve them throughout their lives.

NPS is committed to safeguarding the precious decade of childhood— the years from nursery to sixth grade. The school embraces and seeks to engender in its students five core values: love, respect, honesty, responsibility, and safety.

NOTE: This data applies to the 2009–2010 school year.

THE NEW SCHOOL OF NORTHERN VIRGINIA

est. 1989

John Potter, Headmaster
9431 Silver King Court
Fairfax, VA 22031
703-691-3040
www.newschoolva.com

John Potter
johnp@newschoolva.com

Coed: 4th–12th
Wheelchair accessible

Governance: Proprietary
Accredited by: SACS, SAIS
Memberships: CES, NCISR
Religious affiliation: Nonsectarian

PROFILE
Total enrollment: 151
Graduating class size: 28
Average class size: 12
Number of faculty: 28
Boarding option: No
School day: 9:00–3:55
Extended day hours: 7:30–5:30
Schools three or more graduates have attended over the past five years: American University, Dickinson College, George Mason, Guilford College, Hampshire College, Hiram College, Marymount Manhattan College, St. John's College

APPLICATION PROCESS
Grades with openings (approximate): 4th–9th, limited openings in 10th–11th
Birthday cutoff: N/A
Deadline: Rolling
Fee: $75
Testing required: None
Steps: Meeting with Headmaster or Director, application, student school visit

COSTS
Tuition: $16,600 (4th–6th), $19,500 (7th–8th), $21,600 (9th–12th)
Average additional fees: $350
Financial aid budget: Limited
Average grant size: Varies
% of students receiving aid: N/A
Endowment: N/A

NOTE: This data applies to the 2009–2010 school year.

CURRICULUM

Languages and grades offered: French, German, Spanish (4th–12th)
AP classes/IB program: 5–8 AP classes
Tutors/learning specialists: Privately arranged with teachers
Other resource specialists: N/A
Art programs: Dance, fine arts, music (including instrument lessons), theater (including Cappies)
Sports: Basketball, fitness, soccer, ultimate Frisbee, other
Special features and activities: N/A
Summer programs: Academics, art studio, computer camps

CAMPUS LIFE

Transportation available: To and from Vienna Metro station
Lunch options: Can order from local establishments
Food allergy policy: Students/parents order food independently
Uniform: No

CAMPUS

Facilities: Academic buildings, gym, science center, theater
Long-range plans: N/A

HISTORY AND MISSION STATEMENT

Founded in 1989, the mission of The New School is to develop capable and confident individuals with a passion for living and learning. The New School teaches students the essential skills and habits of mind and body necessary to succeed in life. The school fosters a sense of individual empowerment, tempered by respect and responsibility, that allows students to effect positive change and re-imagine themselves as the people they wish to be. The school is committed to maintaining a vibrant community with small classes where students participate, collaborate and ultimately own their education.

NOTE: This data applies to the 2009–2010 school year.

THE NORA SCHOOL   est. 1964

David Mullen, Head of School
955 Sligo Avenue
Silver Spring, MD 20910
301-495-6672
www.nora-school.org

Janette Patterson, Director of Admissions
janette@nora-school.org

Coed: 9th–12th
Wheelchair accessible

Governance: Nonprofit
Accredited by: MSA
Memberships: AISGW, ASCD, BSF, LDA, NAIS, NASSP
Religious affiliation: Nonsectarian

PROFILE
Total enrollment: 60
Graduating class size: 15
Average class size: 8
Number of faculty: 14
Boarding option: No
School day: 8:45–2:35
Extended day hours: 8:00–4:00
Schools three or more graduates have attended over the past five years: Dickinson College, Drexel, Guilford College, Goucher College, McDaniel College, Montgomery College, Shepherd University, University of Maryland, Washington College

APPLICATION PROCESS
Grades with openings (approximate): 9th (15), 10th (5), 11th (3)
Birthday cutoff: N/A
Deadline: Rolling
Fee: $75
Testing required: None
Steps: Student and parent visit/interview, application

COSTS
Tuition: $21,450
Average additional fees: $800
Financial aid budget: $117,975
Average grant size: $12,600
% of students receiving aid: 15%
Endowment: Yes

NOTE: This data applies to the 2009–2010 school year.

CURRICULUM
Languages and grades offered: German, Spanish
AP classes/IB program: None
Tutors/learning specialists: 1
Other resource specialists: N/A
Art programs: Art, art history, ceramics, craft, design, digital art/graphic art, illustration, photography, studio art
Sports: Basketball, soccer, softball
Special features and activities: Junior and senior retreat, monthly community service, outdoor programs
Summer programs: N/A

CAMPUS LIFE
Transportation available: Metro accessible
Lunch options: Open
Food allergy policy: None
Uniform: No

CAMPUS
Facilities: One building
Long-range plans: Building and enrollment expansion

HISTORY AND MISSION STATEMENT
The Nora School aspires to uncover and strengthen the intelligence and talents of bright students who have been frustrated in school. Their frustration may stem from a variety of sources: learning disabilities, health problems, family circumstances, or simply dealing with large bureaucratic structures. The mission of The Nora School is to assist these students in turning their lives around, to get them excited and confident about learning, to help them take responsibility for their actions and their lives, to help them view the world more critically, and to prepare them for post-secondary education.

NOTE: This data applies to the 2009–2010 school year.

NORWOOD SCHOOL   est. 1952

Richard T. Ewing, Jr., Head of School
8821 River Road
Bethesda, MD 20817
301-841-2130
www.norwoodschool.org

Mimi Mulligan, Director of Admission and Enrollment Management
mmulligan@norwoodschool.org

Coed: K–8th
Wheelchair accessible

Governance: Nonprofit
Accredited by: AIMS, AISGW, NAIS
Memberships: BSF, CAPE, CASE, CDSHA, ERB, ESHA, LSF, SSATB
Religious affiliation: Nonsectarian

PROFILE
Total enrollment: 525
Graduating class size: 56–60
Average class size: 10–15
Number of faculty: 85
Boarding option: No
School day: 8:15–2:30 (K–2nd),
8:15–3:30 (3rd–6th), 8:15–4:15
(7th–8th)
Extended day hours: 8:15–5:50
Schools three or more graduates have attended over the past five years: Georgetown Day, Georgetown Prep, Georgetown Visitation, Holton-Arms, Landon, Maret, National Cathedral, Potomac, St. Albans, St. Andrew's Episcopal, Sidwell Friends

APPLICATION PROCESS
Grades with openings (approximate):
K (48–54), 1st (6–10), 3rd (6),
6th (6)
Birthday cutoff: September 1
Deadline: February 1
Fee: $60
Testing required: WPPSI-III/WISC-IV
(K–4th), SSAT or ISEE (5th–8th)
Steps: Tour or open house, application, parent interview, child visit

COSTS
Tuition: $24,000–$25,500
Average additional fees: $800
Financial aid budget: $1.5M
Average grant size: $15,000
% of students receiving aid: 17%
Endowment: Yes

NOTE: This data applies to the 2009–2010 school year.

CURRICULUM

Languages and grades offered: Chinese (5th–8th), French (5th–8th), Latin (6th–8th), Spanish (K–8th)

AP classes/IB program: N/A

Tutors/learning specialists: 2

Other resource specialists: Lower School and Middle School counselor, school psychologist

Art programs: Art is a core part of the Norwood experience starting in Kindergarten and continuing through 8th grade

Sports: Baseball, basketball, cross-country, dance, field hockey, lacrosse, soccer, softball, strength & conditioning, Summit (Outdoor Adventure), track

Special features and activities: Community service, yearbook, GLOW, newspaper, peer counselors, Model UN, SEED

Summer programs: Art Adventures, chemistry, CIT, cooking, dance, digital photography, French, junior day camp, Magic!, Nuts About Numbers, Outdoor Adventure, Science Explorations, Spanish, sports & games, SSAT & writing prep, technology, theater, Urban Adventures, Writer's Workshop

CAMPUS LIFE

Transportation available: None

Lunch options: Lunch service with a daily hot choice item, salad bar, deli bar and cereal bar (5th–8th)

Food allergy policy: N/A

Uniform: No

CAMPUS

Facilities: 3 academic buildings; art/music building; Athletic Center with 2 full-size basketball courts, locker rooms and fitness center plus additional gym; extensive outdoor space: baseball field, softball field, 2 full-size soccer fields, large playground; 2 libraries, 2 technology labs

Long-range plans: N/A

HISTORY AND MISSION STATEMENT

Norwood School's mission is to ensure that each of its students grows intellectually, morally, physically, socially, emotionally, and spiritually, while preparing to function productively and generously in our pluralistic society. Norwood's challenging educational program and broad-based activities are designed to help students experience joy in learning, develop self-confidence, and learn respect for the rights and feelings of others. Embracing diversity is integral to the school's tradition that recognizes the worth of each member of the community and emphasizes the common values of academic achievement, mutual respect, cooperation, and personal responsibility.

NOTE: This data applies to the 2009–2010 school year.

NYSMITH SCHOOL FOR THE GIFTED   est. 1983

Kenneth Nysmith, Head of School
Carole Nysmith, Founder
13625 EDS Drive
Herndon, VA 20171
703-713-3332 x1004
www.nysmith.com

Marian White
mwhite@nysmith.com

Coed: N–8th
Wheelchair accessible

Governance: Proprietary
Accredited by: CITA, NIPSA, SACS
Memberships:
Religious affiliation: Nonsectarian

PROFILE

Total enrollment: 720
Graduating class size: 54
Average class size: 18–20 max.
Number of faculty: 155
Boarding option: No
School day: 8:30–3:00 (K–8th)
Extended day hours: 7:00–6:30
Schools three or more graduates have attended over the past five years: Episcopal High, Georgetown Day, Landon, Madeira, National Cathedral, Phillips Academy, Phillips Exeter, Potomac, Sidwell Friends, St. Stephen's & St. Agnes, Thomas Jefferson

APPLICATION PROCESS

Grades with openings (approximate):
K (24), 1st–8th (varies)
Birthday cutoff: September 30
Deadline: January 31, then rolling
Fee: $250
Testing required: WPPSI-III/WISC-IV (1st–8th)
Steps: Parent tour, application, student visit

COSTS

Tuition: $24,700 (K–3rd), $28,100 (4th–7th)
Average additional fees: $250
Financial aid budget: N/A
Average grant size: Maximum 25% of tuition
% of students receiving aid: N/A
Endowment: No

NOTE: This data applies to the 2009–2010 school year.

PRESCHOOL PROGRAM

Age	Days	Hours	Tuition	Openings	Class size	Teachers per class	Food provided
3–4 (N)	5	8:30–2:30	$19,070	42	14	2	Snack
4–5 (PK)	5	8:30–2:30	$19,070	22	16	2	Snack

CURRICULUM

Languages and grades offered: French (N–3rd, 7th–8th), Latin (6th–8th), Spanish (4th–5th, 7th–8th)
AP classes/IB program: N/A
Tutors/learning specialists: 1
Other resource specialists: N/A
Art programs: Art, band, drama, Orff music program
Sports: Optional after-school sports club activities
Special features and activities: After-school clubs featuring a variety of interests and activities
Summer programs: 2-week summer camp sessions for ages 3–12, blending sports, music, arts and crafts. Swimming pools provide certified lifeguards; staff offer swimming instruction.

CAMPUS LIFE
Transportation available: Bus service, for additional fee
Lunch options: Yes, for additional fee
Food allergy policy: Optional designated table in lunchroom
Uniform: No

CAMPUS
Facilities: Building divided by age group. Gymnasium, stage, library/media center, computer and science labs, soccer/baseball fields, tennis/basketball courts, outdoor amphitheater
Long-range plans: N/A

HISTORY AND MISSION STATEMENT

The Nysmith School philosophy is to teach children new information as they are ready for it. Small class sizes and low student-to-teacher ratios facilitate the diversified curriculum. By incorporating daily computers, science, logic, and foreign language, we are able to expand the children's academic opportunities and make school fun. By eliminating repetition and diversifying the academics, we accelerate to meet each child's needs. Classes are grouped by children of the same age for a well-rounded and balanced social, emotional and educational experience. Our teachers are highly intelligent and creative. We offer a strong math, science, technology, literature, writing and arts program.

NOTE: This data applies to the 2009–2010 school year.

OAKCREST SCHOOL   est. 1976

Ellen M. Cavanagh, Head of School
850 Balls Hill Road
McLean, VA 22101
703-790-5450
www.oakcrest.org

Holly Hartge, Director of Admission
hhartge@oakcrest.org

Girls: 6th–12th
Wheelchair accessible

Governance: Nonprofit
Accredited by: N/A
Memberships: CASE, SSS
Religious affiliation: Roman Catholic

PROFILE
Total enrollment: 194
Graduating class size: 26
Average class size: 12–15
Number of faculty: 34
Boarding option: No
School day: 7:50–3:00
Extended day hours: N/A
Schools three or more graduates have attended over the past five years: Catholic University, Elon, James Madison, Notre Dame, University of Dallas, University of Mary Washington, University of Maryland–College Park, Villanova, Virginia Tech, William and Mary

APPLICATION PROCESS
Grades with openings (approximate): 6th (22), 9th (7–10), plus attrition
Birthday cutoff: N/A
Deadline: February 2
Fee: $50
Testing required: SSAT or ISEE (6th–12th) or HSPT (9th)
Steps: Student shadow visit day, parent interview, application

COSTS
Tuition: $14,721 (6th–8th), $15,696 (9th–12th)
Average additional fees: N/A
Financial aid budget: $288,000
Average grant size: $5,700
% of students receiving aid: 25+%
Endowment: No

NOTE: This data applies to the 2009–2010 school year.

CURRICULUM

Languages and grades offered: Latin (6th), Spanish (7th–12th)
AP classes/IB program: 11 AP classes
Tutors/learning specialists: N/A
Other resource specialists: College counselor
Art programs: Clarinet ensemble, concert chorus, flute ensemble, liturgical music ensemble, musical theater, string ensemble, studio art, theater arts
Sports: Basketball, cross-country, soccer, softball, swimming, tennis, track & field, volleyball
Special features and activities: One-to-one advising program and character development, college counseling, service opportunities, clubs and traditions, honor societies
Summer programs: N/A

CAMPUS LIFE

Transportation available: Carpool opportunities
Lunch options: Brown bag policy. On certain days, students have the options of Chick-fil-A, Health-e lunch, Domino's Pizza
Food allergy policy: None
Uniform: Yes

CAMPUS

Facilities: Five acres; outdoor tennis, basketball and softball multi-sport courts; 18 classrooms, computer lab, language lab, science lab, gym, music and art rooms, 900-seat theater; 109 computers
Long-range plans: It is our goal to make Oakcrest available to a larger number of girls who would benefit from our program.

HISTORY AND MISSION STATEMENT

Oakcrest is a 32-year-old school that was first located in Washington, DC. After growing out of its space there, it moved to McLean in 2000. In 2007, the school purchased land in western Vienna to provide the facility we need for the program that we offer which prepares our students to be thoughtful, self-assured, creative and compassionate women who will have an impact for the good in every endeavor they pursue.

Oakcrest School in partnership with parents challenges girls in grades 6–12 to develop their intellect, character, faith and leadership potential to succeed in college and throughout their lives.

NOTE: This data applies to the 2009–2010 school year.

OAKWOOD SCHOOL   est. 1971

Robert C. McIntyre, Head of School
7210 Braddock Road
Annandale, VA 22003
703-941-5788
www.oakwoodschool.com

Muriel Jedlicka, Admissions Director
mjedlicka@oakwoodschool.com

Coed: K–8th
Limited wheelchair access

Governance: Nonprofit
Accredited by: VAISEF
Memberships: AISGW
Religious affiliation: Nonsectarian

PROFILE
Total enrollment: 110
Graduating class size: 14
Average class size: 8–12
Number of faculty: 28
Boarding option: No
School day: 8:30–1:45 (M),
8:30–3:00
Extended day hours: 8:30–4:30
Schools three or more graduates have attended over the past five years: Bishop O'Connell, Christchurch, Commonwealth Academy, Lab, McLean, Paul VI

APPLICATION PROCESS
Grades with openings (approximate): All
Birthday cutoff: September 30
Deadline: Rolling
Fee: $50
Testing required: All current psychological and educational testing
Steps: Application, on-campus student educational evaluation ($300 fee), follow-up parent consultation

COSTS
Tuition: $26,500
Average additional fees: $600
Financial aid budget: $140,000
Average grant size: $14,000
% of students receiving aid: 9%
Endowment: No

NOTE: This data applies to the 2009–2010 school year.

CURRICULUM

Languages and grades offered: None
AP classes/IB program: N/A
Tutors/learning specialists: Yes
Other resource specialists: Occupational therapist, speech & language therapist
Art programs: Art and music available
Sports: Adaptive PE instruction
Special features and activities: Meet the needs of students with specific learning disabilities
Summer programs: None

CAMPUS LIFE

Transportation available: Independent van service
Lunch options: Students provide
Food allergy policy: Adapted to specific needs
Uniform: No

CAMPUS

Facilities: Computer lab, gym, music room
Long-range plans: Continuing state-of-the-art technology

HISTORY AND MISSION STATEMENT

Founded in 1971, Oakwood School has made a difference in the lives of thousands of students by helping them understand their unique learning styles and learn how to learn. At the heart of our success is a child-centered program based on a curriculum grounded in traditional academics, and an outstanding faculty well versed in teaching to different learning styles, remediation, and effective compensatory strategies.

Oakwood School provides a multisensory educational program in which students with learning differences are guided to achieve their unique academic and social potential in a nurturing community environment.

NOTE: This data applies to the 2009–2010 school year.

ONENESS-FAMILY SCHOOL　　est. 1988

Andrew Kutt, Head of School
6701 Wisconsin Avenue
Chevy Chase, MD 20815
301-652-7751
www.onenessfamily.org

Lauren Thompson
admissions@onenessfamily.org

Coed: N–8th
Limited wheelchair access

Governance: Nonprofit
Accredited by: AMS, State of Maryland
Memberships: IMC
Religious affiliation: Nonsectarian

PROFILE
Total enrollment: 125
Graduating class size: 5
Average class size: 22
Number of faculty: 28
Boarding option: No
School day: 9:00–3:30
Extended day hours: 7:30–6:00
Schools three or more graduates have attended over the past five years: Field, Sandy Spring Friends, Stone Ridge, Walt Whitman, Walter Johnson

APPLICATION PROCESS
Grades with openings (approximate): All
Birthday cutoff: September 1
Deadline: January 15, then rolling
Fee: $50
Testing required: In-house
Steps: Application, visit, parent/teacher conference

COSTS
Tuition: $17,500 (1st–3rd), $18,100 (4th–6th), $18,600 (7th–8th)
Average additional fees: One-time $1,000 enrollment fee
Financial aid budget: N/A
Average grant size: N/A
% of students receiving aid: 15%
Endowment: No

NOTE: This data applies to the 2009–2010 school year.

PRESCHOOL PROGRAM

Age	Days	Hours	Tuition	Openings	Class size	Teachers per class	Food provided
2	3	8:30–12:00	$9,250	24	12	4	Snack
2	3	8:30–3:30	$14,250			4	Snack
2	5	8:30–12:00	$10,250			4	Snack
2	5	8:30–3:30	$15,250			4	Snack
3–5	3	8:30–3:30	$15,100	24		3	Snack
3–5	5	8:30–12:00	$15,100	24		3	Snack
3–5	5	8:30–3:30	$16,150	24		3	Snack

CURRICULUM

Languages and grades offered: French, Spanish (N–8th)

AP classes/IB program: N/A

Tutors/learning specialists: N/A

Other resource specialists: School counselors, speech & language

Art programs: Creative movement, music

Sports: Basketball, lacrosse, physical fitness, soccer

Special features and activities: Concept-based academics, conflict resolution, United Nations Club of DC and Model UN, Earth-keeper club, peacekeeper club

Summer programs: 2 years through kindergarten

CAMPUS LIFE

Transportation available: None

Lunch options: Students bring their own

Food allergy policy: Nut-free policy

Uniform: No

CAMPUS

Facilities: Leased

Long-range plans: Developing 4-year strategic plan

HISTORY AND MISSION STATEMENT

The mission of the Oneness-Family School is to enable students to be successful adults in today's complex and ever-changing society and, at the same time, to empower them to make a positive contribution toward the betterment of the world. The school has a unique curriculum that is a hybrid of Montessori, Waldorf, and other educational ideas. The school's curriculum teaches students how to become global citizens, and it involves students in many projects that relate to the mission of the United Nations.

NOTE: This data applies to the 2009–2010 school year.

OUR LADY OF GOOD COUNSEL HIGH SCHOOL   est. 1958

Arthur Raimo, President
17301 Old Vic Boulevard
Olney, MD 20832
240-283-3235
www.olgchs.org

Kevin F. Collins, Director of Admissions
collins@olgchs.org

Coed: 9th–12th
Wheelchair accessible

Governance: Nonprofit
Accredited by: MSA
Memberships: N/A
Religious affiliation: Catholic

PROFILE
Total enrollment: 1,200
Graduating class size: 287
Average class size: 22
Number of faculty: 107
Boarding option: No
School day: 8:00–2:45
Extended day hours: N/A
Schools three or more graduates have attended over the past five years: American University, Boston College, University of Delaware, Georgetown, University of Maryland, Villanova, University of Virginia, Virginia Tech

APPLICATION PROCESS
Grades with openings (approximate):
9th (300)
Birthday cutoff: N/A
Deadline: December 10
Fee: $50
Testing required: HSPT (9th)
Steps: Application

COSTS
Tuition: $15,000
Average additional fees: $200
Financial aid budget: N/A
Average grant size: N/A
% of students receiving aid: N/A
Endowment: N/A

NOTE: This data applies to the 2009–2010 school year.

CURRICULUM

Languages and grades offered: French, Latin, Spanish (9th–12th)

AP classes/IB program: 16 AP classes, plus IB

Tutors/learning specialists: N/A

Other resource specialists: Ryken Program for students with mild learning differences

Art programs: Art, band, chorus, music

Sports: Baseball, basketball, cross-country, field hockey, football, golf, ice hockey, lacrosse, soccer, swimming & diving, tennis, track & field, wrestling

Special features and activities: N/A

Summer programs: Basketball, Camp Good Counsel, field hockey, football, lacrosse, soccer

CAMPUS LIFE

Transportation available: Bus service

Lunch options: Included in tuition

Food allergy policy: N/A

Uniform: Yes

CAMPUS

Facilities: New 50-acre campus with new buildings and facilities

Long-range plans: N/A

HISTORY AND MISSION STATEMENT

Our Lady of Good Counsel High School is a Xaverian Brothers Catholic school that is committed to preparing students with diverse learning abilities for the challenges of life by providing programs and activities that advance academic excellence and service to others; fostering spiritual, emotional and social growth; promoting inclusion in all community members; and embodying the Xaverian values of humility, trust, zeal, compassion and simplicity upon which the school is founded.

NOTE: This data applies to the 2009–2010 school year.

PARKMONT SCHOOL   est. 1972

Ron McClain, Head of School
4842 16th Street, NW
Washington, DC 20011
202-726-0740
www.parkmont.org

Gina Duffin, Admissions Coordinator
gduffin@parkmont.org

Coed: 6th–12th
Limited wheelchair access

Governance: Nonprofit
Accredited by: AIMS
Memberships: AIMS, AISGW, NAIS
Religious affiliation: Nonsectarian

PROFILE
Total enrollment: 55
Graduating class size: 9
Average class size: 6–10
Number of faculty: 14
Boarding option: No
School day: 8:30–3:30
Extended day hours: 8:30–4:30
Schools three or more graduates have attended over the past five years: N/A

APPLICATION PROCESS
Grades with openings (approximate):
6th–8th (10), 9th–12th (10)
Birthday cutoff: N/A
Deadline: Rolling
Fee: $50
Testing required: None
Steps: Informal assessment, parent interview, student visit

COSTS
Tuition: $24,560
Average additional fees: None
Financial aid budget: N/A
Average grant size: N/A
% of students receiving aid: 33%
Endowment: N/A

NOTE: This data applies to the 2009–2010 school year.

CURRICULUM
Languages and grades offered: Spanish (9th–12th)
AP classes/IB program: None
Tutors/learning specialists: Yes
Other resource specialists: N/A
Art programs: Art, ceramics, dance, photography
Sports: Basketball, soccer, softball, tennis, volleyball
Special features and activities: Modular scheduling allows three courses at a time and field trips, small classes, multi-age groups with diverse learning styles, internships for Upper School students
Summer programs: Summer school

CAMPUS LIFE
Transportation available: N/A
Lunch options: N/A
Food allergy policy: N/A
Uniform: No

CAMPUS
Facilities: Large house in residential community in northwest DC
Long-range plans: N/A

HISTORY AND MISSION STATEMENT
We help adolescents develop the confidence and skills they need to move ahead energetically with their lives. We create a community where students ally themselves with creative adults whose driving concern is their success and well-being. We provide them with substantial experience in the world beyond school that invites them to see more clearly the possibilities ahead. We challenge them with an academic program that fuses adolescent interests with traditional disciplines and respects the variety of their talents and motivations. They get ready to chart their own course; we make sure they are prepared for the journey.

NOTE: This data applies to the 2009–2010 school year.

PAUL VI CATHOLIC HIGH SCHOOL   est. 1983

Virginia Colwell, Principal
10675 Fairfax Boulevard
Fairfax, VA 22030
703-352-0925 x331
www.paulvi.net

Eileen Hanley, Assistant Principal
ehanley@paulvi.net

Coed: 9th–12th

Governance: N/A
Accredited by: N/A
Memberships: N/A
Religious affiliation: Catholic

PROFILE

Total enrollment: 1,100
Graduating class size: 270
Average class size: 24
Number of faculty: 96
Boarding option: No
School day: 7:45–2:45
Extended day hours: N/A
Schools three or more graduates have attended over the past five years: Boston College, Cornell, George Mason, Georgetown, Holy Cross, James Madison, Notre Dame, University of Virginia, Virginia Tech, Wake Forest

APPLICATION PROCESS

Grades with openings (approximate):
Birthday cutoff: N/A
Deadline: January 31
Fee: $50
Testing required: HSPT (9th)
Steps: Application

COSTS

Tuition: $9,300 (Catholic), $12,000 (non-Catholic)
Average additional fees: $700
Financial aid budget: $600,000
Average grant size: $2,000
% of students receiving aid: 20%
Endowment: N/A

NOTE: This data applies to the 2009–2010 school year.

CURRICULUM
Languages and grades offered: French, German, Latin, Spanish (9th–12th)
AP classes/IB program: 15 AP classes
Tutors/learning specialists: 1
Other resource specialists: Yes
Art programs: Art, band, chorus, drama
Sports: Baseball, basketball, cross-country, drill team, football, golf, ice hockey, lacrosse, soccer, softball, swimming, tennis, track & field, volleyball, wrestling
Special features and activities: Academic Center for Excellence; DeSales Academic Support Program; Options Program for developmentally delayed students (limited enrollment)
Summer programs: Enrichment, remediation, study skills

CAMPUS LIFE
Transportation available: Limited bus service
Lunch options: Available at an additional cost
Food allergy policy: N/A
Uniform: Yes

CAMPUS
Facilities: 16.4 acres, baseball/football and practice fields
Long-range plans: N/A

HISTORY AND MISSION STATEMENT
The mission of Paul VI High School is to provide an excellent Catholic education to young men and women in the Washington metro area by affording them the means to achieve spiritual, intellectual, personal, social and physical development according to the teachings of the Gospel and St. Francis de Sales. Paul VI High School is devoted to graduating responsible, moral young adults so that they will continue to "grow in grace and wisdom."

NOTE: This data applies to the 2009–2010 school year.

THE POTOMAC SCHOOL   est. 1904

Geoffrey Jones, Head of School
1301 Potomac School Road
McLean, VA 22101
703-356-4100
www.potomacschool.org

Charlotte Nelsen, Director of Admission
admission@potomacschool.org

Coed: K–12th

Governance: Nonprofit
Accredited by: VAIS
Memberships: AISGW, ASCD, BSF, CASE, ERB, LSF, NACAC, NAPSG, NAIS, PCW, SSATB
Religious affiliation: Nonsectarian

PROFILE
Total enrollment: 980
Graduating class size: 90–100
Average class size: 16–18
Number of faculty: 150
Boarding option: No
School day: 8:10–3:30 (K–8th), 8:10–5:30 (9th–12th)
Extended day hours: 8:10–6:00 (K–8th)
Schools three or more graduates have attended over the past five years: Brown, Carleton, Harvard, Princeton, Santa Clara University, University of Pennsylvania, University of Virginia, Vanderbilt, William and Mary

APPLICATION PROCESS
Grades with openings (approximate): K (48), 1st (8–10), 4th (10–12), 6th (8–10), 7th (20–24), 9th (25)
Birthday cutoff: September 1
Deadline: January 15
Fee: $65
Testing required: WPPSI-III/WISC-IV (K–6th), SSAT or ISEE (7th–10th), PSAT (11th)
Steps: Application, tour, student interview/visit

COSTS
Tuition: $24,340–$27,445
Average additional fees: $720–$2,000
Financial aid budget: $3M
Average grant size: 67% of tuition
% of students receiving aid: 14%
Endowment: N/A

NOTE: This data applies to the 2009–2010 school year.

CURRICULUM
Languages and grades offered: Chinese (9th–12th), French (7th–12th), Latin (7th–12th), Spanish (4th–12th)

AP classes/IB program: 16 AP classes

Tutors/learning specialists: Specialists in math and language arts

Other resource specialists: Counselors

Art programs: Architecture, art history, band, ceramics, chorus, drawing & design, handbells, jazz band, madrigals, music history, music theory, painting, photography, portfolio—independent study, sculpture, stagecraft, theater

Sports: Baseball, basketball, cross-country, football, golf, lacrosse, outdoor ed, squash, swimming, tennis, track & field, weight training, winter track, wrestling

Special features and activities: K–12th on one campus; long-standing traditions, including a weekly assembly program

Summer programs: Day camp, specialty camps for ages PK–9th grade (please see website)

CAMPUS LIFE
Transportation available: Extensive for DC, Maryland, and Virginia: 22 different bus routes and at least 8 shuttle bus stops throughout the metro area

Lunch options: Buy or bring (K–6th); cafeteria (7th–12th)

Food allergy policy: N/A

Uniform: Yes (4th–8th)

CAMPUS
Facilities: 90-acre campus

Long-range plans: N/A

HISTORY AND MISSION STATEMENT
Potomac seeks to provide an atmosphere which encourages high academic achievement, love of learning, caring for others, delight in creative expression, satisfaction of accomplishment, and an appreciation for diversity among students, faculty, administration, and trustees. The school promotes a firm sense of personal integrity, a solid commitment to high ethical and moral values, and a strong social conscience.

NOTE: This data applies to the 2009–2010 school year.

THE PRIMARY DAY SCHOOL   est. 1944

Louise Plumb, Director
7300 River Road
Bethesda, MD 20817
301-365-4355 x14
www.theprimarydayschool.org

Julie McCaffery, Director of Admission
j.mccaffery@theprimarydayschool.org

Coed: PK–2nd
Wheelchair accessible

Governance: Nonprofit
Accredited by: MSDE
Memberships: AISGW
Religious affiliation: Nonsectarian

PROFILE
Total enrollment: 147
Graduating class size: 36
Average class size: 18, with 2 teachers
Number of faculty: 36
Boarding option: No
School day: 8:15–2:45
Extended day hours: 7:45–2:45
Schools three or more graduates have attended over the past five years: Bullis, Georgetown Day, Green Acres, Holton-Arms, Landon, McLean, Montgomery County Public Schools, Norwood, Sidwell Friends, Stone Ridge, Woods

APPLICATION PROCESS
Grades with openings (approximate): K (4), plus attrition
Birthday cutoff: September 1
Deadline: January 15
Fee: $65
Testing required: WPPSI-III/WISC-IV (1st–2nd)
Steps: Application, visits to school (individual and classroom)

COSTS
Tuition: $16,500–$17,300 (K–2nd)
Average additional fees: None
Financial aid budget: Varies
Average grant size: Varies
% of students receiving aid: Varies
Endowment: Yes

NOTE: This data applies to the 2009–2010 school year.

PRESCHOOL PROGRAM

Age	Days	Hours	Tuition	Openings	Class size	Teachers per class	Food provided
4–5	5	8:15–2:45	$15,500	36	18	2	Snack, milk

CURRICULUM

Languages and grades offered: Some exposure to French and Spanish; no formal language instruction

AP classes/IB program: N/A

Tutors/learning specialists: Math and reading

Other resource specialists: Art, library, music, phonovisual, physical education, science

Art programs: 2 professional art teachers work in small groups with the children

Sports: 2 physical education teachers, and after-school sports programs organized by parents

Special features and activities: Phonovisual, character education program, small nurturing community, rich and engaging curriculum, strong support and guidance to families regarding next school placement

Summer programs: N/A

CAMPUS LIFE

Transportation available: None

Lunch options: Hot lunch available for purchase on Fridays

Food allergy policy: Allergy Awareness Policy

Uniform: No

CAMPUS

Facilities: The school is a one-level building with eight spacious homeroom classrooms and includes art, music, and reading rooms; math, science, and technology labs; auditorium, library, nurse's office; playground with a SportCourt, extensive play structure, playhouse, sandbox, soccer field, and ample play space

Long-range plans: N/A

HISTORY AND MISSION STATEMENT

At the time of publication, the statement was being reviewed by the school's board.

NOTE: This data applies to the 2009–2010 school year.

QUEEN ANNE SCHOOL   est. 1964

J. Temple Blackwood, Headmaster
14111 Oak Grove Road
PO Box 4528
Upper Marlboro, MD 20772
301-249-5000 x305
www.queenanne.org

Courtney Pochet, Admissions Director
cpochet@queenanne.org

Coed: 6th–12th
Limited wheelchair access

Governance: Nonprofit
Accredited by: AIMS
Memberships: AIMS, BSF, CAPE, NAES, NAIS
Religious affiliation: Episcopal

PROFILE
Total enrollment: 156
Graduating class size: 25
Average class size: 12
Number of faculty: 23
Boarding option: No
School day: 8:00–3:30
Extended day hours: 8:00–5:30
Schools three or more graduates have attended over the past five years: Elon, Frostburg, George Washington, University of Maryland, Virginia Tech, Washington College

APPLICATION PROCESS
Grades with openings (approximate): 6th (18), 7th (10), 8th (4), 9th (15), 10th (8)
Birthday cutoff: N/A
Deadline: Rolling
Fee: $50
Testing required: ISEE (6th–12th)
Steps: Application, student shadow visit

COSTS
Tuition: $17,600 (6th–8th), $19,300 (9th–12th)
Average additional fees: None
Financial aid budget: $530,000
Average grant size: $7,000
% of students receiving aid: 49%
Endowment: Yes

NOTE: This data applies to the 2009–2010 school year.

CURRICULUM

Languages and grades offered: French, Spanish (7th–12th)

AP classes/IB program: 8 AP classes

Tutors/learning specialists: By private arrangement

Other resource specialists: By private arrangement

Art programs: Ceramics, digital art, drawing & painting, general art (6th–8th), independent portfolio study, sculpture, 2-D design

Sports: Baseball, basketball, cheerleading, cross-country, soccer, softball, track, volleyball

Special features and activities: Strong community service events and obligations

Summer programs: Full array of academic and sports programs. See website: www.queenanne.org/summerprogram

CAMPUS LIFE

Transportation available: None

Lunch options: Optional hot lunch prepared on campus

Food allergy policy: No peanuts; all teachers EpiPen trained

Uniform: Published dress code focused on school logo

CAMPUS

Facilities: Academic classroom buildings, athletic playing fields, gym, library, space shuttle simulator, woods & wetland sites

Long-range plans: Build a full track & indoor soccer facility and a theater; renovate/replace art facility, additional classroom spaces

HISTORY AND MISSION STATEMENT

Queen Anne School is a college preparatory, coeducational, independent, private day school enrolling approximately 160 students, Grades 6–12. Queen Anne is located on 60 acres midway between Washington, DC, and Annapolis, MD. Affiliated with and owned by St. Barnabas' Episcopal/Anglican Church, the outreach of the school offers a demanding, comprehensive program, including Advanced Placement courses, athletics, community service and strong emphasis on science and arts.

NOTE: This data applies to the 2009–2010 school year.

THE RIVER SCHOOL   est. 2000

Nancy Mellon, Executive Director
4880 MacArthur Boulevard, NW
Washington, DC 20007
202-337-3554
www.riverschool.net

Rachel Goldsten, Assistant Head of School
rgoldsten@riverschool.net

Coed: N–3rd
Wheelchair accessible

Governance: Nonprofit
Accredited by: AIMS (provisional)
Memberships: AIMS, AISGW
Religious affiliation: Nonsectarian

PROFILE
Total enrollment: 240
Graduating class size: 12
Average class size: 14
Number of faculty: 66
Boarding option: No
School day: 8:30–3:00
Extended day hours: 8:00–5:00
Schools three or more graduates have attended over the past five years: Georgetown Day, Holton-Arms, Landon, Maret, Potomac, Sheridan, Sidwell Friends, St. Patrick's Episcopal, Washington International

APPLICATION PROCESS
Grades with openings (approximate): Varies
Birthday cutoff: 18 months by August
Deadline: January 31
Fee: $50
Testing required: WPPSI-III (PK–K), WISC-IV (1st–3rd)
Steps: Parent tour, application, student visit

COSTS
Tuition: $25,525 (K–3rd)
Average additional fees: $100
Financial aid budget: Varies
Average grant size: N/A
% of students receiving aid: N/A
Endowment: No

NOTE: This data applies to the 2009–2010 school year.

PRESCHOOL PROGRAM							
Age	Days	Hours	Tuition	Openings	Class size	Teachers per class	Food provided
18 mo.+	2	8:30–12:00	$12,170		10	2	Snack
2+	3	8:30–12:00	$15,480		12	2	Snack
2.5+	5	8:30–12:00	$18,085		14	2	Snack
3.5+	5	8:30–3:00	$24,470		14	2	Snack

CURRICULUM

Languages and grades offered: N/A

AP classes/IB program: N/A

Tutors/learning specialists: 12

Other resource specialists: Audiologist, occupational therapist, pediatric neuropsychologist, speech pathologist

Art programs: Art, drama, music

Sports: Physical education

Special features and activities: Environmental science program (K–3rd); River REACH: clinical and academic services available to school and Washington-area community; after-school sports, basketball clinics; monthly community meetings; classroom & school-wide community service projects

Summer programs: N/A

CAMPUS LIFE

Transportation available: None

Lunch options: Optional Health-E Lunch Program

Food allergy policy: Nut-free school

Uniform: No

CAMPUS

Facilities: Art, music, and science rooms; gymnasium, library, 3 playgrounds, teaching garden

Long-range plans: Arts and science renovation

HISTORY AND MISSION STATEMENT

The River School was founded January 2000 by Nancy K. Mellon. The River School's philosophy is to encourage children to develop a lifelong love of learning by fostering their growth in self-esteem, independence, communication, creativity, and problem solving. Each classroom is run by an educator and a speech pathologist who work together. The class size is never larger than 14 students, which means there is an average student-teacher ratio of 6:1. The school is theme based, which provides a rich environment for vocabulary and concept development.

NOTE: This data applies to the 2009–2010 school year.

SANDY SPRING FRIENDS SCHOOL   est. 1961

Ken Smith, Head of School
16923 Norwood Road
Sandy Spring, MD 20860
301-774-7455
www.ssfs.org

Linda Cooper, Louise Steinfort, KB Beck, Admissions Team
admissions@ssfs.org

Coed: PK–12th
Wheelchair accessible (limited access in Upper School)

Governance: Nonprofit
Accredited by: AIMS
Memberships: AIMS, AISGW, BSF, LSF, NAIS, SSATB, TABS
Religious affiliation: Society of Friends (Quaker)

PROFILE
Total enrollment: 571
Graduating class size: 67
Average class size: 15
Number of faculty: 75
Boarding option: Yes, 5- or 7-day options (9th–12th)
School day: 8:00–3:20, 8:00–2:20 (W)
Extended day hours: 7:30–6:00
Schools three or more graduates have attended over the past five years: Bryn Mawr, College of Wooster, Dartmouth, Dickinson College, Guilford College, Haverford, Occidental College, St. Mary's College of Maryland, University of Maryland–College Park, Washington University in St. Louis

APPLICATION PROCESS
Grades with openings (approximate): K (18), 6th (16), 9th (25), plus attrition
Birthday cutoff: September 1
Deadline: January 15, then rolling
Fee: $75
Testing required: WPPSI-III/WISC-IV (PK–5th), SSAT or ISEE (6th–12th)
Steps: Application, visit/interview

COSTS
Tuition: $18,600–$24,400 (day), $34,900–$42,900 (boarding)
Average additional fees: Varies
Financial aid budget: $2.1M
Average grant size: $11,850
% of students receiving aid: 31%
Endowment: Yes

NOTE: This data applies to the 2009–2010 school year.

PRESCHOOL PROGRAM

Age	Days	Hours	Tuition	Openings	Class size	Teachers per class	Food provided
4	5	8:10–3:15	$18,600	14	14	2	None

CURRICULUM

Languages and grades offered: French (6th–12th), Spanish (1st–12th)
AP classes/IB program: 9 AP classes
Tutors/learning specialists: 1 full time, 2 part time
Other resource specialists: 4 counselors
Art programs: Art, ceramics, dance, drama, music, painting, photography, stagecraft, weaving
Sports: Baseball, basketball, cross-country, golf, lacrosse, soccer, softball, tennis, track & field, volleyball
Special features and activities: 37% non-European-American diversity, no-cut sports, service trips (Middle & Upper Schools)
Summer programs: Summer camps, summer ESL program

CAMPUS LIFE

Transportation available: Bus options
Lunch options: Hot lunch included in tuition for 1st–12th grades
Food allergy policy: Case by case. Dining hall has a separate peanut butter bar and signs on food containing nuts
Uniform: No

CAMPUS

Facilities: 140-acre wooded campus, 14 academic and 6 residential buildings; Lower, Middle, and Upper Schools; athletic complex, dining hall/dormitory, fine arts center, library/science center, Meetinghouse, performing arts center
Long-range plans: New Upper School building, swimming pool, tennis courts

HISTORY AND MISSION STATEMENT

The Religious Society of Friends, also known as Quakers, cherishes the worth and dignity of each individual because we believe there is that of God in every person. Sandy Spring Friends School develops the trained mind, the skilled hand, and the healthy body within a nurturing community centered in the Life of the Spirit. We provide a challenging academic program combined with stimulating opportunities in the arts, athletics, and community service. Our mission is most clearly stated in our motto "Let Your Lives Speak."

NOTE: This data applies to the 2009–2010 school year.

SENECA ACADEMY/THE CIRCLE SCHOOL   est. 1983

Dr. E. Brooke Carroll, Head of School
15601 Germantown Road
Darnestown, MD 20874
301-869-3728
www.senecaacademy.org

Jennifer Serenyi, Admissions Director
info@senecaacademy.org

Coed: N–8th
Wheelchair accessible

Governance: Nonprofit
Accredited by: AIMS
Memberships: ASCD, WSSA
Religious affiliation: Nonsectarian

PROFILE
Total enrollment: 220
Graduating class size: 7
Average class size: 12
Number of faculty: 15
Boarding option: No
School day: 8:30–3:15
Extended day hours: 8:00–5:30
Schools three or more graduates have attended over the past five years: N/A

APPLICATION PROCESS
Grades with openings (approximate): All
Birthday cutoff: September 1
Deadline: Rolling
Fee: $60
Testing required: None
Steps: School visit, application, student classroom visit

COSTS
Tuition: $9,000 (K–4th), $9,525 (5th–8th)
Average additional fees: $200–$250
Financial aid budget: 6% of tuition
Average grant size: $3,600
% of students receiving aid: 16%
Endowment: No

NOTE: This data applies to the 2009–2010 school year.

PRESCHOOL PROGRAM

Age	Days	Hours	Tuition	Openings	Class size	Teachers per class	Food provided
3	2	9:15–11:45	$2,060		14	2	Snack
3	3	9:15–11:45	$2,960		14	2	Snack
4	4	9:00–11:45	$3,600		16	2	Snack
4	4	12:15–2:45	$3,600		16	2	Snack
4	5	12:00–2:45	$4,550		16	2	Snack
4	5	9:00–2:00	$7,245		16	2	Snack

CURRICULUM
Languages and grades offered: Spanish (N–8th)
AP classes/IB program: N/A
Tutors/learning specialists: 1
Other resource specialists: N/A
Art programs: Band, choir, digital photography, music, sculpting, studio art
Sports: After-school clubs such as field games, golf, soccer
Special features and activities: A variety of after-school clubs, including robotics, theater, yoga
Summer programs: Seneca Camp for age 4–first grade; Arts and Adventure, Band and Adventure

CAMPUS LIFE
Transportation available: None
Lunch options: Hot lunch offered twice weekly
Food allergy policy: Yes
Uniform: Yes

CAMPUS
Facilities: 6.5-acre Federal Wildlife Schoolyard Habitat. Art room, media center, large gathering room; natural light-filled, developmentally appropriate classrooms
Long-range plans: IB Primary Years Program

HISTORY AND MISSION STATEMENT
The Circle School was founded in January 1983 by Jodi Thurmond and Marty Long to provide a program of academic excellence and developmentally appropriate curriculum for their own children. Kindergarten was added in 1985. Seneca Academy, the elementary and intermediate component of the school, has been in existence since 1997.

Our mission is to provide a nurturing environment that meets the intellectual, social, emotional and physical needs of our students and provides varied opportunities for learning.

NOTE: This data applies to the 2009–2010 school year.

SHERIDAN SCHOOL   est. 1927

C. Randall Plummer, Head of School
4400 36th Street, NW
Washington, DC 20008
202-362-7900
www.sheridanschool.org

Julie C. Lewis, Director of Admission
jlewis@sheridanschool.org

Coed: K–8th
Limited wheelchair access

Governance: Nonprofit
Accredited by: AIMS, MSA
Memberships: AIMS, AISGW, ASCD, BSF, CASE, CAPE, NAIS, SSATB
Religious affiliation: Nonsectarian

PROFILE
Total enrollment: 220
Graduating class size: 23
Average class size: 24–26
Number of faculty: 34
Boarding option: No
School day: 8:15–2:30 (K),
8:15–3:30 (1st–8th)
Extended day hours: 7:45–6:00
**Schools three or more graduates
have attended over the past five
years:** Edmund Burke, Field,
Georgetown Day, Georgetown
Prep, Madeira, Maret, St. Andrew's
Episcopal, Sidwell Friends,
Washington International

APPLICATION PROCESS
Grades with openings (approximate):
K (24), plus attrition
Birthday cutoff: September 1
Deadline: January 15
Fee: $60
Testing required: WPPSI-III/WISC-IV
(K–5th), SSAT or ISEE (6th–8th)
Steps: Open house, application, student visit, parent interview

COSTS
Tuition: $23,260–$25,830
Average additional fees: $100
Financial aid budget: $569,500
Average grant size: $12,000
% of students receiving aid: 18%
Endowment: Yes

NOTE: This data applies to the 2009–2010 school year.

CURRICULUM
Languages and grades offered: French, Spanish (K–8th)
AP classes/IB program: N/A
Tutors/learning specialists: 1 learning specialist, tutors at an additional fee
Other resource specialists: Counselor
Art programs: Art, music, music and art electives
Sports: Baseball, basketball, cross-country, soccer, softball, track
Special features and activities: Free music lessons after school; spring musical performed by grades 6–8; monthly art and drama weekend workshops; Student Council provides 4th–8th graders opportunity to serve as leaders; yearbook; 8th grade volunteers; community service
Summer programs: Creative Arts & Summer Adventure (CASA) day camp at city campus (ages 3–14), Shenandoah Summer Camp at Sheridan's Mountain Campus

CAMPUS LIFE
Transportation available: None
Lunch options: Lunch provided
Food allergy policy: Sheridan strives to meet the food allergy needs of students, faculty, and staff
Uniform: No

CAMPUS
Facilities: City campus: central building. Mountain campus: 130 acres, adjacent to Shenandoah National Park near Luray, VA
Long-range plans: Strategic plan 2009–14 in process; ongoing curriculum review

HISTORY AND MISSION STATEMENT
Sheridan School's mission is to educate confident, responsible, and kind children who are well prepared to meet the challenges and demands of a complex and changing world. We believe this goal is best accomplished by faculty, staff, and parents working together as a community, emphasizing high academic standards in a small, diverse, nurturing, and learner-centered environment. The School's two campuses, located in northwest Washington, DC, and the Shenandoah Mountains, provide a unique opportunity for its students and their families to combine academic and experiential learning. Sheridan thrives because its philosophy is as vital today as it was when the school was founded in 1927: that a kindergarten through eighth grade coeducational school provides the intimate and safe environment that children need to fulfill their highest potential.

NOTE: This data applies to the 2009–2010 school year.

SIDWELL FRIENDS SCHOOL　　　　est. 1883

Bruce B. Stewart, Head of School
Tom Farquhar, Head of School (2010)
3825 Wisconsin Avenue, NW
Washington, DC 20016
202-537-8111
www.sidwell.edu

Josh Wolman, Associate Head of School for Admissions and Financial Aid
admissions@sidwell.edu

Coed: PK–12th
Wheelchair accessible
PK–4th: 5100 Edgemoor Lane, Bethesda, MD

Governance: Nonprofit
Accredited by: AIMS, MSA
Memberships: AIMS, AISGW, FCE, NAIS
Religious affiliation: Society of Friends (Quaker)

PROFILE
Total enrollment: 1,097
Graduating class size: 112
Average class size: 24 (K–4th, with 2 teachers), 12–14 (5th–12th)
Number of faculty: 142
Boarding option: No
School day: 8:30–3:00 (K–4th), 8:00–3:20 (5th–8th), 8:00–3:15 (9th–12th)
Extended day hours: 8:00–6:00
Schools three or more graduates have attended over the past five years: Brown, Carnegie Mellon, Columbia, Duke, Georgetown, Harvard, New York University, Princeton, Stanford, Yale

APPLICATION PROCESS
Grades with openings (approximate): K (26), 3rd (16), 6th (16), 7th (16), 9th (22)
Birthday cutoff: September 1
Deadline: December 15
Fee: $60
Testing required: WPPSI-III/WISC-IV (PK–5th), SSAT (6th–11th)
Steps: Application, interview

COSTS
Tuition: $28,442–$29,442
Average additional fees: $300–$600
Financial aid budget: $5M
Average grant size: $19,264
% of students receiving aid: 22.5%
Endowment: Yes

NOTE: This data applies to the 2009–2010 school year.

PRESCHOOL PROGRAM

Age	Days	Hours	Tuition	Openings	Class size	Teachers per class	Food provided
4	5	8:30–3:00	$28,442	22	22	2	

CURRICULUM

Languages and grades offered: Chinese, French, Latin (7th–12th); Spanish (PK–12th)

AP classes/IB program: 15 AP exams

Tutors/learning specialists: 3

Other resource specialists: College counselor, counselor, librarian

Art programs: Chorus, dance, instrumental music, theater, visual arts

Sports: Baseball, basketball, crew (club), cross-country, diving, field hockey, football, golf, indoor soccer, lacrosse, soccer, softball, squash, swimming, tennis, track & field, ultimate Frisbee (club), volleyball, wrestling

Special features and activities: Quaker Meeting for Worship

Summer programs: Alaska travel camp, community service, day camp, England trekking camp, enrichment classes, remediation, sports camp

CAMPUS LIFE

Transportation available: Bus service linking the school's campuses

Lunch options: Lunch provided in cafeteria

Food allergy policy: Daily menu on school website, binder in kitchen with information about all food products used, students submit written Allergy Action Plan

Uniform: No

CAMPUS

Facilities: 15-acre Upper and Middle School campus on Wisconsin Avenue; 5-acre Lower School campus on Edgemoor Lane in Bethesda, MD

Long-range plans: Complete new athletic complex, renovate theater, redesign Quaker Meeting space

HISTORY AND MISSION STATEMENT

Embracing the Quaker belief in the unique worth of each individual, we seek students of diverse cultural, racial, religious, and economic backgrounds—students of ability and promise whose qualities of mind and heart indicate that they will thrive in an atmosphere of intellectual, creative, and physical vitality intended to foster strength of character and concern for others.

NOTE: This data applies to the 2009–2010 school year.

THE SIENA SCHOOL   est. 2006

Jillian Darefsky, School Director
9727 Georgia Avenue
Silver Spring, MD 20910
301-592-0567 x12
www.thesienaschool.org

Bekah Atkinson, Director of Admissions
batkinson@thesienaschool.org

Coed: 4th–12th
Limited wheelchair access

Governance: Proprietary
Accredited by: N/A
Memberships: IDA
Religious affiliation: Nonsectarian

PROFILE
Total enrollment: 62
Graduating class size: 10
Average class size: 10
Number of faculty: 21
Boarding option: No
School day: 8:30–3:30
Extended day hours: 8:30–5:45
Schools three or more graduates have attended over the past five years: N/A

APPLICATION PROCESS
Grades with openings (approximate): All
Birthday cutoff: N/A
Deadline: February 14
Fee: $100
Testing required: Full psycho-educational, including WISC-IV and achievement/academic (WJ-III or similar)
Steps: Tour, application, student visit, parent and/or student interview

COSTS
Tuition: $26,500–$27,500
Average additional fees: $550
Financial aid budget: 15% of budget
Average grant size: $10,000
% of students receiving aid: 33%
Endowment: No

NOTE: This data applies to the 2009–2010 school year.

CURRICULUM
Languages and grades offered: Spanish (9th–12th)
AP classes/IB program: N/A
Tutors/learning specialists: N/A
Other resource specialists: Yes
Art programs: MS, Art I–IV
Sports: Basketball, jujitsu, soccer, softball, track
Special features and activities: After-school homework help, enrichment classes
Summer programs: Flexible weekly academic mornings skill-building summer program in reading, writing, and math

CAMPUS LIFE
Transportation available: Located across from Forest Glen Metro station (Red Line)
Lunch options: Individual
Food allergy policy: N/A
Uniform: No

CAMPUS
Facilities: Located at the Montgomery Hills Baptist Church on Georgia Avenue
Long-range plans: MSA accreditation pending November 2009

HISTORY AND MISSION STATEMENT

The Siena School was established in 2006 by a group of educators, professionals and parents who envisioned a school that would provide students with learning differences, such as dyslexia, a meaningful education preparing them for college and for success in life. The mission became clear to create one of the nation's finest schools for bright students who learn differently.

The school takes its name from the town Siena, Italy, in part to emphasize our strong focus on the arts. In addition, Siena's patron saint, St. Catherine, was a highly regarded Renaissance scholar who only learned to read later in life.

NOTE: This data applies to the 2009–2010 school year.

ST. ALBANS SCHOOL est. 1909

Vance Wilson, Headmaster
Mount St. Alban
Washington, DC 20016
202-537-6440
www.stalbansschool.org

Hart Roper, Director of Admissions and Financial Aid
hroper@cathedral.org

Boys: 4th–12th
Wheelchair accessible

Governance: Nonprofit
Accredited by: AIMS
Memberships: AIMS, AISGW, IBSC, NAES, NAIS, TABS
Religious affiliation: Episcopal

PROFILE
Total enrollment: 570
Graduating class size: 75
Average class size: 13
Number of faculty: 75
Boarding option: Yes
School day: 7:55–3:30 (4th–8th), 8:00–5:30 (9th–12th)
Extended day hours: 7:55–5:00 (4th–8th)
Schools three or more graduates have attended over the past five years: Columbia, Georgetown, Harvard, Princeton, Trinity College, University of Michigan, University of Pennsylvania, University of Virginia, Vanderbilt, Yale

APPLICATION PROCESS
Grades with openings (approximate): 4th (35–40), 6th (4–6), 7th (15–20), 9th (15–20), plus attrition
Birthday cutoff: N/A
Deadline: January 15
Fee: $80
Testing required: SSAT or ISEE (6th–11th)
Steps: Application, interview, tour, informal assessment (4th–5th)

COSTS
Tuition: $31,428 (day), $44,457 (boarding)
Average additional fees: $500
Financial aid budget: $2.8M
Average grant size: $21,000
% of students receiving aid: 26%
Endowment: Yes

NOTE: This data applies to the 2009–2010 school year.

CURRICULUM

Languages and grades offered: Chinese (9th–12th), French (7th–12th), Japanese (7th–12th), Latin (7th–12th), Spanish (4th–12th)

AP classes/IB program: 13 AP classes

Tutors/learning specialists: Yes, including study skills

Other resource specialists: N/A

Art programs: Extensive

Sports: Baseball, basketball, canoeing/kayaking, climbing, crew, cross-country, diving, football, golf, ice hockey, indoor soccer, lacrosse, soccer, swimming, tennis, track & field, water polo

Special features and activities: Cathedral chorister program, Skip Grant Program for students from traditionally underrepresented backgrounds

Summer programs: Academic, athletic; School of Public Service

CAMPUS LIFE

Transportation available: None

Lunch options: Provided by school

Food allergy policy: Full-time nurse

Uniform: Coat and tie

CAMPUS

Facilities: 60-acre campus with 7 buildings including 2 gyms, indoor pool, and theater

Long-range plans: New Upper School building opening in spring of 2009

HISTORY AND MISSION STATEMENT

St. Albans School is a college preparatory school for boys which challenges its students to achieve excellence and to embrace responsibility. It expects them to act always with honor and to respect and care for others.

St. Albans School is a diverse family that welcomes and values individuals from all backgrounds. Such diversity is essential to a vital community of learning and growth. In nurturing the hearts, minds, and bodies of students, St. Albans prepares boys for fulfilling lives of responsibility, leadership, and service to others. Classes and activities may be coordinated with girls from National Cathedral School, which is located next to St. Albans on the Cathedral Close.

NOTE: This data applies to the 2009–2010 school year.

ST. ANDREW'S EPISCOPAL SCHOOL   est. 1978

Robert F. Kosasky, Head of School
8804 Postoak Road
Potomac, MD 20854
301-983-5200 x236
www.saes.org

Julie Jameson, Director of Admission and Financial Aid
jjameson@saes.org

Coed: N–12th
Limited wheelchair access
N–3rd: 10033 River Road, Potomac, MD

Governance: Nonprofit
Accredited by: AIMS, AISGW, MSA, NAES, NAIS
Memberships: N/A
Religious affiliation: Episcopal

PROFILE
Total enrollment: 554
Graduating class size: 88
Average class size: 15
Number of faculty: 82
Boarding option: No
School day: 8:30–3:30 (N–3rd),
8:25–3:25 (4th–8th), 8:25–3:05
(9th–12th)
Extended day hours: 7:15–6:00
(PK–3rd), 7:30–6:00 (4th–5th),
8:25–6:00 (6th–8th)
**Schools three or more graduates
have attended over the past five
years:** Bucknell, Colorado College,
Cornell, Dickinson College,
Hamilton College, Syracuse, Tufts,
University of Maryland–College
Park, Wake Forest, Yale

APPLICATION PROCESS
Grades with openings (approximate):
N–7th, 9th
Birthday cutoff: June 1 (2s),
September 1 (3s-8th)
Deadline: February 1
Fee: $50
Testing required: WPPSI-III/WISC-IV
(N–4th), SSAT or ISEE (6th–12th)
Steps: Application, tour and parent
and student interviews, student visit

COSTS
Tuition: $11,225–$29,960 (K–12th)
Average additional fees: $50–$700
Financial aid budget: N/A
Average grant size: N/A
% of students receiving aid: N/A
Endowment: Yes

NOTE: This data applies to the 2009–2010 school year.

PRESCHOOL PROGRAM

Age	Days	Hours	Tuition	Openings	Class size	Teachers per class	Food provided
2	2	8:30–12:00	$5,380	10	7	2	Snacks
2	3	8:30–12:00	$7,690	10	8	2	Snacks
2	4	8:30–12:00	$9,215	10	8	2	Snacks
3	5	8:30–12:00	$11,225	11	13	2	Snacks

CURRICULUM

Languages and grades offered: French (N–12th), Latin (6th–12th), Spanish (N–12th)

AP classes/IB program: 16 AP classes

Tutors/learning specialists: Learning specialist, tutoring

Other resource specialists: Part-time school counselor

Art programs: Wide array of performing and visual arts

Sports: Baseball, basketball, cross-country, equestrian, golf, lacrosse, soccer, softball, tennis, track, volleyball, wrestling

Special features and activities: The only Episcopal school in the Greater Washington area to offer a continuous education from preschool through high school

Summer programs: www.saes.org/summer_programs

CAMPUS LIFE

Transportation available: Shuttle bus service

Lunch options: Included in tuition (4th–12th)

Food allergy policy: N/A

Uniform: Yes (N–5th)

CAMPUS

Facilities: Preschool–3rd: Art studio, library, science lab, blacktop, playgrounds, field. 4th–12th: 19 acres; 75,000-square foot building; visual arts studios, multipurpose space, darkroom; gymnasium, basketball court, weight room, dance studio/wrestling room, tennis courts, fields

Long-range plans: N/A

HISTORY AND MISSION STATEMENT

St. Andrew's Episcopal School provides a comprehensive coeducational college preparatory program for preschool–12th grade in an environment that embodies the faith and perspective of the Episcopal Church. The school seeks a broadly diverse community and offers programs to serve students of varied interests and abilities capable of achievement in a challenging academic environment. St. Andrew's supports a dedicated faculty and administration who respect and appreciate students.

NOTE: This data applies to the 2009–2010 school year.

ST. ANSELM'S ABBEY SCHOOL   est. 1942

Louis Silvano, Headmaster
4501 South Dakota Avenue, NE
Washington, DC 20017
202-269-2379
www.saintanselms.org

E.V. Downey, Director of Admissions
admissions@saintanselms.org

Boys: 6th–12th
Wheelchair accessible

Governance: Nonprofit
Accredited by: MSA
Memberships: ADW, AIMS, AISGW, NAIS, NCEA
Religious affiliation: Roman Catholic

PROFILE
Total enrollment: 236
Graduating class size: 39
Average class size: 12
Number of faculty: 46
Boarding option: No
School day: 8:00–3:20
Extended day hours: 8:00–6:00
Schools three or more graduates have attended over the past five years: Boston College, Carleton, Catholic University, Georgetown, Morehouse College, New York University, Notre Dame, U.S. Air Force Academy, University of Maryland–College Park, William and Mary

APPLICATION PROCESS
Grades with openings (approximate): 6th (32), 7th (30), 9th (15), plus attrition
Birthday cutoff: N/A
Deadline: Rolling
Fee: $35
Testing required: Entrance exam
Steps: Visit, application, entrance exam, interview

COSTS
Tuition: $19,350 (6th–8th), $19,900 (9th–12th)
Average additional fees: $650–$1,000
Financial aid budget: $575,000
Average grant size: $8,657
% of students receiving aid: 28%
Endowment: Yes

NOTE: This data applies to the 2009–2010 school year.

CURRICULUM

Languages and grades offered: Arabic (11th–12th), French (8th–12th), Greek (11th–12th), Latin (7th–12th), Spanish (8th–12th)

AP classes/IB program: 20+ AP classes

Tutors/learning specialists: None

Other resource specialists: College counseling team, counselor, librarian, publications, school nurse

Art programs: Art history, chorus, computer graphics, general art, jazz band, orchestra, origami, studio art, theater

Sports: Baseball, basketball, cross-country, fencing, golf, soccer, tennis, track & field, wrestling

Special features and activities: Weekly community service, Field Day, House Day, House System, class retreats and field trips, Kairos (11th grade retreat), intramural sports, school-wide community service projects, stress management programs

Summer programs: Academic and athletic programs offered

CAMPUS LIFE

Transportation available: Shuttles to and from Metro

Lunch options: Hot lunch program (optional)

Food allergy policy: Lunch areas are cleaned with hot water and special cleaning products; EpiPens are in both buildings with staff trained in their use

Uniform: Formal dress code

CAMPUS

Facilities: 43-acre urban campus, new cafeteria/gym/performing arts complex; classroom building containing 4 science labs, art room, library, state-of-the-art lecture hall, computer lab

Long-range plans: Small addition to school with faculty lounge, administrative offices, teachers' offices

HISTORY AND MISSION STATEMENT

Our school, serving grades 6 through 12, with its roots in the values of the Christian gospel and Catholic tradition, strives to create a community built on respect for truth, love of learning, regard for human dignity and tolerance.

We pursue this goal by leading our students through a challenging and balanced program of study in the arts, sciences and theology that gives them a solid preparation for the demands of college.

By living and promoting the Benedictine spirit, we strive within our school to create an atmosphere of peace, a sense of service to community and a willingness within our students to work toward a balance in mind, body and spirit.

NOTE: This data applies to the 2009–2010 school year.

ST. JOHN'S COLLEGE HIGH SCHOOL   est. 1851

Brother Thomas Gerrow, President
2607 Military Road, NW
Washington, DC 20015
202-363-2316 x1069
www.stjohns-chs.org

Susan Hinton, Admissions Director
shinton@stjohns-chs.org

Coed: 9th–12th
No wheelchair access

Governance: Nonprofit
Accredited by: MSA
Memberships: College Board, NACAC
Religious affiliation: Roman Catholic

PROFILE

Total enrollment: 1,060
Graduating class size: 248
Average class size: 23
Number of faculty: 84
Boarding option: No
School day: 8:10–2:40
Extended day hours: None
Schools three or more graduates have attended over the past five years: Boston College, Cornell, Duke, Georgetown, University of Maryland, University of Virginia

APPLICATION PROCESS

Grades with openings (approximate): 9th (275), 10th (10–15)
Birthday cutoff: N/A
Deadline: December 15 (9th), then rolling
Fee: $50
Testing required: HSPT (9th)
Steps: N/A

COSTS

Tuition: $13,500
Average additional fees: $500
Financial aid budget: N/A
Average grant size: N/A
% of students receiving aid: N/A
Endowment: Yes

NOTE: This data applies to the 2009–2010 school year.

CURRICULUM

Languages and grades offered: French, Latin, Spanish (9th–12th)

AP classes/IB program: 17 AP classes

Tutors/learning specialists: N/A

Other resource specialists: Benilde Program for academic support for LD students

Art programs: Design, drawing & painting, foundations in art, intro to ceramics and sculpture, portfolio preparation, 2-dimensional and 3-dimensional design

Sports: Baseball, basketball, crew, cross-country, football, golf, ice hockey, lacrosse, rugby, soccer, softball, swimming & diving, tennis, track & field, wrestling

Special features and activities: De La Salle Scholars Program, optional JROTC program

Summer programs: Sports camps

CAMPUS LIFE

Transportation available: Bussing from Montgomery and Prince George's counties, shuttle service from Friendship Heights and Silver Spring Metro stations

Lunch options: Food court-style cafeteria serving breakfast and lunch

Food allergy policy:

Uniform: Yes

CAMPUS

Facilities: 30-acre urban campus adjacent to Rock Creek Park; state-of-the-art science and technology center, new baseball and football stadiums, outstanding art studio

Long-range plans: New cafeteria

HISTORY AND MISSION STATEMENT

St. John's College High School was founded in 1851 by the De La Salle Christian Brothers. As an independent, Catholic college preparatory school, St. John's mission is to provide a human and Christian education to young men and women from diverse socioeconomic and cultural backgrounds. Our Lasallian educators are committed to the spiritual, academic, cultural, physical, and moral development of the students. The Lasallian experience at St. John's prepares young men and women for a life dedicated to leadership, achievement, and service to the community.

NOTE: This data applies to the 2009–2010 school year.

ST. JOHN'S EPISCOPAL SCHOOL   est. 1861

John H. Zurn, Headmaster
3427 Olney-Laytonsville Road
Olney, MD 20832
301-774-6804 x118
www.stjes.com

Trevor Waddington, Director of Admissions
trevor.waddington@stjes.org

Coed: K–8th

Governance: Nonprofit
Accredited by: N/A
Memberships: N/A
Religious affiliation: Episcopal

PROFILE
Total enrollment: 294
Graduating class size: 38
Average class size: 18
Number of faculty: 42
Boarding option: No
School day: 8:15–3:15
Extended day hours: 7:00–6:00
Schools three or more graduates
have attended over the past five
years: N/A

APPLICATION PROCESS
Grades with openings (approximate):
K (36), plus attrition
Birthday cutoff: September 1
Deadline: February 1
Fee: $50
Testing required: None
Steps: N/A

COSTS
Tuition: $14,059
Average additional fees: N/A
Financial aid budget: N/A
Average grant size: N/A
% of students receiving aid: N/A
Endowment: N/A

NOTE: This data applies to the 2009–2010 school year.

CURRICULUM

Languages and grades offered: Latin (7th–8th), Spanish (K–8th)
AP classes/IB program: None
Tutors/learning specialists: Yes, reading
Other resource specialists: Counselor
Art programs: Art, drama, music
Sports: Basketball, soccer, track
Special features and activities: N/A
Summer programs: Summer Activities Program

CAMPUS LIFE

Transportation available: N/A
Lunch options: 3 times per week
Food allergy policy: Yes
Uniform: Yes

CAMPUS

Facilities: Arts center, gymnasium
Long-range plans: N/A

HISTORY AND MISSION STATEMENT

St. John's is a leading private Episcopal school in Olney, Maryland serving students from kindergarten through 8th grade. Founded in 1961, our mission is centered on the three core pillars of academics, character and community. We are dedicated to meeting the intellectual, social and emotional needs of our students within the framework of an inspiring and supportive Christian experience.

NOTE: This data applies to the 2009–2010 school year.

ST. PATRICK'S EPISCOPAL DAY SCHOOL   est. 1956

Peter A. Barrett, Head of School
4700 Whitehaven Parkway, NW
Washington, DC 20007
202-342-2807
www.stpatsdc.org

Jennifer Danish, Director of Admission and Financial Aid
danishj@stpatsdc.org

Coed: N–8th
Wheelchair accessible
7th–8th: 4925 MacArthur Boulevard NW, Washington, DC

Governance: Nonprofit
Accredited by: AIMS, MSA
Memberships: AIMS, AISGW, BSF, LSF, NAES, NAIS, SSATB
Religious affiliation: Episcopal

PROFILE

Total enrollment: 500
Graduating class size: 30
Average class size: 17
Number of faculty: 90 (faculty and administration)
Boarding option: No
School day: 8:15–2:45, 8:15–12:10 (F) (K–3rd); 8:00–2:45 (4th–6th); 8:00–4:00, 8:00–2:30 (Th) (7th–8th)
Extended day hours: 7:30–6:00
Schools three or more graduates have attended over the past five years: Georgetown Day, Holton-Arms, Landon, Maret, National Cathedral, Potomac, Sidwell Friends, St. Albans, St. Andrew's Episcopal

APPLICATION PROCESS

Grades with openings (approximate):
K (10), plus attrition
Birthday cutoff: September 1
Deadline: January 29
Fee: $65; $15 if applying for financial aid
Testing required: WPPSI-III/WISC-IV (K–5th), ISEE or SSAT (6th–8th)
Steps: Parent tour/interview, application, student visit

COSTS

Tuition: $13,828–$26,502
Average additional fees: $654
Financial aid budget: $1.4M
Average grant size: $19,000
% of students receiving aid: 15%
Endowment: Yes

NOTE: This data applies to the 2009–2010 school year.

PRESCHOOL PROGRAM

Age	Days	Hours	Tuition	Openings	Class size	Teachers per class	Food provided
3	5	9:00–12:00		28	14	2.5	Snack, milk, juice
3	5	9:00–2:45		28	14	2.5	Snack, milk, juice
4	5	9:00–12:00		23	16	2.5	Snack, milk, juice
4	5	9:00–2:45		23	16	2.5	Snack, milk, juice

CURRICULUM

Languages and grades offered: Spanish (4th–8th)
AP classes/IB program: N/A
Tutors/learning specialists: 9
Other resource specialists: Art, music, religion, science, technology
Art programs: Music (N–8th), studio art (K–8th)
Sports: Basketball, cross-country, lacrosse, soccer
Special features and activities: Young Singers & Young Ringers (5th–6th), Choir & Handbells (7th–8th), student council (4th–8th), chapel guild (5th–6th), Orff ensemble (5th–6th)
Summer programs: Yes, N–8th

CAMPUS LIFE

Transportation available: None (carpools encouraged)
Lunch options: Mandatory hot lunch (K–8th)
Food allergy policy: Nut-free zones in some classrooms, all individual allergies closely monitored by school nurse
Uniform: No

CAMPUS

Facilities: On 2 campuses, facilities include 34 classrooms, 3 art studios, gymnasium & performance center, 3 libraries, lunch room, mini-gym for 3- and 4-year-olds, 4 music rooms, 3 play parks, playing field, 3 science labs
Long-range plans: Add a high school

HISTORY AND MISSION STATEMENT

Founded in 1956 as a parish day school, St. Patrick's Episcopal Day School strives to create a diverse learning community of students, teachers, and parents who recognize the infinite value of every participant as a child of God. We are committed to developing character, advancing human understanding, and promoting academic excellence in our students in order to prepare them to live with integrity, compassion, and purpose.

NOTE: This data applies to the 2009–2010 school year.

ST. STEPHEN'S AND ST. AGNES SCHOOL   est. 1924

Joan G.O. Holden, Head of School
400 Fontaine Street
Alexandria, VA 22302
703-212-2705
www.sssas.org

Diane Dunning, Director of Admissions and Financial Aid
ddunning@sssas.org

Coed: JK–12th
Wheelchair accessible (Lower School: limited access)
9th–12th: 1000 St. Stephen's Road, Alexandria, VA
6th–8th: 4401 West Braddock Street, Alexandria, VA, 703-212-2706

Governance: Nonprofit
Accredited by: VAIS
Memberships: AISGW, CASE, ERB, MAESA, NACAC, NAIS, VAIS
Religious affiliation: Episcopal

PROFILE

Total enrollment: 1,124
Graduating class size: 100
Average class size: 15
Number of faculty: 160
Boarding option: No
School day: 8:00–3:00
Extended day hours: 7:00–6:00
Schools three or more graduates have attended over the past five years: Boston College, Brown, Georgetown, Princeton, Stanford, University of North Carolina at Chapel Hill, University of Virginia, Virginia Tech, William and Mary, Yale

APPLICATION PROCESS

Grades with openings (approximate): K (48), 4th (10), 6th (25), 9th (30)
Birthday cutoff: September 1 (K)
Deadline: January 15
Fee: $70
Testing required: WPPSI-III/WISC-IV; SSAT or ISEE
Steps: Tour/interview, application

COSTS

Tuition: $22,840–$26,425
Average additional fees: $600
Financial aid budget: $3.5M
Average grant size: $15,402
% of students receiving aid: 20%
Endowment: Yes

NOTE: This data applies to the 2009–2010 school year.

PRESCHOOL PROGRAM					Class size	Teachers per class	Food provided
Age	Days	Hours	Tuition	Openings			
JK	5	8:00–3:00	$20,400				

CURRICULUM

Languages and grades offered: French (4th–12th), Latin (6th–12th), Mandarin Chinese (11th–12th), Spanish (JK–12th)

AP classes/IB program: 22 AP classes

Tutors/learning specialists: 4

Other resource specialists: N/A

Art programs: Visual and performing (JK–12): extensive art, music, and drama classes (see website)

Sports: 19 sports (see website), plus PE and strength & conditioning programs

Special features and activities: Single-gender science and math (6th–8th); leadership, sustainability, and multicultural clubs; Community Service Learning Program (JK–12th); technology integrated in all disciplines

Summer programs: Enrichment classes in academics, arts, athletics and technology, open to community

CAMPUS LIFE

Transportation available: Bus service; free AM and PM shuttle from Metro and between campuses

Lunch options: Available for purchase

Food allergy policy: Varies by campus

Uniform: Yes (Lower School)

CAMPUS

Facilities: 35-acre Upper School campus, 7-acre Middle School campus, 16-acre Lower School campus

Long-range plans: Ten-Year Strategic Plan on file

HISTORY AND MISSION STATEMENT

To help our students succeed in a complex and changing world, we seek to inspire a passion for learning, an enthusiasm for athletic and artistic endeavor, a striving for excellence, a celebration of diversity and a commitment to service. Our mission is to pursue goodness as well as knowledge and to honor the unique value of each of our members as a child of God in a caring community.

NOTE: This data applies to the 2009–2010 school year.

STONE RIDGE SCHOOL OF THE SACRED HEART   est. 1923

Catherine Ronan Karrels, Head of School
9101 Rockville Pike
Bethesda, MD 20814
301-657-4322 x321
www.stoneridge.org

Lori D. Backlund
admission@stoneridge.org

Girls: PK–12th
Wheelchair accessible

Governance: Nonprofit
Accredited by: N/A
Memberships: AIMS, AISGW, MSA, NAIS, NCEA, NSHS
Religious affiliation: Catholic

PROFILE
Total enrollment: 655
Graduating class size: 78
Average class size: 16
Number of faculty: 86
Boarding option: No
School day: 8:00–3:00
Extended day hours: 8:00–6:00
Schools three or more graduates have attended over the past five years: Columbia, Georgetown, University of Maryland, University of Pennsylvania, University of Virginia

APPLICATION PROCESS
Grades with openings (approximate): K, 1st, 3rd, 5th, 6th, 9th
Birthday cutoff: September 1
Deadline: December 11 (9th), then rolling
Fee: $50
Testing required: WPPSI-III/WISC-IV (K–6th), SSAT, ISEE or ERB, HSPT (6th–12th)
Steps: Parent visit, application, student visit

COSTS
Tuition: $18,025–$22,420
Average additional fees: $300–$700
Financial aid budget: $1M
Average grant size: N/A
% of students receiving aid: 23%
Endowment: Yes

NOTE: This data applies to the 2009–2010 school year.

PRESCHOOL PROGRAM

Age	Days	Hours	Tuition	Openings	Class size	Teachers per class	Food provided
4 (PK)	5	8:00–12:00	$11,305	20	20	2	Snack
4 (PK)	5	8:00–3:00	$18,025				

CURRICULUM

Languages and grades offered: French (5th–12th), Latin (7th–12th), Spanish (5th–12th)

AP classes/IB program: 16 AP classes

Tutors/learning specialists: 1

Other resource specialists: Reading specialist

Art programs: Art, dance, drama, music

Sports: Basketball, cross-country, diving, field hockey, lacrosse, soccer, softball, swimming, tennis, track & field, volleyball

Special features and activities: Independent study, career internships, exchange program, coed program PK–K

Summer programs: Yes

CAMPUS LIFE

Transportation available: None

Lunch options: At an additional fee

Food allergy policy: As necessary

Uniform: Yes

CAMPUS

Facilities: Indoor pool

Long-range plans: N/A

HISTORY AND MISSION STATEMENT

Stone Ridge is a Catholic, independent, college preparatory school for girls rooted in the tradition of Sacred Heart education around the world and committed to the contemporary expression of Sacred Heart values. A Stone Ridge education enables young women to develop a personal faith and prepares them to take their places as informed and active members of the Church and society. Consequently, the school provides programs that expose students to the needs of the world, awaken their sense of personal responsibility, and equip them with leadership skills.

NOTE: This data applies to the 2009–2010 school year.

WAKEFIELD SCHOOL   est. 1972

Peter Quinn, Headmaster
4439 Old Tavern Road
The Plains, VA 20198
540-253-7600
www.wakefieldschool.org

Sarah McDonough, Director of Admissions & Financial Aid
smcdonough@wakefieldschool.org

Coed: N–12th
Wheelchair accessible

Governance: Nonprofit
Accredited by: AISGW, VAIS
Memberships: College Board, SSATB
Religious affiliation: Nonsectarian

PROFILE
Total enrollment: 465
Graduating class size: 37
Average class size: 14
Number of faculty: 80
Boarding option: No
School day: 8:30–3:30
Extended day hours: 8:30–6:00
Schools three or more graduates have attended over the past five years: Bucknell, Princeton, University of Mary Washington, University of North Carolina at Chapel Hill, University of Virginia, Ursinus College, Virginia Tech, Washington and Lee, William and Mary

APPLICATION PROCESS
Grades with openings (approximate): K (12), 6th–8th (4–8), 9th (15), 10th–12th (3–5)
Birthday cutoff: September 15
Deadline: January 29, then rolling
Fee: $60
Testing required: In-house (PK–5th), SSAT (6th–12th)
Steps: Application, parent and student interviews

COSTS
Tuition: $15,400– $19,500 (K–12th)
Average additional fees: $750
Financial aid budget: $700,000
Average grant size: 33% of tuition
% of students receiving aid: 19%

NOTE: This data applies to the 2009–2010 school year.

PRESCHOOL PROGRAM

Age	Days	Hours	Tuition	Openings	Class size	Teachers per class	Food provided
3–5 (N)	2	8:30–12:00	$2,500	10	10	1	Snack
3–5 (N)	3	8:30–12:00	$3,500	10	10	1	Snack
3–5 (N)	5	8:30–12:00	$5,500	10	10	1	Snack
PK	5	8:30–3:30	$9,600	20			

CURRICULUM
Languages and grades offered: French (1st–5th, 7th–12th), Latin (6th–12th), Spanish (1st–5th, 7th–12th)
AP classes/IB program: 14 AP classes
Tutors/learning specialists: 3
Other resource specialists: N/A
Art programs: Choir, drama, ensemble, music, visual arts
Sports: Basketball, cross-country, field hockey, golf, lacrosse, soccer, squash, tennis, volleyball
Special features and activities: Senior thesis, interdisciplinary composition, wildlife conservation course in conjunction with the Smithsonian's Conservation Research Center & the Cheetah Conservation Fund
Summer programs: Summer camp—see website

CAMPUS LIFE
Transportation available: Yes
Lunch options: Available for purchase with advance order
Food allergy policy: N/A
Uniform: Yes

CAMPUS
Facilities: Lower and Middle/Upper Schools, art/music & science/technology buildings, gyms
Long-range plans: Theater, field house, Upper School

HISTORY AND MISSION STATEMENT
We provide a rigorous liberal arts education through a content-rich, challenging curriculum and extracurricular activities delivered by skilled, supportive and creative teachers, coaches and advisers. We believe in broad knowledge, the equal importance of character and intellect, the benefits of hard work, and the limitless potential of our students. We foster self-discipline, independence, creativity and curiosity. We welcome families who will embrace our ambitious vision: to develop capable, ethical, and articulate citizens who will seek the challenge, make a difference, and live extraordinary lives . . . each in his or her own way.

NOTE: This data applies to the 2009–2010 school year.

WASHINGTON EPISCOPAL SCHOOL   est. 1985

Stuart Work, Head of School
5600 Little Falls Parkway
Bethesda, MD 20816
301-652-7878 x201
www.w-e-s.org

Debra Duff, Director of Admission and Financial Aid
dduff@w-e-s.org

Coed: N–8th
Wheelchair accessible

Governance: Nonprofit
Accredited by: MSA
Memberships: AIMS, AISGW, BSF, CSEE, LSF, MAESA, NAES, NAIS
Religious affiliation: Episcopal

PROFILE

Total enrollment: 315
Graduating class size: 32
Average class size: 16
Number of faculty: 57
Boarding option: No
School day: 8:10–3:25
Extended day hours: 8:10–6:00
Schools three or more graduates have attended over the past five years: Bullis, Field, Georgetown Day, Landon, Madeira, National Cathedral, Potomac, Sidwell Friends, St. Albans, St. Andrew's Episcopal

APPLICATION PROCESS

Grades with openings (approximate): K (6–8), plus attrition
Birthday cutoff: September 1
Deadline: February 1
Fee: $60
Testing required: WPPSI-III/WISC-IV (K–6th), SSAT or ISEE (7th–8th)
Steps: Open house, parent conference, application, student visits

COSTS

Tuition: $24,635 (K–8th)
Average additional fees: Varies
Financial aid budget: $750,000
Average grant size: $13,000
% of students receiving aid: 18%
Endowment: No

NOTE: This data applies to the 2009–2010 school year.

PRESCHOOL PROGRAM

Age	Days	Hours	Tuition	Openings	Class size	Teachers per class	Food provided
3–4 (N)	5	9:00–12:00	$12,350	14–16	14–16	2	Snack
4–5 (PK)	5	9:00–3:25	$24,050	14–16	14–16	2	Snack; can buy hot lunch

CURRICULUM
Languages and grades offered: French (PK–8th), Latin (5th–8th), Spanish (PK–8th)
AP classes/IB program: N/A
Tutors/learning specialists: 1, plus tutors at an additional fee
Other resource specialists: Counselor, math & reading resource, speech/language
Art programs: Ceramics; studio art in all grades
Sports: Basketball, cross-country, lacrosse, soccer, track & field
Special features and activities: Study trips—Utah (6th), Italy (7th), France & Spain (8th)—included in tuition
Summer programs: Summer at WES: coed PK–8th

CAMPUS LIFE
Transportation available: None
Lunch options: Hot lunch available
Food allergy policy: N/A
Uniform: Yes

CAMPUS
Facilities: 6-acre renovated campus with art & music rooms, multiple gyms, sports field, theater
Long-range plans: Develop adjacent 4 acres for athletics, performing arts

HISTORY AND MISSION STATEMENT
At Washington Episcopal School, learning is joyful because academic excellence and happy children belong together. An independent, coeducational school for students from nursery through grade 8, WES is committed to helping each child develop his or her fullest potential. Our skilled and caring teachers are attentive to the abilities and talents of each student. Our broad and enriched curriculum builds knowledge, moral awareness, self-reliance and leadership. Our supportive community—true to Episcopal tradition—welcomes and celebrates a diversity of faiths and cultures. WES students stride confidently into, delight in and contribute to the world.

NOTE: This data applies to the 2009–2010 school year.

WASHINGTON INTERNATIONAL SCHOOL   est. 1966

Clayton W. Lewis, Head of School
3100 Macomb Street, NW
Washington, DC 20008
202-243-1814
www.wis.edu

Kathleen Visconti-Maleski, Director of Admission and Financial Aid
maleski@wis.edu

Coed: N–12th
Wheelchair accessible
N–5th: 1690 36th Street NW, Washington, DC

Governance: Nonprofit
Accredited by: CIS, Dutch and French Ministries, IB, MSA
Memberships: CIS, NAIS
Religious affiliation: Nonsectarian

PROFILE
Total enrollment: 885
Graduating class size: 56
Average class size: 16
Number of faculty: 100
Boarding option: No
School day: 8:45–3:00 (K),
8:30–3:30 (1st–5th), 8:15–2:50
(6th–12th)
Extended day hours: 7:45–6:00
**Schools three or more graduates
have attended over the past five
years:** N/A

APPLICATION PROCESS
Grades with openings (approximate):
K (30), plus attrition
Birthday cutoff: 3 by June 1;
September 1 for all others
Deadline: January 10
Fee: $50 (domestic), $75 (international), $10 if applying for
financial aid
Testing required: In-house
Steps: Tour, application, visit

COSTS
Tuition: $24,000 (K–5th), $26,000
(6th–12th)
Average additional fees: $400
Financial aid budget: $2.1M
Average grant size: $18,000
% of students receiving aid: 12%
Endowment: Yes

NOTE: This data applies to the 2009–2010 school year.

PRESCHOOL PROGRAM

Age	Days	Hours	Tuition	Openings	Class size	Teachers per class	Food provided
3	5	8:30–12:00		20	12–16	2	Snacks
4	5	8:30–4:00		30	12–16	2	Snacks

CURRICULUM

Languages and grades offered: Chinese, Dutch, French, Italian, Spanish
AP classes/IB program: IB programs for all grades
Tutors/learning specialists: Yes
Other resource specialists: N/A
Art programs: Art, chorus, instruments, theatre arts
Sports: Baseball, basketball, cross-country, golf, soccer, tennis, track & field, volleyball
Special features and activities: Culturally and racially diverse, ESL, dual language curriculum, all 3 programs of IB (PK–12th)
Summer programs: Full summer camp, academic, immersion, bilingual, ESL

CAMPUS LIFE

Transportation available: Yes
Lunch options: Yes
Food allergy policy: Yes
Uniform: No

CAMPUS

Facilities: 9-acre nature trust, mansion grounds
Long-range plans: Primary School expansion

HISTORY AND MISSION STATEMENT

Unique among Washington's independent schools, unusual even among international schools worldwide, WIS offers a demanding, globally focused academic program in an environment that prizes respect for individuals and individual differences. Our students, their families, and the faculty and staff represent nearly ninety countries and bring to the school a breadth of experience and an array of talents. WIS also enrolls American children drawn by the bilingual curriculum, the strength of the academic program, and the rich diversity of the community.

NOTE: This data applies to the 2009–2010 school year.

WASHINGTON WALDORF SCHOOL   est. 1969

Natalie Adams, Faculty Chairperson
4800 Sangamore Road
Bethesda, MD 20816
301-229-6107 x154
www.washingtonwaldorf.org

Lezlie Lawson, Enrollment Director
llawson@washingtonwaldorf.org

Coed: N–12th
Limited wheelchair access (main level is accessible)

Governance: Nonprofit
Accredited by: AWSNA, MSA
Memberships: AISGW, AWSNA
Religious affiliation: Nonsectarian

PROFILE
Total enrollment: 292
Graduating class size: 23
Average class size: 21
Number of faculty: 52
Boarding option: No
School day: 8:15–3:00
Extended day hours: 8:15–6:00
Schools three or more graduates have attended over the past five years: Haverford, Oberlin, University of Maryland, University of Vermont, Vassar

APPLICATION PROCESS
Grades with openings (approximate):
1st, 5th, 6th, 7th, 9th
Birthday cutoff: May 31
Deadline: January 31, then rolling
Fee: $60
Testing required: In-house
Steps: Application, parent/student interview, playgroup (PK–K), 3-day visit/in-house testing (1st–11th)

COSTS
Tuition: $6,500–$21,300
Average additional fees: $300–$550
Financial aid budget: 12% of budget
Average grant size: $10,000
% of students receiving aid: 23%
Endowment: No

NOTE: This data applies to the 2009–2010 school year.

PRESCHOOL PROGRAM

Age	Days	Hours	Tuition	Openings	Class size	Teachers per class	Food provided
3.5–4	3	8:30–12:30		Yes	16	2	
3.5–4	3	8:30–3:00		Yes	16	2	
3.5–K	2	8:30–12:30		Yes	20	2	
3.5–K	2	8:30–3:00		Yes	20	2	
3.5–K	3	8:30–12:30		Yes	20	2	
3.5–K	3	8:30–3:00		Yes	20	2	
3.5–K	5	8:30–12:30		Yes	20	2	
3.5–K	5	8:30–3:00		Yes	20	2	

CURRICULUM

Languages and grades offered: German (7th–12th), Spanish (1st–12th)
AP classes/IB program: None
Tutors/learning specialists: 2
Other resource specialists: Therapeutic eurythmist (movement)
Art programs: Basketry, blacksmithing/metal work, book arts, clay sculpture, drawing (black & white, color pencil, pastel), handwork (knitting, crocheting, sewing, cross-stitch), oil portraiture, printmaking, stone sculpture, watercolor, weaving, woodworking
Sports: Baseball, basketball, cross-country, soccer, softball
Special features and activities: Waldorf or Steiner curriculum
Summer programs: Pre-school camp

CAMPUS LIFE

Transportation available: None
Lunch options: Bring lunch
Food allergy policy: Class-by-class as needed
Uniform: No

CAMPUS

Facilities: 36,000-square-foot building on 5-acre campus
Long-range plans: Building expansion

HISTORY AND MISSION STATEMENT

The Washington Waldorf School cultivates each student's capacity to think clearly, feel compassionately, and act purposefully in the world. We are committed to the educational movement inspired by the pioneering work of Rudolf Steiner and advanced by Waldorf teachers worldwide.

NOTE: This data applies to the 2009–2010 school year.

WESTMINSTER SCHOOL   est. 1962

Ellis Glover, Headmaster
3819 Gallows Road
Annandale, VA 22003
703-256-3620
www.westminsterschool.com

Nancy Schuler, Director of Admissions
admissions@westminsterschool.com

Coed: K–8th
Wheelchair accessible

Governance: Nonprofit
Accredited by: NAIS, VAIS
Memberships: AISGW, NAIS, VAIS
Religious affiliation: Nonsectarian

PROFILE
Total enrollment: 270
Graduating class size: 30
Average class size: 15–18
Number of faculty: 28
Boarding option: No
School day: 8:30–3:00
Extended day hours: 7:45–6:00
Schools three or more graduates have attended over the past five years: Bishop Ireton, Fairfax County Public Schools

APPLICATION PROCESS
Grades with openings (approximate): K (32), others vary
Birthday cutoff: October 31
Deadline: February 6, then rolling
Fee: $100
Testing required: In-house
Steps: Application, in-house testing, student visit, parent interview

COSTS
Tuition: $16,400
Average additional fees: None
Financial aid budget: N/A
Average grant size: N/A
% of students receiving aid: N/A
Endowment: No

NOTE: This data applies to the 2009–2010 school year.

CURRICULUM
Languages and grades offered: French (K–8th), Latin (7th–8th)
AP classes/IB program: N/A
Tutors/learning specialists: All teachers are tutors and they specialize in what they teach. Departmentalized teaching.
Other resource specialists: Reading/writing resource teachers
Art programs: Art, drama, music, orchestra
Sports: Basketball, soccer, softball, track/cross-country
Special features and activities: Classical curriculum emphasizing classical studies and the reading of classic literature, emphasis on the arts, Junior Great Books, multiple field trips, daily PE
Summer programs: Enrichment classes, remedial classes, summer camp

CAMPUS LIFE
Transportation available: Door-to-door bus service to much of Northern Virginia
Lunch options: Bring lunch; order lunch online two days a week
Food allergy policy: N/A
Uniform: Yes

CAMPUS
Facilities: Computer lab, gym
Long-range plans: Add a preschool, turf field

HISTORY AND MISSION STATEMENT

Westminster School, founded in 1962, provides to students in grades K–8 a superior elementary education, based on a structured, classical curriculum; rigorous academic standards; and an emphasis on personal responsibility, courtesy, and upright conduct. Its well-rounded program both nurtures and challenges children's development in all areas: intellectual, physical, and—with its emphasis on the arts—spiritual. With its classical curriculum, challenging academics, and old-fashioned insistence on genuine effort and good manners, Westminster turns out graduates distinguished by their knowledge, study habits, maturity, and self-confidence.

NOTE: This data applies to the 2009–2010 school year.

THE WOODS ACADEMY   est. 1975

Mary Worch, Head of School
6801 Greentree Road
Bethesda, MD 20817
301-365-3080 x130
www.woodsacademy.org

Barbara Snyder, Director of Admission
admissions@woodsacademy.org

Coed: N–8th
Wheelchair accessible

Governance: Nonprofit
Accredited by: AIMS, AMS, MSA
Memberships: AISGW, ERB, NAGC, NAIS, NCEA, NMSA
Religious affiliation: Catholic

PROFILE
Total enrollment: 315
Graduating class size: 31
Average class size: 15
Number of faculty: 55
Boarding option: No
School day: 8:30–3:15
Extended day hours: 7:15–6:00
**Schools three or more graduates
have attended over the past five
years:** Connelly School of the Holy
Child, Georgetown Day,
Georgetown Prep, Georgetown
Visitation, Gonzaga, Good
Counsel, Holy Cross, public IB
programs, St. Andrew's Episcopal,
St. John's College High, Stone
Ridge

APPLICATION PROCESS
Grades with openings (approximate):
1st (5), 6th (9), plus attrition
Birthday cutoff: September 1
Deadline: March 1
Fee: $50
Testing required: Informal assess-
ment (N), in-house (1st), WISC-IV
(2nd–5th), SSAT or ISEE (6th–8th)
Steps: Parent visit, application, stu-
dent visit

COSTS
Tuition: $16,600 (1st–4th), $17,575
(5th–8th)
Average additional fees: $75
Financial aid budget: N/A
Average grant size: N/A
% of students receiving aid: N/A
Endowment: Yes

NOTE: This data applies to the 2009–2010 school year.

PRESCHOOL PROGRAM

Age	Days	Hours	Tuition	Openings	Class size	Teachers per class	Food provided
3	5	8:20–11:30	$11,500	24	28	3	None
4	5	8:20–11:30	$11,500	12	28	3	None
4	5	8:20–2:45	$15,325	12	28	3	None
5	5	8:20–2:45	$16,600	6	28	3	None

CURRICULUM

Languages and grades offered: French, Spanish (K–8th)

AP classes/IB program: N/A

Tutors/learning specialists: 2

Other resource specialists: Guidance counselors

Art programs: Drama, fine art (ceramics), music (band, choir, guitar), technology (graphic art)

Sports: Baseball, basketball, cross-country, lacrosse, soccer, softball, track & field

Special features and activities: Montessori program for 3–6 year olds, continuing into more traditional grades 1–8; French and Spanish instruction begin with 5 year olds.

Summer programs: N/A

CAMPUS LIFE

Transportation available: None

Lunch options: Hot catered lunch (1st–8th)

Food allergy policy: Peanut-free tables at lunch

Uniform: Yes (1st–8th)

CAMPUS

Facilities: 6-acre campus with art studio, basketball & tennis courts, chapel, computer labs, courtyards, library, music studio, playing fields, regulation-size gym, science labs, stage, student activity center

Long-range plans: Renovate Upper School (5th–8th) to create a state-of-the-art facility

HISTORY AND MISSION STATEMENT

An independent, Catholic school, offering boys and girls from Montessori pre-school through traditional grades 1–8, a challenging and supportive educational program that encourages all students to reach their full intellectual, spiritual, emotional, social, and physical potential.

NOTE: This data applies to the 2009–2010 school year.

Independent School
Maps, Table, and Worksheet

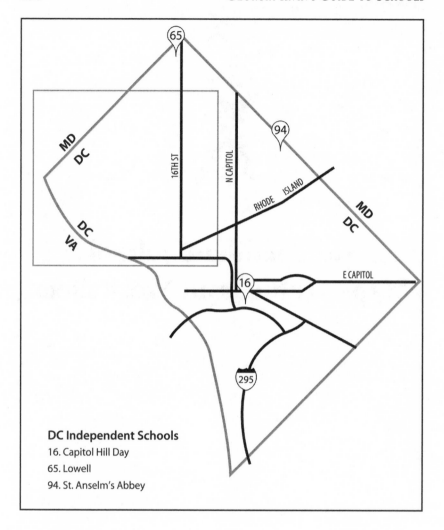

DC Independent Schools

16. Capitol Hill Day
65. Lowell
94. St. Anselm's Abbey

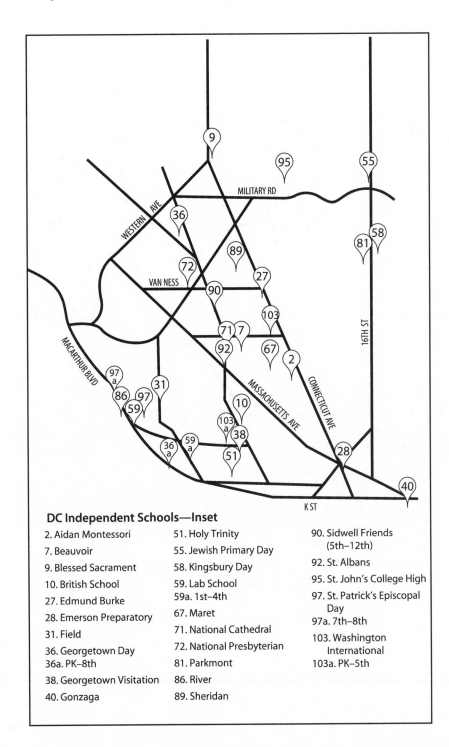

DC Independent Schools—Inset

2. Aidan Montessori

7. Beauvoir

9. Blessed Sacrament

10. British School

27. Edmund Burke

28. Emerson Preparatory

31. Field

36. Georgetown Day
36a. PK–8th

38. Georgetown Visitation

40. Gonzaga

51. Holy Trinity

55. Jewish Primary Day

58. Kingsbury Day

59. Lab School
59a. 1st–4th

67. Maret

71. National Cathedral

72. National Presbyterian

81. Parkmont

86. River

89. Sheridan

90. Sidwell Friends
(5th–12th)

92. St. Albans

95. St. John's College High

97. St. Patrick's Episcopal
Day
97a. 7th–8th

103. Washington
International
103a. PK–5th

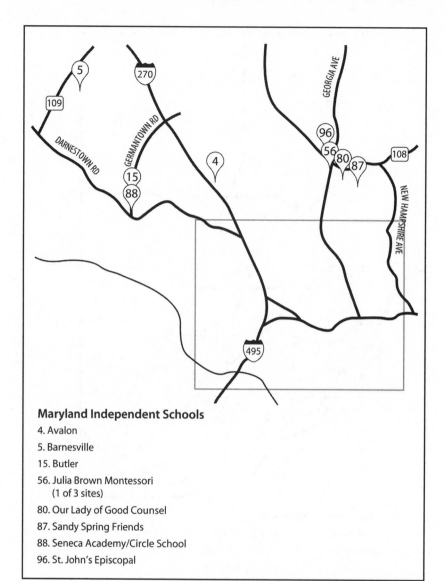

Maryland Independent Schools

4. Avalon

5. Barnesville

15. Butler

56. Julia Brown Montessori
    (1 of 3 sites)

80. Our Lady of Good Counsel

87. Sandy Spring Friends

88. Seneca Academy/Circle School

96. St. John's Episcopal

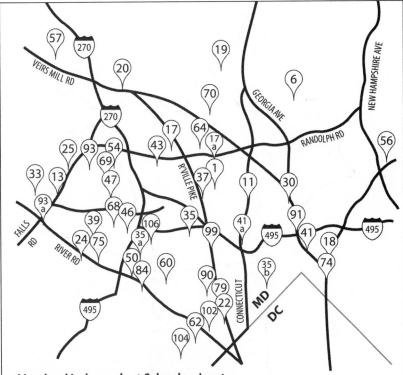

Maryland Independent Schools—Inset

1. Academy of the Holy Cross
6. Barrie
11. Brookwood
13. Bullis
17. Charles E. Smith
17a. 7th–12th
18. Chelsea
19. Children's Learning Center
20. Christ Episcopal
22. Concord Hill
24. Connelly
25. Diener
30. Evergreen
33. Fourth Presbyterian
35. French International
35a. N–K
35b. 1st–4th

37. Georgetown Preparatory
39. German
41. Grace Episcopal Day
41a. 1st–8th
43. Green Acres
46. Harbor
47. Heights
50. Holton-Arms
54. Ivymount
56. Julia Brown Montessori (1 of 3 sites)
57. Katherine Thomas
60. Landon
62. Little Flower
64. Lourie Center
68. Mater Dei
69. McLean

70. Melvin J. Berman Hebrew Academy
74. Nora
75. Norwood
79. Oneness-Family
84. Primary Day
90. Sidwell Friends (PK-4th)
91. Siena
93. St. Andrew's Episcopal
93a. PS–3rd
99. Stone Ridge
102. Washington Episcopal
104. Washington Waldorf
106. Woods Academy

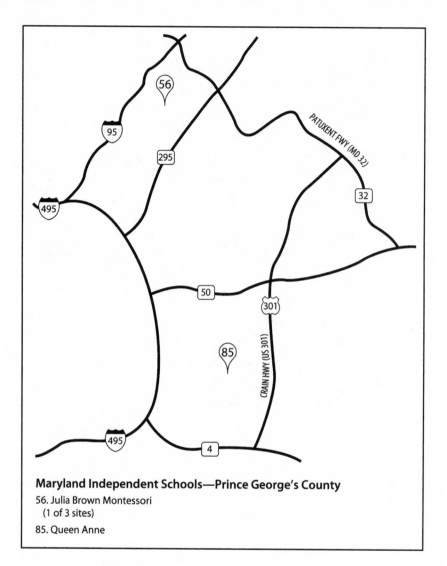

Maryland Independent Schools—Prince George's County

56. Julia Brown Montessori
   (1 of 3 sites)

85. Queen Anne

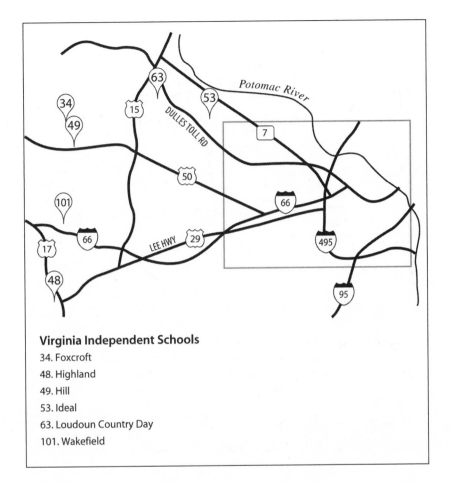

Virginia Independent Schools

34. Foxcroft
48. Highland
49. Hill
53. Ideal
63. Loudoun Country Day
101. Wakefield

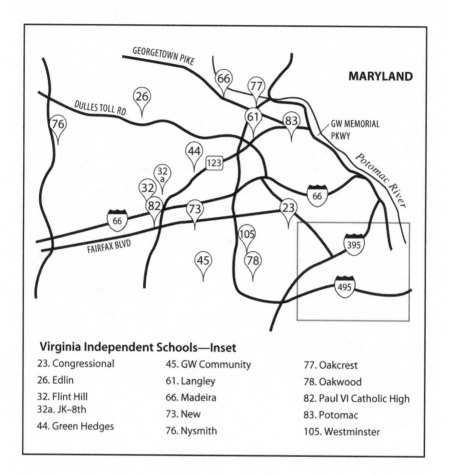

Virginia Independent Schools—Inset

23. Congressional	45. GW Community	77. Oakcrest
26. Edlin	61. Langley	78. Oakwood
32. Flint Hill	66. Madeira	82. Paul VI Catholic High
32a. JK–8th	73. New	83. Potomac
44. Green Hedges	76. Nysmith	105. Westminster

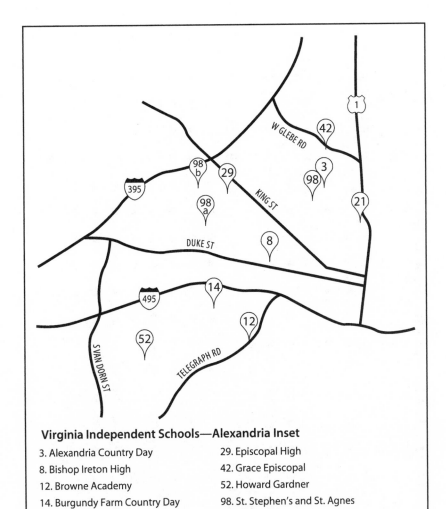

Virginia Independent Schools—Alexandria Inset

3. Alexandria Country Day

8. Bishop Ireton High

12. Browne Academy

14. Burgundy Farm Country Day

21. Commonwealth Academy

29. Episcopal High

42. Grace Episcopal

52. Howard Gardner

98. St. Stephen's and St. Agnes
98a. 9th–12th
98b. 6th–8th

Table 1.2 Alphabetical List of Independent Schools with Grade Range

Name of School	State	Gender	N	PK	K	1st	2nd	3rd	4th	5th	6th	7th	8th	9th	10th	11th	12th	Page
Academy of the Holy Cross	MD	G												●	●	●	●	46
Aidan Montessori School	DC	C	●	●	●	●	●	●	●	●	●							48
Alexandria Country Day School	VA	C		●	●	●	●	●	●	●	●	●	●					50
Avalon School	MD	B			●	●	●	●	●	●	●	●	●	●	●	●	●	52
Barnesville School	MD	C	●	●	●	●	●	●	●	●	●	●	●					54
Barrie School	MD	C	●	●	●	●	●	●	●	●	●	●	●	●	●	●	●	56
Beauvoir School	DC	C		●	●	●	●	●										58
Bishop Ireton High School	VA	C												●	●	●	●	60
Blessed Sacrament School	DC	C			●	●	●	●	●	●	●	●	●					62
British School of Washington	DC	C	●	●	●	●	●	●	●	●	●	●	●	●	●	●	●	64
Brookewood School	MD	G		●	●	●	●	●	●	●	●	●	●	●	●	●	●	66
Browne Academy	VA	C	●	●	●	●	●	●	●	●	●	●	●					68
Bullis School	MD	C			●	●	●	●	●	●	●	●	●	●	●	●	●	70
Burgundy Farm Country Day School	VA	C		●	●	●	●	●	●	●	●	●	●					72
Butler School	MD	C	●	●	●	●	●	●	●	●	●							74
Capitol Hill Day School	DC	C		●	●	●	●	●	●	●	●	●	●					76

Key: C = coed; B = boys; G = girls; N = nursery (three years old or younger); PK = pre-kindergarten (four years old); K = kindergarten (five years old)
*boarding only; **day and boarding

Name of School	State	Gender	N	PK	K	1st	2nd	3rd	4th	5th	6th	7th	8th	9th	10th	11th	12th	Page
Charles E Smith Jewish Day School	MD	C			●	●	●	●	●	●	●	●	●	●	●	●	●	78
Chelsea School	MD	C								●	●	●	●	●	●	●	●	80
Children's Learning Center	MD	C	●	●	●	●	●	●	●	●								82
Christ Episcopal School	MD	C	●	●	●	●	●	●	●	●	●	●	●					84
Commonwealth Academy	VA	C									●	●	●	●	●	●	●	86
Concord Hill School	MD	C	●	●	●	●	●	●										88
Congressional Schools of Virginia	VA	C	●	●	●	●	●	●	●	●	●	●	●					90
Connelly School of the Holy Child	MD	G									●	●	●	●	●	●	●	92
Diener School	MD	C			●	●	●	●	●	●								94
Edlin School	VA	C	●	●	●	●	●	●	●	●	●	●	●					96
Edmund Burke School	DC	C									●	●	●	●	●	●	●	98
Emerson Preparatory School	DC	C												●	●	●	●	100
Episcopal High School*	VA	C												●	●	●	●	102
Evergreen School	MD	C	●	●	●	●	●	●	●	●	●							104
Field School	DC	C									●	●	●	●	●	●	●	106
Flint Hill School	VA	C			●	●	●	●	●	●	●	●	●	●	●	●	●	108
Fourth Presbyterian School	MD	C		●	●	●	●	●	●	●	●	●						110
Foxcroft School**	VA	G												●	●	●	●	112

Key: C = coed; B = boys; G = girls; N = nursery (three years old or younger); PK = pre-kindergarten (four years old); K = kindergarten (five years old)

*boarding only; **day and boarding

Name of School	State	Gender	N	PK	K	1st	2nd	3rd	4th	5th	6th	7th	8th	9th	10th	11th	12th	Page
French International School	MD	C	●	●	●	●	●	●	●	●	●	●	●	●	●	●	●	114
Georgetown Day School	DC	C	●	●	●	●	●	●	●	●	●	●	●	●	●	●	●	116
Georgetown Preparatory School**	MD	B												●	●	●	●	118
Georgetown Visitation Preparatory School	DC	G												●	●	●	●	120
German School, Washington, DC	MD	C		●	●	●	●	●	●	●	●	●	●	●	●	●	●	122
Gonzaga College High School	DC	B												●	●	●	●	124
Grace Episcopal Day School	MD	C		●	●	●	●	●	●	●	●	●	●					126
Grace Episcopal School	VA	C	●	●	●	●	●	●	●	●								128
Green Acres School	MD	C		●	●	●	●	●	●	●	●	●	●					130
Green Hedges School	VA	C	●	●	●	●	●	●	●	●	●	●	●					132
GW Community School	VA	C											●	●	●	●	●	134
Harbor School	MD	C	●	●	●	●	●	●	●	●	●	●	●					136
Heights School	MD	B						●	●	●	●	●	●	●	●	●	●	138
Highland School	VA	C	●	●	●	●	●	●	●	●	●	●	●	●	●	●	●	140
Hill School	VA	C		●	●	●	●	●	●	●	●	●	●					142
Holton-Arms School	MD	G			●	●	●	●	●	●	●	●	●	●	●	●	●	144
Holy Trinity School	DC	C		●	●	●	●	●	●	●	●	●	●					146
Howard Gardner School	VA	C												●	●	●	●	148

Key: C = coed; B = boys; G = girls; N = nursery (three years old or younger); PK = pre-kindergarten (four years old); K = kindergarten (five years old)
*boarding only; **day and boarding

Name of School	State	Gender	N	PK	K	1st	2nd	3rd	4th	5th	6th	7th	8th	9th	10th	11th	12th	Page
Ideal Schools	VA	C												●	●	●	●	150
Ivymount School	MD	C		●	●	●	●	●	●	●	●	●	●	●	●	●	●	152
Jewish Primary Day School	DC	C		●	●	●	●	●	●	●	●							154
Julia Brown Montessori School	MD	C	●	●	●	●	●	●										156
Katherine Thomas School	MD	C		●	●	●	●	●	●	●	●	●	●	●	●	●	●	158
Kingsbury Day School	DC	C			●	●	●	●	●	●	●	●	●	●	●	●	●	160
Lab School of Washington	DC	C				●	●	●	●	●	●	●	●	●	●	●	●	162
Landon School	MD	B			●	●	●	●	●	●	●	●	●	●	●	●	●	164
Langley School	VA	C	●	●	●	●	●	●	●	●	●	●	●					166
Little Flower School	MD	C		●	●	●	●	●	●	●	●	●	●					168
Loudoun Country Day School	VA	C		●	●	●	●	●	●	●	●	●	●					170
Lourie Center School	MD	C	●	●	●	●	●	●	●	●								172
Lowell School	DC	C	●	●	●	●	●	●	●	●	●							174
Madeira School**	VA	G												●	●	●	●	176
Maret School	DC	C			●	●	●	●	●	●	●	●	●	●	●	●	●	178
Mater Dei School	MD	B				●	●	●	●	●	●	●	●					180
McLean School of Maryland	MD	C			●	●	●	●	●	●	●	●	●	●	●	●	●	182
Melvin J. Berman Hebrew Academy	MD	C	●	●	●	●	●	●	●	●	●	●	●	●	●	●	●	184

Key: C = coed; B = boys; G = girls; N = nursery (three years old or younger); PK = pre-kindergarten (four years old); K = kindergarten (five years old)
*boarding only; **day and boarding

Name of School	State	Gender	N	PK	K	1st	2nd	3rd	4th	5th	6th	7th	8th	9th	10th	11th	12th	Page
National Cathedral School	DC	G							●	●	●	●	●	●	●	●	●	186
National Presbyterian School	DC	C	●	●	●	●	●	●	●	●	●							188
New School of Northern Virginia	VA	C			●				●	●	●	●	●	●	●	●	●	190
Nora School	MD	C												●	●	●	●	192
Norwood School	MD	C		●	●	●	●	●	●	●	●	●	●					194
Nysmith School for the Gifted	VA	C	●	●	●	●	●	●	●	●	●	●	●					196
Oakcrest School	VA	G									●	●	●	●	●	●	●	198
Oakwood School	VA	C			●	●	●	●	●	●	●	●	●					200
Oneness-Family School	MD	C	●	●	●	●	●	●	●	●	●	●	●					202
Our Lady of Good Counsel	MD	C												●	●	●	●	204
Parkmont School	DC	C									●	●	●	●	●	●	●	206
Paul VI Catholic High School	VA	C												●	●	●	●	208
Potomac School	VA	C			●	●	●	●	●	●	●	●	●	●	●	●	●	210
Primary Day School	MD	C		●	●	●	●											212
Queen Anne School	MD	C									●	●	●	●	●	●	●	214
River School	DC	C	●	●	●	●	●	●										216
Sandy Spring Friends School**	MD	C	●	●	●	●	●	●	●	●	●	●	●	●	●	●	●	218
Seneca Academy/Circle School	MD	C	●	●	●	●	●	●	●	●								220

Key: C = coed; B = boys; G = girls; N = nursery (three years old or younger); PK = pre-kindergarten (four years old); K = kindergarten (five years old)
*boarding only; **day and boarding

Name of School	State	Gender	N	PK	K	1st	2nd	3rd	4th	5th	6th	7th	8th	9th	10th	11th	12th	Page
Sheridan School	DC	C			•	•	•	•	•	•	•	•	•					222
Sidwell Friends School	MD/DC	C		•	•	•	•	•	•	•	•	•	•	•	•	•	•	224
Siena School	MD	C							•	•	•	•	•	•	•	•	•	226
St. Albans School**	DC	B							•	•	•	•	•	•	•	•	•	228
St. Andrew's Episcopal School	MD	C		•	•	•	•	•	•	•	•	•	•	•	•	•	•	230
St. Anselm's Abbey School	DC	B									•	•	•	•	•	•	•	232
St. John's College High School	DC	C												•	•	•	•	234
St. John's Episcopal School	MD	C			•	•	•	•	•	•	•	•	•					236
St. Patrick's Episcopal Day School	DC	C	•	•	•	•	•	•	•	•	•	•	•					238
St. Stephen's and St. Agnes School	VA	C	•	•	•	•	•	•	•	•	•	•	•	•	•	•	•	240
Stone Ridge School of the Sacred Heart	MD	G	•	•	•	•	•	•	•	•	•	•	•	•	•	•	•	242
Wakefield School	VA	C	•	•	•	•	•	•	•	•	•	•	•	•	•	•	•	244
Washington Episcopal School	MD	C	•	•	•	•	•	•	•	•	•	•	•					246
Washington International School	DC	C	•	•	•	•	•	•	•	•	•	•	•	•	•	•	•	248
Washington Waldorf School	MD	C	•	•	•	•	•	•	•	•	•	•	•	•	•	•	•	250
Westminster School	VA	C	•	•	•	•	•	•	•	•	•	•	•					252
Woods Academy	MD	C	•	•	•	•	•	•	•	•	•	•	•					254

Key: C = coed; B = boys; G = girls; N = nursery (three years old or younger); PK = pre-kindergarten (four years old); K = kindergarten (five years old)
*boarding only; **day and boarding

Admission Worksheet

Name of School: _____ Telephone: _____

Location: _____ Contact Person: _____ Tuition: _____

Deadline for receipt of application: _____ Fee: _____

Date application and fee submitted: _____ Deadline for completion of file: _____

Date & time of appointment for open house/tour: _____ Student included: Yes _____ No _____

Parent interview required?:   Yes _____ No _____ Date & time: _____

Student essay required?:   Yes _____ No _____

Photo required?:   Yes _____ No _____

Parent essay required?:   Yes _____ No _____ Other: _____

Name of required test(s): _____ Date & time of test(s): _____

Test site: _____ Test fee: _____

Date transcript requested: _____

Recommendation forms: Date given _____ to _____ (Usually English)
                                                            Name of teacher

                                  Date given _____ to _____ (Usually Math)
                                                            Name of teacher

                                  Date given _____ to _____ (Optional)
                                                                      Name

Date & time of play date, school visit, and/or interview: _____

Deadline for financial aid information: _____ Date completed, if appropriate: _____

Other requirements:

Date that schools notify of decision: _____ Date enrollment contract is due: _____

Notes, impressions or special concerns:

Preschools

There are no crystal balls to tell us exactly what a child will definitely need when he or she is only about a thousand days old, but there are steps you can take to be sure you find the right preschool program. Your focus should be on something that is vitally important: finding a place that will provide an excellent beginning that fosters joy, stimulates curiosity, and encourages respect for oneself and others in a developmentally appropriate environment. Teaching the Three R's comes later!

BASIC EARLY EDUCATION INFORMATION

As you begin your search for a preschool, it is helpful to understand the basic terminology most frequently used with children this age.

Early childhood education refers to programs designed to meet the needs of children before compulsory education begins, which is five years old in local jurisdictions. These are basic definitions of terms used in early childhood education:

- *Nursery school* is most often defined as a school that enrolls children who are younger than five years old, or before compulsory education begins, follows a regular school calendar, and offers an abbreviated day or number of days per week.
- *Preschool* often refers to a school for children younger than the age at which compulsory education begins, follows a regular school calendar, has abbreviated days, and also continues with classes for older children. Both nursery schools and preschools are staffed by qualified teachers who encourage educational play rather than providing childcare. In some programs, limited before- and after-school care is available.
- *Daycare* is a program providing full-day, year-round supervision that has childcare and the same elements of early education.
- *Playgroups* are just as implied: a parent or a group of parents or nannies arrange for and supervise a few hours of play.
- *Pre-kindergarten* is a program for four- and five-year-olds and often runs the length of an academic day.
- *Kindergarten* is for five- and six-year-olds and usually runs the length of an academic day.

At each preschool, the age of eligibility may be different.

The terms *nursery school* and *preschool* are often used interchangeably. In this book I use the word *preschool* to refer to the precompulsory education programs. Daycare programs, of which there are many, require a different set of licenses and supervision and are not included in this book.

Most preschools that end at age four are proprietary and for-profit. They are owned and operated by individuals who pay taxes, like any other business. For additional information, check out www.daycareindc.org.

CONSIDER YOUR AND YOUR CHILD'S NEEDS

It is appropriate to begin thinking about preschools a year before you want to use one. Since most preschools begin with children in the two- to three-year-old range, you can begin to gather information when your child is about a year old. Infant care is limited, and arrangements should be considered even during pregnancy.

Good questions are:

- What is important to me in a preschool?
- What is a reasonable commute? Young children should not be cooped up in a car for unnecessarily extended periods; you want to be available in case of an emergency; and it is nice if there are friends nearby for play dates and snow days. It seems that children choose as a best friend the person who lives the greatest distance from home and from school, which means being close to the school can be an asset.
- What length of a school day do I need? For two- and three-year-olds, many schools have a choice of either a morning or an afternoon session and a two- or three-day option. For four- and five-year-olds, the length of the school day may be the same as that of an elementary school. If your child needs care for the entire day, additional caregivers will be required, or a daycare program might be a better option.
- Do I want a religious orientation? Some schools that are located in churches or synagogues witness to the values of those faiths; other programs are located in a church's facilities but have no affiliation with the religious institution.
- Do I need a program that accepts children in diapers?
- Does my child have any special needs?
- How much can I afford to pay? Prices vary; many programs have tuition assistance.
- Is my child ready for preschool? This question needs to be addressed in the context of the age of the child, but in general, the following are good indicators:
  - Uses words to express basic needs
  - Listens to and follows simple directions
  - Transitions from a parent or caregiver with relative ease

- Enjoys the pace and activities of the group
- Looks forward to each day at school

If, after a period of adjustment, this is not the case, perhaps he or she is too young and should continue in playgroups.

YOUR OPTIONS

Choice: A Preschool Only or a Preschool within a School that Continues to Higher Grades?

To the extent that geographic proximity permits, parents have a choice in selecting their child's first learning environment. One option is a nursery school, a program designed for children younger than five years old, without classes for older children. The other option is a school that begins with a nursery program and continues through second or third or sixth or eighth grades, or through twelfth grade. This book includes some of each, with charts that indicate the age range and grade levels available.

Types of Preschools

The governance of all schools is either nonprofit or for-profit. Among nonprofit schools, some are nonsectarian and governed by a board of trustees with a head of school selected by the board. Other nonprofits are religious schools that are governed by selected members of the congregation. Others are devoted to the tenets of a denomination, but have a separate board of governors. All are tax-exempt and subject to state and federal laws.

For-profit schools can be privately owned and operated. These are often called *proprietary schools*. Other for-profits are owned by a corporation or are part of a chain of schools owned by a corporation, with a head of school employed by the corporation.

Teaching Methods and Styles

Some terms that are used to describe teaching styles and methods in preschools are self-explanatory, and there are obviously many overlaps. It is difficult to make discrete comparisons. For instance, traditional schools often employ some of the same teaching methods as progressive schools, religious schools may use the Montessori method, and so on. Nonetheless, this is a generalized list that provides some insights into how schools differ. I have supplied websites when available.

- Religious—a curriculum or culture that is associated with an established faith
- Traditional—orderly, predictable, clear expectations
- Progressive—active learning, flexible curriculum, multiple resources
- Developmental—attuned to explicit or subtle age-appropriate differences
- Special needs—teachers have additional course work or graduate degrees that enable them to use divergent methods of instruction to remediate underdeveloped skills
- International—students from around the globe bring a mix of cultures; focus on foreign languages and global issues
- Foreign language immersion—catering to a proficiency in specific languages
- Co-op—refers to parental leadership and involvement
- Montessori—see www.montessori.org
- Reggio Emilia—North American Reggio Emilia Alliance; see www.reggioalliance.org
- Phonovisual—see www.phonovisual.com/steps.php
- Waldorf—see www.whywaldorfworks.org

Programmatically, all of these schools are focused on helping children gain a love of learning, independence, and social skills among a small group of peers and adults from outside of the home. Some programs may appear more academic, but most educators agree that truly noble goals for teachers in preschool are to enable children to:

- Use a wide range of materials creatively.
- Share and play cooperatively.
- Enhance large and fine motor skills through activities and play.
- Whet curiosity and instill a love of learning.

DO YOUR HOMEWORK

Begin the application process one year or more prior to enrollment. No two schools have identical procedures. It is important to know each school's process, but the following is a general outline. It is similar to the independent school timetable; however, there are significant differences.

- Preschools are more apt to have rolling admission, meaning spaces may occur during the school year and applications are accepted as spaces develop.
- A few schools accept students according to the chronological receipt of applications, which means it is even more important to know the application procedure. A few have a lottery system.
- Most schools have specific deadlines for the receipt of applications and the completion of steps in the process. After the deadline for receipt of an application, and dependent upon the length of a waiting list, many preschools have rolling admission.
- Begin by researching schools in your neighborhood or near your workplace, or, if you intend to move, near where you will relocate. Talk to neighbors and other parents who have children in preschools. Read local parenting magazines and visit school websites.
- Determine which schools seem appropriate and add a few others to explore the options.
- Visit the schools in which you are interested.
- Submit applications.
- Schedule a visit or play date, if applicable. Most schools do not meet children younger than two and a half prior to enrollment. For children two and a half or older, schools often invite the child to accompany his or her parents for a brief visit during which parents and child may remain together throughout the session. Often, there is a small group of other children with whom your child can play; it is equally permissible for the child to remain in your lap the entire time. Teachers or an admission officer or head of school will observe the child's language development, interests, and attention span. Everyone usually has a good time.

- Preschools do not require an admission test or letters of recommendation.
- Decisions are generally made in February or as spaces become available. The process is much less complicated than for older students. Like other schools, preschools try to maintain a balance of boys and girls and create a diverse group of students who learn from each other. Most give priority to siblings or, in religious affiliated programs, to the children of members of the congregation.
- If accepted, read the contract carefully, sign, and return promptly. If you do not want the space, notify the school immediately so that someone else may have the place.
- Waiting lists are an indication that space is not immediately available. Spaces may develop throughout the summer or even during the school year. If your child is on a waiting list, inform the school either that you have made another decision and do not wish to remain on the list, or that you would like to be considered if a space develops. It is appropriate to contact the school periodically (about once a month) to show your continued interest.
- If you have signed a contract with a school and you break the contract, you may be held responsible for the tuition.

PREPARE TO APPLY

What to Look for During Your Visits

Compare the preschool's description of its program and goals with your personal observations. If it appears confusing, tactfully inquire about the differences.

School Community

- Size of school, ages included, size of each group
- Length of school day and before- and after-school options
- Pupil/teacher ratio
- Nonsectarian with a focus on character education

- Religious affiliation: prayers, chapel; religious holidays that are celebrated; spiritual climate
- Governance: for-profit (proprietary), nonprofit
- Accreditation, memberships, or licenses, as applicable
- Urban or suburban location
- General ambiance of the institution: atmosphere, more formal or informal style
- Enrichment opportunities, including field trips
- Demeanor of the children: engaged, happy, alert, playing together, resting
- Supervision of playgrounds and free time
- Additional personnel (nurse, resource teachers, therapists)
- School calendar, holidays, snow-day policies
- Celebration of multiculturalism
- Property: owned or leased, terms of the lease
- Future plans for programs or facilities
- Financial stability; endowment, if any

Student Body

- Age at which a student is eligible for admission (different preschools have different birthday cut-off dates)
- Racial diversity or multicultural composition
- Percentage of families who receive financial aid
- Evidence that your child will be comfortable in the social setting

Faculty and Staff

- Academic background and qualifications
- Use of and qualifications for teacher aides
- Special part-time staff for music, art, or physical therapies
- Background security check on all staff and employees
- Age range, experience, average years teaching

- Male/female ratio
- Racial diversity or multicultural composition
- Average number of children for whom each teacher is responsible
- Responsibilities: classroom and extracurricular
- Professional mentoring and development opportunities and resources
- Evidence of affectionate, energetic, and skillful nurture of young children
- Evidence of excitement and commitment
- Camaraderie among teachers
- Rapport with parents

Facilities

- A safe, clean, and welcoming climate in the halls and classrooms
- Equipment and supplies that are appropriate and accessible for each age group and encourage discovery and exploration
- Labeled cubbies, with hooks for coats, for children to store their belongings
- Clean, accessible, age-appropriate bathrooms (most are coed)
- Fresh, attractive classroom materials, books, and games
- Classrooms: arrangement of furniture; content and format of bulletin boards; availability of space for arts, crafts, blocks, puzzles, imaginative play, music, dance
- Appropriate space and arrangement for quiet time, rest, and naps
- Use of other space: adequate indoor and outdoor fenced play space; playground that is well maintained, safe, and age appropriate; library, science or media center, faculty room and supplies, conference room
- Food service: optional, required, additional expense; nutritional value; ability to accommodate special diets; atmosphere of eating area
- Diaper-changing area that is clean, user friendly, and properly licensed for children who are not potty trained

Teaching Methods

- Teaching methodology, training, and curriculum
- Classroom behavior management: teacher's tone of voice, methods of gaining attention, ability to engage all children, assistance with transitions, awareness of the whole group and individuals
- Organized schedule of daily activities and long-range goals
- Accommodation or remediation for special learning and developmental needs
- Opportunities for children to try new activities, pursue individual interests, explore new ideas, reflect
- Quality time out-of-doors
- Use of field trips for exploration and information

School Policies

- Costs, availability of financial aid, projected annual tuition increase
- Hidden costs: activity fees, field trips
- Safety issues: measures in place to handle emergencies
- Disciplinary measures
- Method and frequency of communicating with parents
- Parent participation: opportunities in the classroom, for membership on the board of trustees or committees, to accompany on field trips, or other activities
- Opportunities to meet other parents
- Special speakers or programs of interest to parents of young children
- Library with books on child development for parents and faculty

Being organized helps. Many families use the worksheet on page 272 as a model to create their own spreadsheet, adapting it to include the points pertinent to their child's age.

SUBMIT APPLICATIONS

If the school provides options, you will need to decide the number of days and hours per week that you want, based on what is available at each school. Most families prefer a morning program, especially if the child naps in the afternoon. Some parents with a younger child think the afternoon sessions are more convenient.

Sometimes the application process can be very simple. You submit the application and the fee, have a talk with the admission officer or school director, and within a few days or weeks, you are advised that your child is admitted.

A few preschools have a larger number of applicants to consider, which means the wait for a decision may be longer. Because you cannot be sure of a place until the deadlines for submitting other applications have passed, you may need to submit multiple applications.

Preschools that are a part of a larger school with higher grade levels often notify the families of all applicants at the same time, usually in March.

PARENT RESPONSES

When you have decided on a preschool and the days and hours that your child will attend, notify any other schools to which you applied that you will not accept the places offered. Also, advise them if you do or do not want to remain on a waiting list.

When my first-born went off for his first day of nursery school, I went home and wept the entire morning! It was the beginning of something big and he was in the care of others. Yes! I had to grow up too! Other mothers in the nursery school became my friends for life as we watched our children blossom and shared our mutual interests and concerns. Those were wondrous years and I can only hope your experience will be as rewarding.

Preschool Directory

ABINGDON MONTESSORI SCHOOL   est. 1970

Lynn Prosten, Director
5144 Massachusetts Avenue
Bethesda, MD 20816
301-320-3646
www.abingdonschool.org

2.5–6 years
No wheelchair access

Governance: Proprietary
Accredited by: Montgomery County Board of Education, MSDE
Memberships: N/A
Religious affiliation: Nonsectarian

PROFILE
Total enrollment: 50
Number of faculty: 7
Number of teaching assistants: 6
Schools three or more children attend next: Beauvoir, Maret, St. Patrick's Episcopal, Washington Episcopal, Washington International

APPLICATION PROCESS
Birthday cutoff: Most turn 3 by March of the next year
Deadline: N/A
Fee: None
Testing required: None
Steps: Visit/tour, application

COSTS
Average additional fees: N/A
Financial aid: Yes
% of children receiving aid: 5%

NOTE: This data applies to the 2009–2010 school year.

Age	Days	Hours	Tuition	Openings	Class size	Teachers per class	Food provided
2.5–6	5	8:45–11:50	$8,400				
2.5–6	5	8:45–2:15	$11,000				

DAILY LIFE
Before- or after-school care: 8:00–8:45 AM
Food allergy policy: Careful about allergies
Resource specialists: Psychologist, speech pathologist
Summer programs: None
Special features: Art, computers, gym, music

FACILITIES AND LONG-RANGE PLANS
Church location

HISTORY AND PHILOSOPHY

At Abingdon we combine Dr. Montessori's theories of human development with the contemporary child's world. While devoted to the Montessori method, we are not bound by it. We are open to and eager to apply new complementary concepts, as evidenced in our instruction in science, social studies, music, art, computer skills, and physical development. Our basic function is to help children learn whenever they are ready. We do not stress the acquisition of a body of knowledge, but rather the development of independence and self-esteem that benefits the child physically, emotionally, and intellectually. The teacher serves as a learning "guide."

NOTE: This data applies to the 2009–2010 school year.

ADAS ISRAEL'S GAN HAYELED   est. 1972

Shelley Remer, Director
2850 Quebec Street, NW
Washington, DC 20008
202-362-4491
www.adasisrael.org/gan

Shelley Remer
shelley.remer@adasisrael.org

18 months–5 years
Wheelchair accessible

Governance: Nonprofit
Accredited by: NAEYC
Memberships: PJLL, Zero to Three: Infants and Toddlers
Religious affiliation: Jewish

PROFILE
Total enrollment: 200
Number of faculty: 40
Number of teaching assistants: 14
Schools three or more children attend next: Charles E. Smith Jewish Day, DC Public Schools, Georgetown Day, Jewish Primary Day, Montgomery County Public Schools, Sidwell Friends

APPLICATION PROCESS
Birthday cutoff: 2 by September 1
Deadline: January 16
Fee: $50 registration, $250 advance tuition payment
Testing required: None
Steps: Open house (optional), application

COSTS
Average additional fees: None
Financial aid: Yes
% of children receiving aid: 2–5%

NOTE: This data applies to the 2009–2010 school year.

Age	Days	Hours	Tuition	Openings	Class size	Teachers per class	Food provided
2–2.5	2	8:50–11:50	$4,030		12	3	Snack
2.5–3	3	8:50–11:50	$6,075		12	3	Snack
3–4	5	8:50–11:50	$7,070		14	2	Snack
4–5	5	8:50–2:50, 8:50–11:50 (M/F)	$10,920		14	2	Snack
4–5	5	8:50–2:50	$11,410		14	2	Snack

DAILY LIFE

Before- or after-school care: 8:30–8:50 AM

Food allergy policy: Nut-free policy

Resource specialists: N/A

Summer programs: Yes

Special features: Active parent body, dedicated staff, discount for synagogue members, high teacher/pupil ratio, inclusion program, Lunch Bunch & Enrichment programs, resource programs, small class size, wonderful facility

FACILITIES AND LONG-RANGE PLANS

Continue to enhance playground and indoor facilities

HISTORY AND PHILOSOPHY

We believe that each child is unique. Our developmental approach allows our children to learn and grow at their own pace and in their own way. Our warm and nurturing environment fosters self-confidence and independence. It also encourages children to develop the cognitive, language, motor and social skills that will serve them well later in schooling, and in life. When one goes from room to room you will notice small classes decorated with children's artwork and staffed with a high teacher-to-student ratio. As early childhood professionals, we aim to provide the best possible early learning experience for our students and their families.

NOTE: This data applies to the 2009–2010 school year.

AMAZING LIFE GAMES   est. 1971

Deborah Kline, Managing Director
4300 16th Street, NW
Washington, DC 20011
202-265-0114
www.amazinglifegames.org

Deborah Kline
deborah@amazinglifegames.org

2.5–5 years
No wheelchair access

Governance: Nonprofit
Accredited by: N/A
Memberships: N/A
Religious affiliation: N/A

PROFILE
Total enrollment: 38
Number of faculty: 6
Number of teaching assistants: N/A
Schools three or more children attend next: N/A

APPLICATION PROCESS
Birthday cutoff: 2.5 by start of school
Deadline: February 1, rolling
Fee: $50
Testing required: None
Steps: Sign up for tour on website

COSTS
Average additional fees: Negligible
Financial aid: Yes
% of children receiving aid: 15%

NOTE: This data applies to the 2009–2010 school year.

Age	Days	Hours	Tuition (monthly)	Openings	Class size	Teachers per class	Food provided
2.5–5	2	8:45–1:00	$345	Varies	30 at most	6–7	None
2.5–5	2	8:45–3:00	$466	Varies	30 at most	6–7	None
2.5–5	2	8:45–6:00	$621	Varies	30 at most	6–7	None
2.5–5	3	8:45–1:00	$492	Varies	30 at most	6–7	None
2.5–5	3	8:45–3:00	$664	Varies	30 at most	6–7	None
2.5–5	3	8:45–6:00	$886	Varies	30 at most	6–7	None
2.5–5	4	8:45–1:00	$621	Varies	30 at most	6–7	None
2.5–5	4	8:45–3:00	$839	Varies	30 at most	6–7	None
2.5–5	4	8:45–6:00	$1,119	Varies	30 at most	6–7	None
2.5–5	5	8:45–1:00	$690	Varies	30 at most	6–7	None
2.5–5	5	8:45–3:00	$932	Varies	30 at most	6–7	None
2.5–5	5	8:45–6:00	$1,243	Varies	30 at most	6–7	None

DAILY LIFE

Before- or after-school care: 3:00–6:00 PM

Food allergy policy: Case by case

Resource specialists: Dramatic play, music, Spanish, yoga

Summer programs: Three 2-week summer camp sessions

Special features: ALG is a cooperative preschool, where parents are involved in the classroom. Partial and no co-op options available, as well as extended day at an hourly rate.

FACILITIES AND LONG-RANGE PLANS

Two fully fenced outdoor spaces, one with a garden and woodland path, the other an enclosed courtyard where children can ride bikes and have picnics. Two large open classrooms, with a science area, reading nooks, art and building areas, and space and equipment for large motor play.

HISTORY AND PHILOSOPHY

ALG was founded on the principle that children learn best through play. Our dedicated, long-term teachers get to know children as individuals, and help them learn to function successfully as members of a group while maintaining their individuality. We encourage children to be independent, to learn to care for their own needs, and to be sensitive to the needs and feelings of others. The involvement of parents helps to foster a strong community spirit, which for many families continues long after their children have left ALG.

NOTE: This data applies to the 2009–2010 school year.

APPLE MONTESSORI SCHOOL   est. 1983

Sandra Gaddy, Director
The Concord Center
7210 Hidden Creek Road
Bethesda, MD 20817
301-320-8832
www.applems.com

Erin Yost, Assistant Director
applemontessori@aol.com

2–6 years
Wheelchair accessible

Governance: Nonprofit
Accredited by: MSDE
Memberships: AMS
Religious affiliation: Nonsectarian

PROFILE
Total enrollment: 64
Number of faculty: 8
Number of teaching assistants: 4
Schools three or more children attend next: Christ Episcopal, Green Acres, Potomac, St. Elizabeth Parish School, Stone Ridge, Thomas Jefferson Preparatory, Washington Episcopal

APPLICATION PROCESS
Birthday cutoff: 2 by date of entry, 3 by December
Deadline: Rolling
Fee: $50
Testing required: None
Steps: School tour, application

COSTS
Average additional fees: $650
Financial aid: No
% of children receiving aid: N/A

NOTE: This data applies to the 2009–2010 school year.

Age	Days	Hours	Tuition	Openings	Class size	Teachers per class	Food provided
2	3	9:00–12:00	$7,010	7	10	2	Snack
2	3	9:00–3:00	$8,500	7	10	2	Snack
2	5	9:00–12:00	$8,389	7	10	2	Snack
2	5	9:00–3:00	$10,122	7	10	2	Snack
3–6	5	9:00–12:00	$8,389	10	36	4	Snack
3–6	5	9:00–3:00	$10,122	10	36	4	Snack
Apple Seed Option							
3–6	5	8:45–11:45	$15,000	5	8	2	Snack
3–6	5	12:45–3:15	$12,500	5	8	2	Snack
3–6	5	8:45–3:15	$21,000	5	8	2	Snack

DAILY LIFE
Before- or after-school care: 8:00–9:00 AM, 3:00–6:00 PM
Food allergy policy: Policy adjusted as needed; all teachers trained in use of EpiPen
Resource specialists: Dance, music, and Spanish specialists; occupational therapist, speech therapist
Summer programs: June Summer Camp, Monday–Friday 9:00–3:00
Special features: The Apple Seed Option at Apple Montessori School, serving children ages 3–6 challenged by educational or developmental delays. Unique Montessori program, small class size, inclusive therapies.

FACILITIES AND LONG-RANGE PLANS
Athletic field, garden, large playground, library

HISTORY AND PHILOSOPHY
Apple Montessori School has provided an outstanding learning environment and a caring community for children since 1983. A dedicated staff guided by the philosophy and materials developed by Maria Montessori strive to help each child reach his/her potential. The staff knows that the process of learning is more important than the product and guide the children as they follow their natural curiosity. While working in the classroom the children develop independence, self-discipline, respect for others and the love of learning.

NOTE: This data applies to the 2009–2010 school year.

BETHESDA-CHEVY CHASE COOPERATIVE NURSERY SCHOOL   est. 1955

Kathy D'Alelio, Director
4700 Norwood Drive
Chevy Chase, MD 20815
301-986-0677
www.bccnurseryschool.org

bccnurseryadmissions@gmail.com

3–5 years
No wheelchair access

Governance: Nonprofit
Accredited by: MSDE
Memberships: N/A
Religious affiliation: Nonsectarian

PROFILE
Total enrollment: 26
Number of faculty: 2
Number of teaching assistants: 2
(co-oping parents)
Schools three or more children attend next: Bethesda Elementary, Rosemary Hills Primary, Somerset Elementary

APPLICATION PROCESS
Birthday cutoff: 3 by September 1
Deadline: Rolling, beginning December 1
Fee: $45
Testing required: None
Steps: Tour, application

COSTS
Average additional fees: $95
Financial aid: Yes
% of children receiving aid: 4%

NOTE: This data applies to the 2009–2010 school year.

Age	Days	Hours	Tuition	Openings	Class size	Teachers per class	Food provided
3	3	9:00–12:00	$3,350	13	13	1	Snack
3	4	9:00–12:00	$3,450	13	13	1	Snack
3	5	9:00–12:00	$3,550	13	13	1	Snack
4	3	9:00–12:00	$3,350	13	13	1	Snack
4	4	9:00–12:00	$3,450	13	13	1	Snack
4	5	9:00–12:00	$3,550	13	13	1	Snack

DAILY LIFE

Before- or after-school care: 12:00–2:30 PM

Food allergy policy: We can commit to being peanut- and tree nut-free when needed. All teachers trained in use of EpiPen, CPR, and first aid.

Resource specialists: Kathy D'Alelio holds a masters degree in Special Education and has several years of experience in Special Education.

Summer programs: Parent-arranged weekly playgroups

Special features: Our teachers have worked together for over twenty years. Flexible curriculum developed yearly around current interests, featuring cooperation, friendships, listening, social skills, questioning, outside play each day. We have a dynamic and culturally diverse parent community.

FACILITIES AND LONG-RANGE PLANS

Located in beautiful Norwood Park with three newly renovated playgrounds and space to explore. Montgomery County owns and maintains our school building and Norwood Park.

HISTORY AND PHILOSOPHY

Founded in 1955 as a parent co-operative and has remained one with a clear mission to stay as such for over 50 years. The school is run by the parents and each family assumes a job responsibility for the school. We believe children are naturally curious and eager to learn. We think many skills are best learned through play. Our task is preparing children to recognize the wonders of the world; to be free to question the ideas and concepts of others, and to treat everyone respectfully. Our children enjoy discovering "how? and why?" through discussion, observation and experimentation.

NOTE: This data applies to the 2009–2010 school year.

BETHESDA COUNTRY DAY SCHOOL   est.

Judy McClimans, Principal
5615 Beech Avenue
Bethesda, MD 20814
301-530-6999
www.bethesdacountrydayschool.com

Judy McClimans
judith.mcclimans@nlcinc.com

2–5 years
Limited wheelchair access

Governance: Proprietary
Accredited by: MSDE Department of Child Care
Memberships: N/A
Religious affiliation: Nonsectarian

PROFILE
Total enrollment: 259
Number of faculty: 35
Number of teaching assistants: N/A
Schools three or more children attend next: Ashburton Elementary, British, French International, German, McLean, Norwood, St. Jane de Chantal, Stone Ridge, Wyngate

APPLICATION PROCESS
Birthday cutoff: At age by first day of school
Deadline: None
Fee: $100
Testing required: None
Steps: Tour, application

COSTS
Average additional fees: $630, plus $80 registration fee
Financial aid: No
% of children receiving aid: N/A

NOTE: This data applies to the 2009–2010 school year.

Age	Days	Hours	Tuition	Openings	Class size	Teachers per class	Food provided
2	2	9:00–12:00	$497	10	12	2	Snack
2	3	9:00–12:00	$610	10	12	2	Snack
2	5	9:00–12:00	$807	24	12	2	Snack
2	5	9:00–3:00	$1,062	36	12	2	Snack, lunch
3	5	9:00–12:00	$711	20	20	2	Snack
3	5	9:00–3:00	$1,021	60	20	2	Snack, lunch
4	5	9:00–12:00	$711	20	20	2	Snack
4	5	9:00–3:00	$1,021	60	20	2	Snack, lunch

DAILY LIFE

Before- or after-school care: 7:30–9:00 AM, 3:00–6:00 PM

Food allergy policy: No peanuts; children with allergies may bring their own lunch and snack

Resource specialists: N/A

Summer programs: Mid-June through end of August. Swimming, in-house activities, sports, arts & crafts

Special features: On-site librarian, music teacher; Spanish

FACILITIES AND LONG-RANGE PLANS

Computers—age 3 and up; library/music room, multipurpose room, two playgrounds

HISTORY AND PHILOSOPHY

Bethesda Country Day School provides an environment where children are safe, nurtured and ready to absorb what the world has to offer. Our well-trained, dedicated and caring teachers nurture your child through their educational journey. Children are inspired to explore, experience and make connections with the world around them. Our Links to Learning curriculum gives the structure and guidance children need to grow. Our curriculum is an integrated series of programs that incorporate preparation for reading and math as well as building social skills and confidence. Spanish, Art, Music and Library are a part of each day at BCDS.

NOTE: This data applies to the 2009–2010 school year.

BEVERLEY HILLS CHURCH PRESCHOOL   est. 1939

Kelley Organek, Director
3512 Old Dominion Boulevard
Arlington, VA 22305
703-549-7441
www.bhcpnet.org

Kelley Organek
bhcp@comcast.net

2.5–5 years
No wheelchair access

Governance: Nonprofit
Accredited by: NECPA
Memberships: NAREA
Religious affiliation: United Methodist Church

PROFILE
Total enrollment: 59
Number of faculty: 9
Number of teaching assistants:
None
Schools three or more children attend next: Alexandria City Public Schools, Alexandria Country Day, Arlington County Public Schools, Burgundy Farm, St. Mary's Catholic, St. Rita, St. Stephen's & St. Agnes, St. Thomas More Cathedral

APPLICATION PROCESS
Birthday cutoff: 2 by March 31
Deadline: End of Open House in January
Fee: $50
Testing required: None
Steps: Open house; lottery in February to fill available openings. Priority admission granted to siblings, alumni families, church families

COSTS
Average additional fees: $200
Financial aid: Yes
% of children receiving aid: 5%

NOTE: This data applies to the 2009–2010 school year.

Age	Days	Hours	Tuition	Openings	Class size	Teachers per class	Food provided
2.5–3	2	9:15–12:15	$2,220	Varies	12	2	Snack
3	3	9:00–12:15	$3,400	Varies	13	2	Snack
3–4	4	9:00–12:15	$4,080	Varies	14	2	Snack
4–5 (PK)	4	9:00–12:15	$4,080	Varies	17	2	Snack

DAILY LIFE

Before- or after-school care: None

Food allergy policy: Nut-free facility, allergy lists distributed for the purpose of parents bringing snacks

Resource specialists: Music enrichment teacher, studio teacher

Summer programs: Camp, three 2-week sessions, 9:00–1:00 daily

Special features: Parent co-operative preschool, Reggio Emelia arts focus

FACILITIES AND LONG-RANGE PLANS

Construction of a Natural Elements Playground anticipated in the next 5 years.

HISTORY AND PHILOSOPHY

The mission of Beverley Hills Church Preschool is to celebrate the wonder and breadth of children, linking them, their families and our educators in a community of mutual learning and care. Our school deeply honors the potential of children, supports their eagerness and capacities to make sense of and transform the world, and nurtures their individual and collective contributions to the learning and well-being of others.

At BHCP, young children, their families, teachers and others come together to enjoy the process of discovery, learning and becoming. Our learning environment is marked by great respect for young learners; a spirit of inquiry; the willingness to take risks; the expectation of sustained effort; and attentiveness to reflection, relationships, dialogue and growth. Together, we experience joy, wonder and satisfaction in meaningful work.

NOTE: This data applies to the 2009–2010 school year.

BRADLEY HILLS PRESBYTERIAN CHURCH NURSERY SCHOOL

est. 1957

Hilah Gaba, Director
6601 Bradley Boulevard
Bethesda, MD 20817
301-365-2909
www.bhpcns.org

Hilah Gaba
bhpcns@yahoo.com

2–4 years
No wheelchair access

Governance: Nonprofit
Accredited by: MSDE
Memberships: N/A
Religious affiliation: Presbyterian

PROFILE
Total enrollment: 320
Number of faculty: 32 (includes teaching assistants)
Number of teaching assistants: N/A
Schools three or more children attend next: Ashburton Elementary, Bannockburn Elementary, Bradley Hills Elementary, Norwood, Primary Day, St. Bartholomew Catholic, St. Jane de Chantal, Woods, Wyngate Elementary

APPLICATION PROCESS
Birthday cutoff: September 1
Deadline: Rolling
Fee: $50
Testing required: None
Steps: Application

COSTS
Average additional fees: None
Financial aid: Yes
% of children receiving aid: 2%

NOTE: This data applies to the 2009–2010 school year.

Age	Days	Hours	Tuition	Openings	Class size	Teachers per class	Food provided
2	1	9:00–11:30	$1,000		8	2	Snack
2	2	9:00–11:30	$1,950		8–12	2	Snack
3	2	9:00–12:30	$2,200		13–14	2	Snack
3	3	9:00–12:30	$3,200		13–14	2	Snack
4	3	9:00–12:30	$3,200		12–17	2	Snack
4	5	9:00–12:30	$5,100		12–19	2	Snack

DAILY LIFE
Before- or after-school care: 12:30–2:30 PM
Food allergy policy: Handled on a case-by-case basis
Resource specialists: Aerobics, literature, music, science
Summer programs: June camp
Special features: N/A

FACILITIES AND LONG-RANGE PLANS
N/A

HISTORY AND PHILOSOPHY
Established in 1957 the Bradley Hills Presbyterian Church Nursery School provides a relaxed, loving and caring atmosphere in which a child is encouraged to develop his/her own talents, uniqueness and self-esteem.

NOTE: This data applies to the 2009–2010 school year.

CHEVY CHASE-BETHESDA COMMUNITY CHILDREN'S CENTER (CCBC)   est. 1971

Lisa McAuliffe, Director
5671 Western Avenue, NW
Washington, DC 20015
202-966-3299
www.ccbccc.org

Lisa McAuliffe
ccbc@verizon.net

18 months–5 years
No wheelchair access

Governance: Nonprofit
Accredited by: N/A
Memberships: N/A
Religious affiliation: Nonsectarian

PROFILE
Total enrollment: 160
Number of faculty: 18 teachers, 4 administrative, 4 aides
Number of teaching assistants: 3
Schools three or more children attend next: Beauvoir, Blessed Sacrament, Janney, Lafayette, Murch, National Presbyterian, Rosemary Hills, Sidwell Friends, Somerset, Washington Episcopal

APPLICATION PROCESS
Birthday cutoff: 18 months by September 1
Deadline: First Thursday in February
Fee: $50
Testing required: None
Steps: N/A

COSTS
Average additional fees: None
Financial aid: Yes
% of children receiving aid: 4%

NOTE: This data applies to the 2009–2010 school year.

Age	Days	Hours	Tuition	Openings	Class size	Teachers per class	Food provided
18–23 mo.	2	9:00–12:30	$3,456	12	6	2	Healthy snack
18–23 mo.	3	9:00–12:30	$5,180	12	6	2	Healthy snack
2–2.5	2	9:00–12:30	$3,236	24	8	2	Healthy snack
2–2.5	3	9:00–12:30	$4,844	24	8	2	Healthy snack
2.5–3	2	9:00–12:30	$3,236	30	10	2	Healthy snack
2.5–3	3	9:00–12:30	$4,844	30	10	2	Healthy snack
3–3.5	2	9:00–12:30	$3,236	24	12	2	Healthy snack
3–3.5	3	9:00–12:30	$4,844	24	12	2	Healthy snack
3.5–4	5	9:00–12:30	$7,490	30	15	3	Healthy snack
4–5	5	9:00–12:30	$7,490	40	20	3	Healthy snack

DAILY LIFE

Before- or after-school care: 8:00–9:00 AM, 12:30–2:45 PM

Food allergy policy: Peanut free; we are sensitive to individual allergies

Resource specialists: Art, movement, music, early intervention

Summer programs: 3 sessions (June–mid-August), ages 2–5

Special features: Water and outside play, music, arts & crafts, special visitors, neighborhood field trips, snack provided

FACILITIES AND LONG-RANGE PLANS

Lease agreement with church until 2028; great indoor facilities, including 2 playrooms for inclement weather, music & movement room, library, kitchen

HISTORY AND PHILOSOPHY

CCBC began in 1971 as a mother's morning out program and has grown into nine classrooms of children 18 months to 5 years old. The philosophy is learning through play. A developmentally appropriate curriculum is planned to enhance the development of the whole child—socially, emotionally, cognitively, and physically. There are two experienced teachers in each classroom and the staff-to-child ratio is kept low. The school thrives on parental involvement and parents are encouraged to assist at the school four times a year.

NOTE: This data applies to the 2009–2010 school year.

CHEVY CHASE PRESBYTERIAN CHURCH   est. 1958
WEEKDAY NURSERY SCHOOL

Cindy Walsh, Director
1 Chevy Chase Circle, NW
Washington, DC 20015
202-363-2209
www.chevychasepc.org

Cindy Walsh
cindy@chevychasepc.org

1–5 years
Wheelchair accessible

Governance: Nonprofit
Accredited by: N/A
Memberships: NAEYC
Religious affiliation: Presbyterian but open to all races,
ethnic backgrounds, and religious affiliations

PROFILE
Total enrollment: 180
Number of faculty: 10
Number of teaching assistants: 16
Schools three or more children attend next: Beauvoir, Blessed Sacrament, Concord Hill, Lafayette, Murch, Rosemary Hills, Washington Episcopal

APPLICATION PROCESS
Birthday cutoff: September 30
Deadline: Last day of February
Fee: $50
Testing required: None
Steps: N/A

COSTS
Average additional fees: N/A
Financial aid: Yes
% of children receiving aid: 1%

NOTE: This data applies to the 2009–2010 school year.

Age	Days	Hours	Tuition (monthly)	Openings	Class size	Teachers per class	Food provided
1	1	9:00–12:00	$150		12	4	Snack
2	2	9:00–12:00	$315		10–12	3	Snack
3	2	9:00–12:00	$315		15	2	Snack
3	3	9:00–12:00	$420		15	2–3	Snack
3	5	9:00–12:00	$630		15	2	Snack
4	5	9:00–12:00	$630		17	2–3	Snack
5	5	9:00–12:00	$630		14	2	Snack

DAILY LIFE
Before- or after-school care: 8:30–9:00 AM, 12:00–2:30 PM
Food allergy policy: No nuts or related foods, school-wide; others by class if needed
Resource specialists: Music
Summer programs: Camp, mid-June through July
Special features: N/A

FACILITIES AND LONG-RANGE PLANS
Renovations done 5 years ago

HISTORY AND PHILOSOPHY
CCPC WNS provides a safe and loving environment where children are encouraged to explore their world. The staff plans and implements a play-based developmentally appropriate curriculum and commits to nurture the physical, emotional, intellectual, spiritual, and social growth of each child.

NOTE: This data applies to the 2009–2010 school year.

CHEVY CHASE UNITED METHODIST CHURCH PRESCHOOL   est. 1967

Annette Fitzpatrick, Director
7001 Connecticut Avenue
Chevy Chase, MD 20815
301-652-7660
www.ccumcpreschool.org

Lauren Bailey, Program Administrator
ccumcpreschool@verizon.net

2–5 years
Wheelchair accessible

Governance: Nonprofit
Accredited by: MSDE
Memberships: N/A
Religious affiliation: Methodist

PROFILE
Total enrollment: 136
Number of faculty: 8
Number of teaching assistants: 8
Schools three or more children attend next: Beauvoir, Blessed Sacrament, Grace Episcopal, Lafayette, Norwood, Primary Day, Rosemary Hills, St. Patrick's Episcopal, Stone Ridge, Washington Episcopal

APPLICATION PROCESS
Birthday cutoff: September 1
Deadline: January 30
Fee: $25
Testing required: None
Steps: Open house, lottery application

COSTS
Average additional fees: Early Bird $5/morning; Lunch Bunch $16/day; Adventure Afternoon $27/day
Financial aid: Yes
% of children receiving aid: 1–2%

NOTE: This data applies to the 2009–2010 school year.

Age	Days	Hours	Tuition	Openings	Class size	Teachers per class	Food provided
2	2	9:15–12:15	$2,710	30	10	2	None
2	3	9:15–12:15	$3,595	10	10	2	None
3	3	9:00–12:00	$3,595	24	12	2	None
3	5	9:00–12:00	$6,070	24	12	2	None
4	5	9:00–12:00	$6,070	48	16	2	None

DAILY LIFE
Before- or after-school care: 8:30–9:00 AM, 12:00–2:30 PM
Food allergy policy: Some classrooms may be designated peanut-free, as needed; all staff trained in first aid & CPR, including use of EpiPen.
Resource specialists: 2 specialists; consultants engaged on as-needed basis
Summer programs: None
Special features: Parent involvement—participation in classrooms, field trips, and events

FACILITIES AND LONG-RANGE PLANS
Spacious, well-equipped facility, including 8 classrooms, staff resource room, all-purpose hall for indoor play; 2 large, newly renovated playgrounds

HISTORY AND PHILOSOPHY
CCUMC Preschool is a non-profit, self-supporting program operating under the auspices of the Chevy Chase United Methodist Church. The school was established in 1967. The preschool believes that young children learn best through play and that parental involvement is good both for the parent and for the child.

Mission Statement: We are a school community within a Christian faith community, committed to helping children develop a belief in God's world, an awareness of their role in this world, and an ability to deal compassionately with all people.

NOTE: This data applies to the 2009–2010 school year.

THE CHILDREN'S HOUSE OF WASHINGTON　est. 1981

Patti Harburger, Director
3133 Dumbarton Street, NW
Washington, DC 20007
202-342-2551
www.thechildrenshouseofwashington.com

Patti Harburger
pharburger@verizon.net

2.5–6 years
Wheelchair accessible

Governance: Nonprofit
Accredited by: District of Columbia
Memberships: N/A
Religious affiliation: Nonsectarian

PROFILE
Total enrollment: 27–29
Number of faculty: 2 trained
Montessori teachers
Number of teaching assistants: 3
**Schools three or more children
attend next:** Aidan Montessori,
Georgetown Day, Horace Mann,
Hyde, Maret, St. Patrick's
Episcopal, Washington
International

APPLICATION PROCESS
Birthday cutoff: 3 by December 31
Deadline: February 15
Fee: $55
Testing required: None
Steps: Parent visit/classroom obser-
vation, application, child visit

COSTS
Average additional fees: $6–$8 per
hour for extended care
Financial aid: Yes
% of children receiving aid: 20%

NOTE: This data applies to the 2009–2010 school year.

Age	Days	Hours	Tuition	Openings	Class size	Teachers per class	Food provided
2.5–4	5	8:45–12:00	$8,000		27	3	None
5	5	8:45–3:00	$9,000		27	3	None

DAILY LIFE

Before- or after-school care: 8:20–8:45 AM, 12:00–6:00 PM
Food allergy policy: No peanut products allowed
Resource specialists: Part-time dance and music teachers
Summer programs: N/A
Special features: "Arts and Play Program" extended-day option: indoor traditional pre-school play, outdoor playground, art activities. Half-hour dance classes by age once a week. Music teacher twice a week for storytelling, drama, world instruments, songs, and movement work.

FACILITIES AND LONG-RANGE PLANS

We are located in the Dumbarton United Methodist Church. We have our own playground attached to the church. We have no plans for expansion.

HISTORY AND PHILOSOPHY

The Children's House of Washington is a Montessori preschool, offering children an academic approach to preschool. In a mixed-aged class children explore, through the use of manipulative materials, the basics of language, mathematics, geography, sensorial differentiation and independence skills. Ideally each child remains in this special environment for three years.

NOTE: This data applies to the 2009–2010 school year.

CLARA BARTON CENTER FOR CHILDREN   est. 1975

Linda Owen, Director
7425 MacArthur Boulevard
Cabin John, MD 20818
301-320-4565
www.clarabartoncenter.org

Linda Owen
info@clarabartoncenter.org

2–5 years
Limited wheelchair access

Governance: Nonprofit
Accredited by: MSDE
Memberships: N/A
Religious affiliation: Nonsectarian

PROFILE
Total enrollment: 80
Number of faculty: 15
Number of teaching assistants:
None
Schools three or more children attend next: Bannockburn, Carderock Springs, Georgetown Day, Green Acres, Norwood, St. Bartholomew, Little Flower, Washington Episcopal, Washington International, Wood Acres

APPLICATION PROCESS
Birthday cutoff: 2 by August 31
Deadline: November 30
Fee: $40
Testing required: None
Steps: Tour, application

COSTS
Average additional fees: $250
Financial aid: Yes
% of children receiving aid: 15%

NOTE: This data applies to the 2009–2010 school year.

Age	Days	Hours	Tuition (monthly)	Openings	Class size	Teachers per class	Food provided
2	3	8:00–12:30	$640		8–12	2	Snack
2	3	8:00–3:30	$775		8–12	2	Snack
2	3	8:00–6:00	$890		8–12	2	Snack
2	4	8:00–12:30	$730		8–12	2	Snack
2	4	8:00–3:30	$925		8–12	2	Snack
2	4	8:00–6:00	$1,055		8–12	2	Snack
2	5	8:00–12:30	$820		8–12	2	Snack
2	5	8:00–3:30	$1,035		8–12	2	Snack
2	5	8:00–6:00	$1,215		8–12	2	Snack
3	3	8:00–12:30	$570		14–15	2	Snack
3	3	8:00–3:30	$705		14–15	2	Snack
3	3	8:00–6:00	$825		14–15	2	Snack
3	4	8:00–12:30	$660		14–15	2	Snack
3	4	8:00–3:30	$855		14–15	2	Snack
3	4	8:00–6:00	$985		14–15	2	Snack
3	5	8:00–12:30	$750		14–15	2	Snack
3	5	8:00–3:30	$970		14–15	2	Snack
3	5	8:00–6:00	$985		14–15	2	Snack
4–5	5	8:00–12:30	$750		16–17	2	Snack
4–5	5	8:00–3:30	$970		16–17	2	Snack
4–5	5	8:00–6:00	$1,145		16–17	2	Snack

DAILY LIFE

Before- or after-school care: None
Food allergy policy: None
Resource specialists: Creative movement, music, Spanish
Summer programs: Yes
Special features: Low student-to-teacher ratios

FACILITIES AND LONG-RANGE PLANS

Large, spacious classrooms and playgrounds

HISTORY AND PHILOSOPHY

We provide a language-rich, socially nurturing environment where children can play and learn. Children are encouraged to take risks, solve problems, and gain trust and confidence in their own abilities. Parents are the child's first and most important teacher, and we encourage parent involvement.

NOTE: This data applies to the 2009–2010 school year.

COMMUNITY PRESCHOOL OF THE PALISADES   est. 1986

Amelia Clark, Director
5200 Cathedral Avenue, NW
Washington, DC 20016
202-364-8424
www.palisadescommunitychurch.org/preschool.html

Amelia Clark
palisadespreschl@aol.com

2–4 years
No wheelchair access

Governance: Nonprofit
Accredited by: N/A
Memberships: N/A
Religious affiliation: Nonsectarian

PROFILE
Total enrollment: N/A
Number of faculty: 7
Number of teaching assistants: 3
Schools three or more children attend next: Beauvoir, Georgetown Day, Key Elementary, Lowell, National Presbyterian, St. Patrick's Episcopal, Washington Episcopal, Washington International

APPLICATION PROCESS
Birthday cutoff: 2 by August 31
Deadline: November 1–February 15
Fee: $40
Testing required: None
Steps: Contact director

COSTS
Average additional fees: N/A
Financial aid: Yes
% of children receiving aid: Currently none; most years 5–10%

NOTE: This data applies to the 2009–2010 school year.

Age	Days	Hours	Tuition	Openings	Class size	Teachers per class	Food provided
2	2	9:00–12:00	$3,600		12	3	Snack
3	3	9:00–12:00	$4,500		16	3	Snack
4	5	9:00–12:00	$6,700		15	2	Snack

DAILY LIFE
Before- or after-school care: 8:30–9:00 AM, 12:00–2:00 PM
Food allergy policy: Nut and peanut restricted
Resource specialists:
Summer programs: 6-week summer camp, 9:00–1:00 daily
Special features: Neighborhood play-based preschool

FACILITIES AND LONG-RANGE PLANS
2 classrooms, large playground, large indoor play space

HISTORY AND PHILOSOPHY

The Community Preschool of the Palisades is a ministry of The Palisades Community Church. Its primary focus is the emotional, social, physical, intellectual, and spiritual well-being and development of its students. The preschool provides an atmosphere and context for children that will promote intellectual, social, emotional, physical, and spiritual health; help form habits of respect, safety, courtesy, self-confidence, responsibility, independence, and cooperation; stimulate natural curiosity; create a basic readiness for later school experiences and cultural activities; and nurture tolerance, appreciation, growth, and diversity.

NOTE: This data applies to the 2009–2010 school year.

THE COUNTRY DAY SCHOOL   est. 1964

Dr. Suzanne Nichols
6418 Georgetown Pike
McLean, VA 22101
703-356-9149
www.countryday.org

Lorrie Hallahan, Admission Director
lhallahan@countryday.org

2–5 years
Limited wheelchair access

Governance: Nonprofit
Accredited by: NAEYC
Memberships: NAEYC
Religious affiliation: Nonsectarian

PROFILE
Total enrollment: 280
Number of faculty: 27
Number of teaching assistants:
None
Schools three or more children attend next: Beauvoir, Flint Hill, Langley, Norwood, Nysmith, Potomac, St. Luke's, St. Patrick's Episcopal, Washington Episcopal

APPLICATION PROCESS
Birthday cutoff: 2 by September 30
Deadline: January 15
Fee: $70
Testing required: None
Steps: Parent tour, application

COSTS
Average additional fees: N/A
Financial aid: Yes
% of children receiving aid: 5%

NOTE: This data applies to the 2009–2010 school year.

Age	Days	Hours	Tuition	Openings	Class size	Teachers per class	Food provided
2	3	9:30–11:00	$6,600		9	2	Snack
3	4	9:00–12:00	$6,980		13	2	Snack
3	4	1:00–4:00	$6,980		13	2	Snack
4	4	8:30–12:00	$7,124		15	2	Snack
4	4	12:30–4:00	$7,124		15	2	Snack
4	5	8:30–11:30	$7,124		15	2	Snack
5 (K)	5	8:30–3:30	$14,000		15	2	Snack, lunch

DAILY LIFE

Before- or after-school care: None

Food allergy policy: Allergy-aware school

Resource specialists: Learning specialists

Summer programs: 3- or 6-week part-day camp, outdoor, nature-based, camp sing-alongs, water safety instruction

Special features: 10 playgrounds, located in center of McLean, low student-teacher ratios, Parent/Child program

FACILITIES AND LONG-RANGE PLANS

Two buildings on 4 wooded acres, art studio, children's garden, library, movement/music room, on-site pool, outdoor amphitheater, science/nature room

HISTORY AND PHILOSOPHY

With its developmental approach to learning, warm and nurturing faculty and an appreciation of each child's individual strengths, The Country Day School offers young children an environment which fosters their excitement for learning, development of thought processes and strong conceptual understanding, and ability to be constructive and contributing members of a group. The curriculum encourages children to initiate exploration of topics of interest to them and kindles an appreciation of their natural surroundings while focusing on interactive and creative learning. CDS is committed to a strong parent-child relationship where parents are active partners in their child's education and development.

NOTE: This data applies to the 2009–2010 school year.

DOLLEY MADISON PRESCHOOL   est. 1976

Anne Schwartz, Director
1125 Savile Lane
McLean, VA 22101
703-356-1351
www.dolleymadisonpreschool.org

Anne Schwartz
info@dolleymadisonpreschool.org

2.5–5 years
Wheelchair accessible

Governance: Nonprofit
Accredited by: State of Virginia
Memberships: NAEYC
Religious affiliation: Nonsectarian

PROFILE
Total enrollment: 66
Number of faculty: 6
Number of teaching assistants: 12
Schools three or more children attend next: Churchill, Franklin Sherman, Chesterbrook, Potomac, Kent Gardens

APPLICATION PROCESS
Birthday cutoff: 2.5 by September 1
Deadline: Rolling
Fee: $100 registration
Testing required: None
Steps: N/A

COSTS
Average additional fees: Field trips $3–$6 per trip
Financial aid: No
% of children receiving aid: N/A

NOTE: This data applies to the 2009–2010 school year.

Age	Days	Hours	Tuition (monthly)	Openings	Class size	Teachers per class	Food provided
2.5	2	9:15–12:00	$260		12	3	Snack
2.5	2	12:30–3:00	$235		12	3	Snack
2.5	3	12:30–3:00	$270		12	3	Snack
3	2	9:15–12:00	$260		15	3	Snack
3	2	12:30–3:00	$235		12	3	Snack
3	3	9:15–12:00	$310		15	3	Snack
3	3	12:30–3:00	$270		12	3	Snack
3	4	9:15–12:00	$350		15	3	Snack
4	2	9:15–12:00	$260		18	3	Snack
4	2	12:30–3:00	$235		17	3	Snack
4	3	9:15–12:00	$310		18	3	Snack
4	3	12:30–3:00	$270		17	3	Snack
4	4	9:15–12:00	$350		18	3	Snack
4	4	12:30–3:00	$295		17	3	Snack
4	5	9:15–12:00	$375		18	3	Snack
PK	5		$400		14	3	Snack

DAILY LIFE
Before- or after-school care: None
Food allergy policy: Bring own food
Resource specialists: Occupational therapist, speech-language pathologist
Summer programs: Summer camp
Special features: Art, music

FACILITIES AND LONG-RANGE PLANS
N/A

HISTORY AND PHILOSOPHY
Dolley Madison Preschool, founded in 1976, is a traditional nonsectarian preschool, located on the grounds of the Immanuel Presbyterian Church. The facility consists of bright, sunny rooms and a spacious outdoor play area. The philosophy of the school is to provide a challenging environment that nurtures self-esteem, fosters friendships, and encourages each child's unique abilities.

NOTE: This data applies to the 2009–2010 school year.

EMMANUEL LUTHERAN PRESCHOOL   est. 1960

Jenny Reinhart, Administrator
2589 Chain Bridge Road
Vienna, VA 22181
703-938-6187
www.elcvienna.org/elcpreschool.html

Jenny Reinhart
emmanuelpreschool@verizon.net

2.5–5 years
Limited wheelchair access

Governance: Nonprofit
Accredited by: State of Virginia
Memberships: ELEA
Religious affiliation: Lutheran

PROFILE
Total enrollment: 86
Number of faculty: 20
Number of teaching assistants:
Schools three or more children attend next: Flint Hill Elementary, Flint Hill Prep, Good Counsel, Lorien Woods, Oakton Elementary, Vienna Elementary, Waples Mill Elementary

APPLICATION PROCESS
Birthday cutoff: 2.5 by March 30; all others September 30
Deadline: N/A
Fee: N/A
Testing required: None
Steps: N/A

COSTS
Average additional fees: $75 registration fee, $35–$65 activity fee
Financial aid: Yes
% of children receiving aid: 2%

NOTE: This data applies to the 2009–2010 school year.

Age	Days	Hours	Tuition	Openings	Class size	Teachers per class	Food provided
2.5	2	9:00–12:00	$160		10	2	Snack
3	3	9:00–12:00	$260		12	2	Snack
4	4	9:00–12:00	$345		12–16	2	Snack

DAILY LIFE

Before- or after-school care: N/A

Food allergy policy: Peanut-free classrooms if needed, all staff trained in EpiPen administration

Resource specialists: Creative movement, music, science. Special needs referred to Child Find

Summer programs: N/A

Special features: Developmental curriculum; creative movement, music, science enrichment, integrated chapel program

FACILITIES AND LONG-RANGE PLANS

6 classrooms, large space for creative movement class, enclosed playground

HISTORY AND PHILOSOPHY

ELP was established in 1960 for the purpose of Christian outreach within the congregation to the community. Our goal, for each student, is to instill a love of God, love of learning, and love of self and others.

NOTE: This data applies to the 2009–2010 school year.

THE FRANKLIN MONTESSORI SCHOOL   est. 2002

Randy Crowley, Head of School
4473 Connecticut Avenue, NW
Washington, DC 20008
202-966-7747
www.franklinmontessori.com

Randy Crowley
mail@franklinmontessorischool.com

2–6 years
Wheelchair accessible
Second campus: 10500 Darnestown Road, Rockville, MD

Governance: Proprietary
Accredited by: N/A
Memberships: AMS
Religious affiliation: Nonsectarian

PROFILE
Total enrollment: 194
Number of faculty: 8
Number of teaching assistants: 14
Schools three or more children attend next: Beauvoir, Georgetown Day, Maret, Norwood, Sheridan, Sidwell Friends

APPLICATION PROCESS
Birthday cutoff: 2 by September 1
Deadline: Rolling
Fee: $50
Testing required: None
Steps: Tour, application, playdate/interview (primary classes only)

COSTS
Average additional fees: $500
Financial aid: Yes
% of children receiving aid: 3%

NOTE: This data applies to the 2009–2010 school year.

Age	Days	Hours	Tuition	Openings	Class size	Teachers per class	Food provided
2	5	7:30–3:30			12	2	Snack
3	5	7:30–6:00			25–30	3	Snack

DAILY LIFE
Before- or after-school care: 7:30–9:30 AM, 3:30–6:00 PM
Food allergy policy: Case by case
Resource specialists: Art, drama, music, nature
Summer programs: 10- or 11-month school year option. School is closed in August
Special features: N/A

FACILITIES AND LONG-RANGE PLANS
Franklin Montessori has a beautiful, warm and inviting facility. There are two 2-year-old classrooms and six primary classrooms. To complement these spaces we have a library, a large gymnasium, an art studio and an outside playground.

HISTORY AND PHILOSOPHY
Established in 1977 and in the Washington, DC, area since 2002, The Franklin Montessori School nurtures each child's natural love of learning. The children are encouraged to challenge themselves through a variety of multi-disciplinary materials and activities. Each day at Franklin offers numerous opportunities to develop academic proficiency, independence, leadership and self-respect. Most importantly, each day at Franklin is filled with the joy and excitement of childhood.

NOTE: This data applies to the 2009–2010 school year.

FRIENDSHIP CHILDREN'S CENTER   est. 1989

Lisa Danahy, Executive Director
5411 Western Avenue, NW
Washington, DC 20015
202-244-5115
www.friendshipchildren.org

Lisa Danahy
ldanahy@friendshipchildren.org

3 months–5 years
Wheelchair accessible
Second campus: 5310 43rd Street NW, Washington, DC, 202-244-1402

Governance: Nonprofit
Accredited by: N/A
Memberships: NAEYC, WACCC, WCDC
Religious affiliation: Nonsectarian

PROFILE
Total enrollment: 75
Number of faculty: 20
Number of teaching assistants: 10
Schools three or more children attend next: Janney, Lafayette, Murch, Sheridan, Westbrook

APPLICATION PROCESS
Birthday cutoff: Placement is determined by developmental readiness
Deadline: Rolling
Fee: $50
Testing required: None
Steps: Application, classroom visit for placement evaluation

COSTS
Average additional fees: $300–$650
Financial aid: Yes
% of children receiving aid: None

NOTE: This data applies to the 2009–2010 school year.

Age	Days	Hours	Tuition	Openings	Class size	Teachers per class	Food provided
3–12 mo.	5	7:30–6:00	$1,675		6–9	2–3	AM & PM snacks, whole milk
1–2	5	7:30–6:00	$1,675		12	4	AM & PM snacks, whole milk
2–3	5	7:30–6:00	$1,465		16	4	AM & PM snacks
3–4	5	7:30–6:00	$1,355		12	2	AM & PM snacks
4–6	5	7:30–6:00	$1,250		13	2	AM & PM snacks

DAILY LIFE

Before- or after-school care: Daily 7:30 AM–6:00 PM

Food allergy policy: No current exclusion for peanuts, dairy, wheat, egg; allergen-free foods provided for student from home

Resource specialists: Outsourced

Summer programs: Included in regular full-time program; includes 10-week creative movement class, weekly field trips & special visitors, daily outdoor play, water play, art activities, museum visits

Special features: Creative curriculum—learning through real-life experiences & hands-on play; literacy-based teaching; year-round program; Spanish, music & dance classes.

FACILITIES AND LONG-RANGE PLANS

The school opened its new preschool facility in the fall of 2007, more than doubling its capacity from 31 to 75 students. At this time, there are no plans to further expand the program.

HISTORY AND PHILOSOPHY

We are a nonprofit school for children between the ages of three months and five years. Using the Creative Curriculum, the school provides developmentally appropriate programs and experiences that enhance each child's social, emotional, physical, and cognitive growth within an atmosphere of warmth and understanding where children can develop as individuals and as part of a group. Teachers design experiences to broaden and deepen children's use of the ideas they are developing naturally and aid each child in developing respect for others, a sense of responsibility, self-discipline, and independent learning. Each child is encouraged to grow and learn at his or her own pace in an environment filled with respect and support.

NOTE: This data applies to the 2009–2010 school year.

GENEVA DAY SCHOOL   est. 1965

Suzanne Funk, Director
11931 Seven Locks Road
Potomac, MD 20854
301-340-7704
www.genevadayschool.org

Amanda White, Administrator
office@genevadayschool.org

2–5 years
Limited wheelchair access

Governance: Nonprofit
Accredited by: MSDE
Memberships: NAEYC
Religious affiliation: Nonsectarian

PROFILE
Total enrollment: 250
Number of faculty: 9
Number of teaching assistants: 17
Schools three or more children attend next: Christ Episcopal, French International, German School, McLean, Norwood, Our Lady of Mercy, Primary Day, Stone Ridge, St. John's, St. Raphael's

APPLICATION PROCESS
Birthday cutoff: 2 by entry date for 2s; September 1 for all others
Deadline: Ongoing registration; re-enrollment and new admissions in January
Fee: $75
Testing required: None
Steps: Tour, application, class visit

COSTS
Average additional fees: $250 registration
Financial aid: Yes
% of children receiving aid: Varies

NOTE: This data applies to the 2009–2010 school year.

Age	Days	Hours	Tuition	Openings	Class size	Teachers per class	Food provided
2	2	9:00–11:30	$2,153		12	3	Snack
2	2	12:15–2:45	$2,153		12	3	Snack
2–3	3	9:00–11:30	$3,230		12	3	Snack
2–3	3	12:15–2:45	$3,230		12	3	Snack
3–4	5	9:00–11:30	$5,354		18	2–3	Snack
3–4	5	12:15–2:45	$5,354		18	2–3	Snack
3–4	5	9:00–3:00	$10,900		18	3	Snack
K	5	9:00–3:00	$10,900		16	2	Snack

DAILY LIFE

Before- or after-school care: 7:00–9:00 AM, 3:00–6:00 PM

Food allergy policy: No peanuts or peanut products; other allergies and dietary considerations on a case-by-case basis

Resource specialists: Literacy resource consultant, occupational therapist, speech/language pathologist

Summer programs: Camp, 1-week sessions from early June to August, 9:00–1:00 or 9:00–3:00

Special features: Arts & crafts, cooking, flannel stories, games, My Gym fun, playground activities, water play

FACILITIES AND LONG-RANGE PLANS

Self-contained and open-space classrooms, two playgrounds, music/movement and art specialty classes, cultural events; optional extended care, lunch and enrichment classes

HISTORY AND PHILOSOPHY

Learning occurs through freedom and flexibility of center time, organized circle activities, emerging curriculum, and the "teachable moment." A large, well-equipped playground and library support this endeavor. Each child is scheduled into activities to maximize learning strengths, interests and various intelligences in developmentally appropriate activities. Themes, projects, discussions, and literature, together with art and music, promote learning for all students. This takes place in a warm and supportive yet challenging and stimulating environment. Geneva staff understands the development of young children and enjoy working with them. The school provides all staff with continuing education, plus pediatric CPR and first-aid training.

NOTE: This data applies to the 2009–2010 school year.

GEORGETOWN MONTESSORI SCHOOL   est. 1983

Lee Allard, Administrator
1041 Wisconsin Avenue, NW
Washington, DC 20007
202-337-8058
www.georgetownmontessori.net

Lee Allard
gms20007@aol.com

2–5 years
Wheelchair accessible

Governance: Proprietary
Accredited by: N/A
Memberships: N/A
Religious affiliation: Nonsectarian

PROFILE
Total enrollment: 48
Number of faculty: 8
Number of teaching assistants: 2
Schools three or more children attend next: Beauvoir, Georgetown Day, Washington International

APPLICATION PROCESS
Birthday cutoff: 2 by September 1 for toddler class; 3 by December 31 for primary class
Deadline: March 15
Fee: N/A
Testing required: None
Steps: N/A

COSTS
Average additional fees: N/A
Financial aid: No
% of children receiving aid: N/A

NOTE: This data applies to the 2009–2010 school year.

Age	Days	Hours	Tuition	Openings	Class size	Teachers per class	Food provided
2–3	3	9:00–12:00	$6,600				
2–3	5	9:00–12:00	$8,800				
3–5	5	9:00–12:00	$7,700				
3–5	5	9:00–3:00	$10,800				

DAILY LIFE

Before- or after-school care: Beginning at 8:15 AM
Food allergy policy: No nuts
Resource specialists: N/A
Summer programs: None
Special features: N/A

FACILITIES AND LONG-RANGE PLANS

N/A

HISTORY AND PHILOSOPHY

We have maintained an international population of both students and teachers for 25 years. We are located in a quiet oasis in the historic Georgetown waterfront district. We have a high teacher/student ratio with many years' teaching experience. Children leave Georgetown Montessori after three years being very academically advanced and ready to achieve success in their next school. Independence and self-confidence are fostered. We strive to offer a cozy, nurturing environment. We have a wonderful playground.

NOTE: This data applies to the 2009–2010 school year.

THE JEFFERSON MONTESSORI SCHOOL   est. 1987

Penny Glover, Head of School
8507 Emory Grove Road
Gaithersburg, MD 20877
301-840-8448
www.thejeffersonschool.com

Meredith Shankle
admin@thejeffersonschool.com

2–6 years
Wheelchair accessible

Governance: Proprietary
Accredited by: N/A
Memberships: AMS, NAGC
Religious affiliation: Nonsectarian

PROFILE
Total enrollment: 190
Number of faculty: 43
Number of teaching assistants: N/A
Schools three or more children attend next: Barnesville, Mater Amoris, St. John's Episcopal, Thomas Jefferson Prep

APPLICATION PROCESS
Birthday cutoff: 2 by entry
Deadline: N/A
Fee: $50
Testing required: None
Steps: Tour, application, child visit

COSTS
Average additional fees: $400
Financial aid: No
% of children receiving aid: N/A

NOTE: This data applies to the 2009–2010 school year.

Age	Days	Hours	Tuition	Openings	Class size	Teachers per class	Food provided
2–3	2	9:15–12:15	$4,380		12–14		Snack
2–3	2	9:15–3:15	$5,290		12–14		Snack
2–3	3	9:15–12:15	$6,520		12–14		Snack
2–3	3	9:15–3:15	$7,940		12–14		Snack
2–3	5	9:15–12:15	$9,120		12–14		Snack
2–3	5	9:15–3:15	$11,025		12–14		Snack
3–6	5	9:15–12:15	$7,970		28–30		Snack
3–6	5	9:15–3:15	$9,820		28–30		Snack

DAILY LIFE

Before- or after-school care: 7:15–9:15 AM, 3:15–6:15 PM

Food allergy policy: N/A

Resource specialists: Art, Mandarin Chinese, music, physical education, Spanish

Summer programs: Yes

Special features: "Beyond the Walls" outdoor education program, 11-month expanded school year option

FACILITIES AND LONG-RANGE PLANS

10 classrooms, all-purpose room, art room, 4 playgrounds

HISTORY AND PHILOSOPHY

The Jefferson Montessori School, established in 1987, provides the "prepared environment" essential to Montessori education. This prepared classroom environment is comprised of six interrelated areas: Practical Life, Sensorial, Language, Math, Social Studies, and Science. A full range of cultural experiences including drama, music, poetry, cooking, art, storytelling, and field trips complement the daily routine.

Children are free to talk and move around, are stimulated by purposeful learning activities of their own choosing, can discover and correct their own errors, and are treated with respect and trust. All these factors help the children to develop an inner discipline and a sense of responsibility. The Jefferson Montessori School strives to instill in each child a sense of acceptance and understanding through our diverse learning environment.

NOTE: This data applies to the 2009–2010 school year.

THE JENNY WAELDER HALL CENTER FOR CHILDREN　　　est. 2005

Dr. Kathleen Miller, Director
3150 Chesapeake Street, NW
Washington, DC 20008
202-237-1550
www.jwhcenter.org

Kathleen Miller
jwhcenter@gmail.com

3–6 years
No wheelchair access

Governance: Nonprofit
Accredited by: N/A
Memberships: N/A
Religious affiliation: Nonsectarian

PROFILE
Total enrollment: 8
Number of faculty: 4
Number of teaching assistants: None
Schools three or more children attend next: Public and private kindergarten

APPLICATION PROCESS
Birthday cutoff: 3 by date of admission
Deadline: Rolling
Fee: $75
Testing required: None
Steps: Application, school visit/meeting with director, child play visit

COSTS
Average additional fees: None
Financial aid: Yes
% of children receiving aid: Varies

NOTE: This data applies to the 2009–2010 school year.

Age	Days	Hours	Tuition	Openings	Class size	Teachers per class	Food provided
3–6	5	8:30–12:15	$19,000		8	2	Snack

DAILY LIFE
Before- or after-school care: None
Food allergy policy: We work with parents to accommodate children with food allergies
Resource specialists: N/A
Summer programs: The school year runs from September through the end of July
Special features: Close collaboration with parents; exclusively master's-level teachers; extended school year; low child-to-teacher ratio; small class size

FACILITIES AND LONG-RANGE PLANS
Spacious, light-filled classroom; large playground

HISTORY AND PHILOSOPHY
The center uses personalized teacher-child relationships in a play-based learning model to promote each child's cognitive, social, emotional, and physical development. We believe each child's strengths can be harnessed to optimize development. Play facilitates problem solving, consolidates learning experiences, and is critical for abstract thinking and creativity in work and relationships. The small size of our program allows us to serve children who may have social difficulties or mild delays in development. These difficulties may include sensory integration, communication, emotional expressions (shyness or overly boisterous), peer relationships, or ordinary challenges such as toileting, sleeping, eating, or listening.

NOTE: This data applies to the 2009–2010 school year.

LITTLE FOLKS SCHOOL   est. 1973

Gay Cioffi, Director
3224 N Street, NW
Washington, DC 20007
202-333-6571
www.littlefolks.org

Helen Hagerty, Assistant Director
littlefolks@littlefolks.org

2.5–5 years
No wheelchair access

Governance: Nonprofit
Accredited by: N/A
Memberships: N/A
Religious affiliation: Nonsectarian

PROFILE
Total enrollment: 50
Number of faculty: 8
Number of teaching assistants: 2
Schools three or more children attend next: Beauvoir, Georgetown Day, Holy Trinity, Hyde, Maret, Potomac, St. Patrick's Episcopal, Sheridan, Sidwell Friends, Washington International

APPLICATION PROCESS
Birthday cutoff: 2.5 by September 1
Deadline: February 15
Fee: $50
Testing required: None
Steps: Open house, application, play date

COSTS
Average additional fees: None
Financial aid: Yes
% of children receiving aid: 5%

NOTE: This data applies to the 2009–2010 school year.

Age	Days	Hours	Tuition	Openings	Class size	Teachers per class	Food provided
2.5–5	5	8:45–11:45	$12,750		Varies	2	Parents provide snack
2.5–5	5	8:45–2:45	$15,500		Varies	2	Snack

DAILY LIFE
Before- or after-school care: None
Food allergy policy: Nut free
Resource specialists: Speech and language therapy
Summer programs: 8-week summer camp
Special features: Large outdoor playground, excellent individual attention to children and parents

FACILITIES AND LONG-RANGE PLANS
School is housed in charming historical Georgetown townhouse

HISTORY AND PHILOSOPHY
While highly regarded for its approach to the needs of the "whole" child, Little Folks School is also known as a wonderful resource for the parents of the children who attend. At Little Folks we prepare the environment for children to learn through active exploration and interaction with teachers, other children, equipment, and materials. We approach the whole child: developing the social, the cognitive, the physical, and the aesthetic.

NOTE: This data applies to the 2009–2010 school year.

THE MADDUX SCHOOL   est. 2004

Andrea A. Mullins, Director
11614 Seven Locks Road
Rockville, MD 20854
301-469-0223 x109
www.madduxschool.org

Lucy L. Cohen, Program Specialist
lcohen@madduxschool.org

3–7 years
Wheelchair accessible

Governance: Nonprofit
Accredited by: MSDE
Memberships: N/A
Religious affiliation: Nonsectarian

PROFILE
Total enrollment: 43
Number of faculty: 16
Number of teaching assistants: N/A
Schools three or more children attend next: Grace Episcopal, Green Acres, Harbor, Jewish Primary Day, Kingsbury, Lab School, McLean, Primary Day, St. Andrew's Episcopal, Sheridan, Washington Episcopal

APPLICATION PROCESS
Birthday cutoff: September 1
Deadline: February 15, then rolling
Fee: $75
Testing required: None
Steps: Open house/parent tour, application, child visit, informal assessment

COSTS
Average additional fees: None
Financial aid: No
% of children receiving aid: N/A

NOTE: This data applies to the 2009–2010 school year.

Age	Days	Hours	Tuition	Openings	Class size	Teachers per class	Food provided
3–4	5	9:00–12:00	$17,200		8–10	2	Snack
4–5	5	12:30–3:30	$17,200		8–10	2	Snack
5–6	5	8:30–2:30	$23,300		10–12	2	Snack
6–7	5	8:30–2:30	$23,300		12–14	2	Snack

DAILY LIFE
Before- or after-school care: None
Food allergy policy: Teachers trained in use of EpiPen
Resource specialists: Occupational therapists, speech/language pathologists
Summer programs: None
Special features: Small classes, small student-to-teacher ratios, nurturing environment, individualized programming, integration of speech/language and occupational therapy, art, music, PE, yoga

FACILITIES AND LONG-RANGE PLANS
Art studio, children's library, computers in all classrooms, gym, music room, playground. Long range plans: Expand through second grade

HISTORY AND PHILOSOPHY
The Maddux School celebrates the different personalities, interests and learning styles of young children. The school is committed to establishing strong academic, communication and social skill foundations through individualized, interactive and innovative activities and small student-to-teacher ratios. The Maddux School reaches out to competent children who may need support developing social language, fine motor and play skills within the framework of a regular education program. Our school strives, at all times, to complement the strengths, meet the needs and promote the self-esteem of each child.

NOTE: This data applies to the 2009–2010 school year.

NATIONAL CHILD RESEARCH CENTER   est. 1928

Liz Barclay, Head of School
3209 Highland Place, NW
Washington, DC 20008
202-363-8777
www.ncrcpreschool.org

Katherine Vazquez, Admissions Director
kvazquez@ncrcpreschool.org

2.5–5 years
Wheelchair accessible

Governance: Nonprofit
Accredited by: NAEYC
Memberships: AISGW, BSF, LSF
Religious affiliation: Nonsectarian

PROFILE
Total enrollment: 171
Number of faculty: 40
Number of teaching assistants: 6
Schools three or more children attend next: Beauvoir, Georgetown Day, Holy Trinity, John Eaton, Lowell, Maret, Norwood, Potomac, Sheridan, Sidwell Friends

APPLICATION PROCESS
Birthday cutoff: 2.5 by September 15
Deadline: January 31
Fee: $75
Testing required: None
Steps: Parent tour, application, applicant play session

COSTS
Average additional fees: $80
Financial aid: Yes
% of children receiving aid: 12%

NOTE: This data applies to the 2009–2010 school year.

Age	Days	Hours	Tuition	Openings	Class size	Teachers per class	Food provided
2.5	2	8:30–11:30	$5,060	9	9	3	Snack
2.5	3	8:30–11:30	$6,750	9	9	3	Snack
2.5	3	12:40–3:30	$6,750	9	9	3	Snack
3	5	8:30–11:30	$10,890	16	16	3	Snack
3	5	12:40–3:30	$10,890	16	16	3	Snack
3.5	5	8:30–11:30	$10,890	Varies	16	3	Snack
3.5	5	12:40–3:30	$10,890	Varies	16	3	Snack
4	5	8:30–11:30	$10,890	Varies	18	3	Snack
4	5	12:40–3:30	$10,890	Varies	18	3	Snack
4.5	5	8:30–3:00	$21,615	Varies	22	3	Snack

DAILY LIFE

Before- or after-school care: 8:00–8:30 AM, 3:00–5:00 PM

Food allergy policy: Peanut-free school

Resource specialists: Occupational therapist, school counselor, speech and language pathologist

Summer programs: 6-week camp, mid-June through July

Special features: Early Intervention Program for 2.5-year-old class, Lunch Bunch Program for 4-year-old class, specials (library, motor, music) built into curriculum

FACILITIES AND LONG-RANGE PLANS

Major renovation completed fall 2008

HISTORY AND PHILOSOPHY

Founded in 1928, the National Child Research Center provides a collaborative approach to preschool education in an environment that nurtures the whole child, fosters partnerships with families and is committed to the inclusion of children with special needs. A highly trained, multi-disciplinary faculty employs developmentally appropriate practices, supported by ongoing professional development and sound research. Essential to its role as a model of early childhood education is the creation of a diverse, respectful community. Both within and beyond the school community, NCRC seeks opportunities to advocate for all children and their families.

NOTE: This data applies to the 2009–2010 school year.

OUTDOOR NURSERY SCHOOL   est. 1933

Barbara Hutchinson
8922 Spring Valley Road
Chevy Chase, MD 20815
301-656-8871

2.5–5 years
No wheelchair access

Governance: Nonprofit
Accredited by: State of Maryland
Memberships: N/A
Religious affiliation: Nonsectarian

PROFILE
Total enrollment: 75
Number of faculty: 5
Number of teaching assistants: 5
Schools three or more children attend next: Blessed Sacrament, Lafayette, Maret, Norwood, Rosemary Hills, Sidwell Friends

APPLICATION PROCESS
Birthday cutoff: 2.5 by the end of August
Deadline: Visits mid-October to mid-December, decisions by first week of February
Fee: $50
Testing required: None
Steps: Parent visit, application

COSTS
Average additional fees: None
Financial aid: No
% of children receiving aid: N/A

NOTE: This data applies to the 2009–2010 school year.

Age	Days	Hours	Tuition (monthly)	Openings	Class size	Teachers per class	Food provided
2.5–3	2	9:00–11:45	$225	14	15	2	Snack
3–3.5	3	9:00–11:45	$335	Attrition	15	2	Snack
3.5–4	5	9:00–11:45	$560	Attrition	15	2	Snack
4–4.5	5	9:00–11:45	$560	Attrition	15	2	Snack
4.5–5	5	9:00–11:45	$560	Attrition	15	2	Snack

DAILY LIFE
Before- or after-school care: 11:45 AM–2:00 PM
Food allergy policy: None
Resource specialists: None
Summer programs: 4 weeks in July
Special features: N/A

FACILITIES AND LONG-RANGE PLANS
Historic building, no changes planned

HISTORY AND PHILOSOPHY
N/A

NOTE: This data applies to the 2009–2010 school year.

PETER PIPER PRESCHOOL OF MCLEAN   est. 1954

Lynda K. O'Bryan, Director
1351 Scotts Run Road
McLean, VA 22102
703-356-5811

3–5 years
Limited wheelchair access

Governance: Proprietary
Accredited by: N/A
Memberships: NAEYC, NVAEYC
Religious affiliation: Nonsectarian

PROFILE
Total enrollment: 42
Number of faculty: 8
Number of teaching assistants:
None
**Schools three or more children
attend next:** N/A

APPLICATION PROCESS
Birthday cutoff: 3 by October 1
Deadline: First-come acceptance
Fee: $35
Testing required: None; however, hearing, vision, and developmental screening is done in our school for individual development/educational planning
Steps: Submit enrollment form

COSTS
Average additional fees: $50 maximum
Financial aid: No
% of children receiving aid: N/A

NOTE: This data applies to the 2009–2010 school year.

Age	Days	Hours	Tuition	Openings	Class size	Teachers per class	Food provided
3	2	8:50–11:45	$2,032				
4–5 (JK)	3	8:50–11:45	$2,656				
4–5 (JK)	4*	8:50–11:45	$3,600				
4–5 (JK)	5	8:50–11:45	$4,691				

*4-day JK is 3 mornings and one afternoon

DAILY LIFE

Before- or after-school care: None
Food allergy policy: Child brings own snacks
Resource specialists: County and private specialists
Summer programs: None
Special features: N/A

FACILITIES AND LONG-RANGE PLANS

Modern facilities with radiant-heated floors. Architect-designed for Preschool, located on 2.5 acres along with large playground with outdoor equipment. Qualified and experienced teachers.

HISTORY AND PHILOSOPHY

A three year old's first school experience in a relaxed atmosphere for developing social interactions and planned experiences for motor and intellectual growth. Exposures to music, rhythms, art, literature and discovering the world "around him."

Our program for four year olds is geared to meet each child's needs and to promote growth by providing language development, beginning phonics, number concepts, physical activities, music, art and learning to participate as a member in a group.

Field trips and special class activities provide additional enrichment.

NOTE: This data applies to the 2009–2010 school year.

POTOMAC GLEN DAY SCHOOL   est. 1992

Angela Tranquill, Principal
9908 South Glen Road
Potomac, MD 20854
301-299-9193
www.potomacglendayschool.com

Karen Crocker
pgds@comcast.net

2–5 years
Wheelchair accessible

Governance: Proprietary
Accredited by: MSDE
Memberships: N/A
Religious affiliation: Christian, non-denominational

PROFILE
Total enrollment: 130
Number of faculty: 18
Number of teaching assistants: 2
Schools three or more children attend next: Bells Mill, Norwood, Our Lady of Mercy, Potomac Elementary, St. Elizabeth, Wayside, Woods Academy

APPLICATION PROCESS
Birthday cutoff: 2 by first day of school
Deadline: January registration
Fee: $100 registration
Testing required: None except for incoming kindergartners
Steps: Tour, registration, orientation

COSTS
Average additional fees: N/A
Financial aid: No
% of children receiving aid: N/A

NOTE: This data applies to the 2009–2010 school year.

Age	Days	Hours	Tuition	Openings	Class size	Teachers per class	Food provided
2	2	7:30–12:15	Online		10–12	2	None
2	3	7:30–12:15	Online		10–12	2	None
2	5	7:30–12:15	Online		10–12	2	None
2	2	7:30–3:30	Online		10–12	2	None
2	3	7:30–3:30	Online		10–12	2	None
2	5	7:30–3:30	Online		10–12	2	None
3	2	7:30–12:15	Online		11–13	2	None
3	3	7:30–12:15	Online		11–13	2	None
3	5	7:30–12:15	Online		11–13	2	None
3	2	7:30–3:30	Online		11–13	2	None
3	3	7:30–3:30	Online		11–13	2	None
3	5	7:30–3:30	Online		11–13	2	None
4	5	7:30–12:15	Online		13–16	1–2	None
4	5	7:30–3:30	Online		13–16	1–2	None
PK	5	7:30–12:15	Online		11	1	None
PK	5	7:30–3:30	Online		11	1	None
K	5	7:30–3:30	Online		16	1–2	None

DAILY LIFE

Before- or after-school care: None
Food allergy policy: Cannot accommodate severe nut allergy
Resource specialists: N/A
Summer programs: 8 weeks, age 2–2nd grade
Special features: Computer, religion, Spanish

FACILITIES AND LONG-RANGE PLANS
N/A

HISTORY AND PHILOSOPHY

Our classrooms are set up for a traditional style of learning, where children are being educated while they are having fun. We provide a sound, safe, and secure environment that will enable the child to develop both educational and social skills, promote self-concept, and encourage a sense of responsibility and an increasing sense of independence. We are a Christian school that teaches Christian values and the Golden Rule. We are a school that builds pride and respect for a great nation.

NOTE: This data applies to the 2009–2010 school year.

RESTON CHILDREN'S CENTER   est. 1967

Fahemeh Pirzadeh, Executive Director
11825 Olde Crafts Drive
Reston, VA 20191
703-476-8150
www.restonchildren.org

Fahemeh Pirzadeh
rccfrontdesk@aol.com

6 weeks–12 years (before- and after-school care)
Limited wheelchair access

Governance: Nonprofit
Accredited by: NAEYC
Memberships: NAEYC
Religious affiliation: Nonsectarian

PROFILE
Total enrollment: 272
Number of faculty: 35
Number of teaching assistants: 25
Schools three or more children attend next: N/A

APPLICATION PROCESS
Birthday cutoff: N/A
Deadline: None
Fee: $50
Testing required: None
Steps: Tour, parent interview, application

COSTS
Average additional fees: $100
Financial aid: Yes
% of children receiving aid: 6%

NOTE: This data applies to the 2009–2010 school year.

Age	Days	Hours	Tuition	Openings	Class size	Teachers per class	Food provided
6 wk.–11 mo.	5	6:30–6:30	$1,490		12	8	Yes
11–16 mo.	5	6:30–6:30	$1,465		12	5	Yes
16–24 mo.	5	6:30–6:30	$1,465		12	5	Yes
2–2.5	5	6:30–6:30	$1,275		15	5	Yes
2.5–5	5	6:30–6:30	$1,275		7–10	5	Yes

DAILY LIFE
Before- or after-school care: 6:30–9:00 AM, 3:30–6:30 PM
Food allergy policy: All food prepared in-house in RCC's full-size commercial kitchen; nut-free policy; all staff are first aid and CPR trained
Resource specialists: Dance, field trips, music & movement
Summer programs: School-age 10-/11-week Summer Camp Program
Special features: 6:30 AM–6:30 PM; before-/after-school care through age 12; swimming 3 days a week; Big Wednesday field trips, including Luray Caverns, Baltimore Science Center, Mount Vernon/Reynolds Museum & Education Center, Washington Mystics WNBA games

FACILITIES AND LONG-RANGE PLANS
Computers, playground, large collections of children's literature
Long-range plans: Add new playground equipment

HISTORY AND PHILOSOPHY
Reston Children's Center is a nonprofit, parent-owned cooperative dedicated to the developmental and educational needs of children and to provide quality support systems for families. A variety of parent education and support programs are offered. We stress cooperation, independence and interaction among children of various ages and caring adults. Children are allowed choices while being guided to take advantage of all facilities and opportunities offered at RCC and in the community.

NOTE: This data applies to the 2009–2010 school year.

RIDGEMONT MONTESSORI SCHOOL   est. 1965

Mary Beth Humen, Director
6519 Georgetown Pike
McLean, VA 22101
703-356-1970
www.ridgemontmontessori.com

Mary Beth Humen
info@ridgemontmontessori.com

18 months–6 years
No wheelchair access

Governance: Nonprofit
Accredited by: Virginia Department of Social Service
Memberships: AMI, NAMTA
Religious affiliation: Nonsectarian

PROFILE
Total enrollment: 66
Number of faculty: 7
Number of teaching assistants: 3
Schools three or more children attend next: Chesterbrook Elementary, Churchill, Franklin Sherman, Kent Gardens Elementary, Langley, Mater Dei, Norwood, Potomac, Washington International

APPLICATION PROCESS
Birthday cutoff: 18 months by September 1
Deadline: Rolling
Fee: $75
Testing required: None
Steps: Parent visit/classroom observation, application, child school visit

COSTS
Average additional fees: $125
Financial aid: No
% of children receiving aid: N/A

NOTE: This data applies to the 2009–2010 school year.

Age	Days	Hours	Tuition	Openings	Class size	Teachers per class	Food provided
18 mo. –3	3	9:00–11:45	$7,150	7	9	2	Parents provide snack
3–4	5	9:00–12:00	$9,300	15–20	18	2	Parents provide snack
5–6	5	9:00–3:00	$11,550	15–20	18	2	Parents provide snack

DAILY LIFE

Before- or after-school care: None
Food allergy policy: Nut-free school
Resource specialists: N/A
Summer programs: None
Special features: AMI-trained teachers, music, Spanish

FACILITIES AND LONG-RANGE PLANS

HISTORY AND PHILOSOPHY

Ridgemont was founded in McLean, Virginia, in 1965 and has served McLean and its surrounding areas since that time. We adhere to the Montessori principles established by Dr. Maria Montessori and the Association Montessori Internationale. At Ridgemont, we foster a love of learning within our students and create a setting where children learn at their own pace in a cooperative atmosphere. We feel fortunate to have a sense of community present not only within our classrooms, but also within our parent group. We believe that the experience our children have today will shape tomorrow.

NOTE: This data applies to the 2009–2010 school year.

SCHOOL FOR FRIENDS   est. 1981

Jim Clay, Director
2121 Decatur Place, NW
Washington, DC 20008
202-328-1789
www.schoolforfriends.org

Jim Clay
jclay@schoolforfriends.org

2–5 years
Limited wheelchair access
Second campus: 2201 P Street NW, Washington, DC, 202-328-7237

Governance: Nonprofit
Accredited by: NAEYC
Memberships: FCE
Religious affiliation: Society of Friends (Quaker)

PROFILE
Total enrollment: 57
Number of faculty: 5
Number of teaching assistants: 6
Schools three or more children attend next: British, Eaton, Georgetown Day, Haynes, Lafayette, Lowell, Murch, Oyster, Sidwell Friends, Stoddart

APPLICATION PROCESS
Birthday cutoff: 2 by September 1
Deadline: March 1
Fee: $50
Testing required: None
Steps: Open house, application

COSTS
Average additional fees: None
Financial aid: Yes
% of children receiving aid: 15–20%

NOTE: This data applies to the 2009–2010 school year.

Age	Days	Hours	Tuition	Openings	Class size	Teachers per class	Food provided
2	5	8:00–1:00	$925	2	8	2	Snack
2	5	1:00–6:00	$925	2	8	2	Snack
2	5	8:00–6:00	$1,435	6	8	2	Snack
3	5	8:00–1:00	$925		13	3	Snack
3	5	1:00–6:00	$925		12	2	Snack
3	5	8:00–6:00	$1,435		12	3	Snack
4	5	8:00–1:00	$925		20	4	Snack
4	5	8:00–6:00	$1,435		20	4	Snack

DAILY LIFE

Before- or after-school care: None

Food allergy policy: Peanut-free classroom if a student has a peanut allergy; all teachers trained in use of EpiPen

Resource specialists: Center for outreach in education

Summer programs: Regular program is 12 months

Special features: Music, Spanish

FACILITIES AND LONG-RANGE PLANS

Playgrounds

Long-range plans: New playground equipment and ground cover

HISTORY AND PHILOSOPHY

School for Friends is a preschool that provides a loving, caring, and supportive educational environment for children. We are committed to creating a diverse community of children and families. The curriculum reflects the Quaker values of cooperation, equality, and nonviolence.

The school encourages all aspects of a child's development—social, emotional, physical, and cognitive—in a setting that is safe, warm, and cheerful. The teachers help the children develop positive self-concepts and understand others from different cultural and economic backgrounds. The program is committed to the inclusion of children with special needs.

NOTE: This data applies to the 2009–2010 school year.

ST. COLUMBA'S NURSERY SCHOOL   est. 1958

Julia Berry, Director
4201 Albemarle Street, NW
Washington, DC 20016
202-742-1980
www.stcolumbadc.org

Karen Smyers, Office Administrator
school@columba.org

3–5 years
Wheelchair accessible

Governance: Nonprofit
Accredited by: NAEYC
Memberships: MAESA, NAES, NAEYC
Religious affiliation: Protestant Episcopal

PROFILE
Total enrollment: 125–135
Number of faculty: 15
Number of teaching assistants:
None
Schools three or more children attend next: Beauvoir, Georgetown Day, Maddux, National Presbyterian, Norwood, Potomac, Sheridan, St. Patrick's Episcopal, Washington Episcopal, Washington International

APPLICATION PROCESS
Birthday cutoff: November 1
Deadline: N/A
Fee: $50
Testing required: None
Steps: Open house, application, playdate (if child has special needs)

COSTS
Average additional fees: N/A
Financial aid: Yes
% of children receiving aid: 20%

NOTE: This data applies to the 2009–2010 school year.

Age	Days	Hours	Tuition	Openings	Class size	Teachers per class	Food provided
3	5	8:30–11:30	$8,480	28	14	2	Snack
3	5	12:30–3:30	$8,480	28	14	2	Snack
4	5	8:30–11:30	$8,480	14	14	2	Snack
4	5	12:30–3:30	$8,480	14	14	2	Snack
3–4	5	8:30–2:10	$13,100	34	14–18	2	Snack

DAILY LIFE

Before- or after-school care: 8:00–8:30 AM, 2:00–3:30 PM

Food allergy policy: Nut-free/allergen-free classrooms where children have allergies

Resource specialists: Will facilitate occupational, speech & language, physical, and other private therapies during the school day

Summer programs: None

Special features: Active, vigorous outdoor play on our fabulous and spacious playgrounds; socially focused, developmentally based program; inclusive practices for a variety of special needs; many school pets; weekly science and environmental education; twice-weekly music and movement classes; full-time playground teacher/coordinator; out every day in all kinds of weather

FACILITIES AND LONG-RANGE PLANS

N/A

HISTORY AND PHILOSOPHY

St. Columba's is a haven for the unhurried child. We believe that children learn most effectively when they can be active, and at St. Columba's, we provide children with an array of hands-on experiences both in and out of the classroom that challenge their senses, minds, and bodies as it teaches them about the wider world. St. Columba kids spend nearly half their day outdoors playing, digging, climbing, riding, and learning. Our integrated approach to learning allows children to broaden and deepen their social, cognitive, motor, language, and emotional skills at their own pace while preparing them for school ahead.

NOTE: This data applies to the 2009–2010 school year.

ST. JOHN'S EPISCOPAL PRESCHOOL

Marley Joyce, Head of School
3240 O Street, NW
Washington, DC 20007
202-338-2574
www.stjohnsdc.org

Marley Joyce
info@stjohnsdc.org

2–5 years
Wheelchair accessible

Governance: Nonprofit
Accredited by: N/A
Memberships: MAESA, NAES
Religious affiliation: Episcopal

PROFILE
Total enrollment: 45
Number of faculty: 8
Number of teaching assistants:
None
Schools three or more children attend next: Beauvoir, St. Patrick's Episcopal, Sidwell Friends

APPLICATION PROCESS
Birthday cutoff: 2.5 by September 30
Deadline: January 30
Fee: $50
Testing required: None
Steps: Tour/information session, application, playdate

COSTS
Average additional fees: None
Financial aid: Yes
% of children receiving aid: 0% this year

NOTE: This data applies to the 2009–2010 school year.

Age	Days	Hours	Tuition	Openings	Class size	Teachers per class	Food provided
2.5–3	3	8:00–12:00	$7,046	14	14	2	Snack
2.5–3	4	8:00–12:00	$9,750	14	14	2	Snack
3–4	5	8:00–3:00	$10,995	1	15	2	Snack
4–5	5	8:00–3:00	$10,995	1–2	16	2	Snack

DAILY LIFE
Before- or after-school care: 8:00–9:00 AM, 12:30–3:00 PM
Food allergy policy: Nut-free school if one or more children are allergic; parents approve ingredients in snacks provided
Resource specialists: Part-time studio consultant, part-time Early Childhood Educator Series Coordinator; parents may also arrange for in-class observation
Summer programs: 6-week program for children aged 2.5–9 years
Special features: Early Childhood Educators Series: a series of programs to support colleagues in their individual and professional development

FACILITIES AND LONG-RANGE PLANS
Preschool consists of three classrooms, including dedicated studio space, and an outdoor classroom. Preschool is located on the second floor of St. John's Episcopal Church Parish Hall.

HISTORY AND PHILOSOPHY
Our mission is to celebrate children's depth of wonder and joy in the world and to engage with them and their families in their explorations. In a rich environment, children collaborate with experienced teachers to extend their thinking and develop their unique abilities. We seek to form a bridge to the wider community, reflect its diversity, and support the full potential of childhood. We are inspired by the philosophy of teaching young children that originates in Reggio Emilia, Italy.

NOTE: This data applies to the 2009–2010 school year.

TEMPLE SINAI NURSERY SCHOOL   est. 1992

Perri Iger-Silversmith, Director
3100 Military Road, NW
Washington, DC 20015
202-362-3836
www.templesinaidc.org/study/nursery

Alyssa Policarpio, Admissions Coordinator
nurseryschool@templesinaidc.org

2–5 years
Wheelchair accessible

Governance: Nonprofit
Accredited by: NAEYC, PJLL
Memberships: NAEYC, NAREA, PJLL
Religious affiliation: Jewish

PROFILE
Total enrollment: 150
Number of faculty: 31
Number of teaching assistants:
Team approach (co-teachers in every classroom)
Schools three or more children attend next: Beauvoir, Concord Hill, Georgetown Day, Green Acres, Jewish Primary Day, Lowell, Norwood, Sheridan, Sidwell Friends

APPLICATION PROCESS
Birthday cutoff: September 1
Deadline: January 1, then rolling
Fee: $50
Testing required: None
Steps: Tour/school visit, application

COSTS
Average additional fees: Parent Association dues, classroom fees
Financial aid: No
% of children receiving aid: N/A

NOTE: This data applies to the 2009–2010 school year.

Age	Days	Hours	Tuition (non-members)	Openings	Class size	Teachers per class	Food provided
2	2	9:15–11:45	$4,350	24	8	2	Snacks
2.5	3	9:15–12:15	$5,290	24	12	2	Snacks
3	3	9:15–12:15	$6,000	24	12	2	Snacks
3.5	5	9:15–12:15	$6,765	28	14	2	Snacks
4	5	9:15–12:15	$6,765	42	14	2	Snacks
5	5	9:15–2:15	$11,905	14	14	2	Snacks

DAILY LIFE
Before- or after-school care: 8:15–9:10 AM
Food allergy policy: Nut-free
Resource specialists: In-house occupational therapist, Ivymount C.O.R.E. team (includes behavior management specialist, occupational therapist, speech-language pathologist), music specialist
Summer programs: Camp, 2-week sessions
Special features: Afternoon enrichment program, C.O.R.E. consultants on site, Jewish, Reggio-inspired

FACILITIES AND LONG-RANGE PLANS
Garden, kitchen, playground

HISTORY AND PHILOSOPHY
Temple Sinai Nursery School was founded in 1992 by the temple community under the leadership of Perri Iger-Silversmith, who has remained the director since the school's inception. The school philosophy is based on established theories of early childhood education, including the Bank Street Model, and is inspired by the Reggio Emilia approach. TSNS's philosophy emphasizes the importance of social-emotional development in a hands-on, play-based learning environment. Most important to the nature of our approach is our teachers' style of gentle facilitation, attention to individual needs, and respect for unique learning styles. All classes are co-taught by teachers, emphasizing small group ratios.

NOTE: This data applies to the 2009–2010 school year.

WALDEN MONTESSORI ACADEMY   est. 1981

Linda Grodin, Director
7730 Bradley Boulevard
Bethesda, MD 20817
301-469-8123

Linda Grodin
grodinl@aol.com

2–6 years
Limited wheelchair access

Governance: Proprietary
Accredited by: MSDE
Memberships: AMS
Religious affiliation: Nonsectarian

PROFILE
Total enrollment: 68
Number of faculty: 8
Number of teaching assistants: 5
Schools three or more children attend next: Christ Episcopal, Norwood, St. Jane de Chantal, Sidwell Friends

APPLICATION PROCESS
Birthday cutoff: September 1
Deadline: First come, first served
Fee: $50
Testing required: None
Steps: Parent visit

COSTS
Average additional fees: None
Financial aid: Occasionally
% of children receiving aid: 19%

NOTE: This data applies to the 2009–2010 school year.

Age	Days	Hours	Tuition	Openings	Class size	Teachers per class	Food provided
2	2	9:00–12:00	$3,700		12	2	Snack
2	3	9:00–12:00	$5,000		12	2	Snack
2	5	9:00–12:00	$8,000		12	2	Snack
2	5	9:00–3:00	$10,000		12	2	Snack
2	5	8:00–4:00	$13,000		12	2	Snack
3–6	5	9:00–12:00	$8,000		25	3	Snack
3–6	5	9:00–3:00	$10,000		25	3	Snack
3–6	5	8:00–4:00	$13,000		25	3	Snacks

DAILY LIFE
Before- or after-school care: 8:00–9:00 AM, 3:00–4:00 PM
Food allergy policy: Nut-free
Resource specialists: Art, drama, music, Spanish, yoga
Summer programs: None
Special features: Individualized teaching; personalized instruction following Montessori theory; special programs of art, drama, music, Spanish, yoga. Acceptance is based on availability only: families choose us, we don't choose them.

FACILITIES AND LONG-RANGE PLANS
New equipment on playground and classrooms always added; no changes planned for our facilities

HISTORY AND PHILOSOPHY
Walden Montessori Academy has provided a quality early learning program for nearly 2,000 children since 1981. We encourage socialization and cognitive learning in a nurturing environment. Our Montessori program for 3–6 year olds follows Dr. Montessori's philosophy that "the most important period of life is not the university studies, but the period from birth to the age of six."

From the chaos of a child's world full of sights and sounds, the child gradually creates order. He/she learns to distinguish among the impressions that assail his environment. Walden Montessori is prepared to take advantage of these sensitive periods, allowing the child to develop at a non-competitive rate.

NOTE: This data applies to the 2009–2010 school year.

THE WASHINGTON HEBREW   est. 1979
CONGREGATION EARLY CHILDHOOD CENTER

Phyllis Shankman, Director
Julia Bindeman Suburban Center
11810 Falls Road
Potomac, MD 20854
301-279-7505
www.whcecc.org

Bea Langel, Registrar
pshankman@whctemple.org

2–6 years
Wheelchair accessible
Second campus: 3935 Macomb Street NW, Washington, DC, 202-895-6334

Governance: Nonprofit
Accredited by: MSDE, PJLL
Memberships: N/A
Religious affiliation: Jewish

PROFILE
Total enrollment: 462
Number of faculty: 37
Number of teaching assistants: 42
Schools three or more children attend next: Concord Hill, Georgetown Day, Green Acres, Maret, Norwood, Primary Day, Sidwell Friends

APPLICATION PROCESS
Birthday cutoff: September 1
Deadline: N/A
Fee: $55
Testing required: None
Steps: Open house/tour, application

COSTS
Average additional fees: Enrichment and ACE
Financial aid: Yes
% of children receiving aid: 2%

NOTE: This data applies to the 2009–2010 school year.

Age	Days	Hours	Tuition	Openings	Class size	Teachers per class	Food provided
2	2	9:30–11:30	$2,364		10	3	Snack
2	3	9:15–11:45	$4,414		12	3	Snack
3	4	9:15–11:45	$5,381		16	3	Snack
3	5	9:15–11:45	$5,996		16	3	Snack
4	5	9:15–11:45	$5,996		16	3	Snack
5 (K)	5	8:45–3:00	$13,786		18	2	Snack, lunch

DAILY LIFE
Before- or after-school care: 8:30–9:30 AM
Food allergy policy: Peanut-free school
Resource specialists: Art, creative movement, drama, Hebrew, Judaic studies, language arts, media, music, physical education, science; full-time nurse
Summer programs: Camp Keetov
Special features: N/A

FACILITIES AND LONG-RANGE PLANS
Computer room, discovery/science room, media center, 5 playgrounds

HISTORY AND PHILOSOPHY
We believe that children are our most precious resource. We recognize that it is incumbent upon us to create a warm, positive environment for their learning. We recognize that every child is a unique individual, and that we must strive to assist our children in discovering themselves as well as the world around them. We believe that group experience is part of life and that each child should have the opportunity to discover the meaning of sharing and be conscious of his/her own rights, as well as the prerogatives of others.

NOTE: This data applies to the 2009–2010 school year.

WESTMORELAND CHILDREN'S CENTER   est. 1970

Kim Mohler, Executive Director
5112 Allan Terrace
Bethesda, MD 20816
301-229-7161
www.westmorelandchildrenscenter.com

Clare Cahill, Office Manager
wccmain@aol.com

2–4 years
Limited wheelchair access
Multiple campuses: 1 Westmoreland Circle, Bethesda, MD, 301-320-2020
5500 Massachusetts Avenue, Bethesda, MD, 301-229-7161

Governance: Nonprofit
Accredited by: MSDE, NAEYC
Memberships: N/A
Religious affiliation: Nonsectarian

PROFILE
Total enrollment: 156
Number of faculty: 25
Number of teaching assistants: N/A
Schools three or more children attend next: Georgetown Day, Montgomery County Public Schools, Norwood, Primary Day, Sidwell Friends

APPLICATION PROCESS
Birthday cutoff: September 1
Deadline: Rolling
Fee: $50
Testing required: None
Steps: Tour, application, optional child visit

COSTS
Average additional fees: $100
Financial aid: Yes
% of children receiving aid: 3%

NOTE: This data applies to the 2009–2010 school year.

Age	Days	Hours	Tuition (monthly)	Openings	Class size	Teachers per class	Food provided
2	3	9:00–12:00	$390	24	12	2	Snack
2	5	9:00–12:00	$790	2	12	2	Snack
2	5	7:30–6:00	$1,365	10	12	2	Breakfast, lunch
3	3	9:00–12:00	$480	30	15	2	Snack
3	5	9:00–12:00	$740	10	15	2	Snack
3	5	7:30–6:00	$1,185	20	15	2	Breakfast, lunch
4	5	9:00–12:00	$740	20	20	2	Snack
4	5	9:00–2:45	$955	20	20	2	Snack, lunch
4	5	7:30–6:00	$1,185	20	20	2	Breakfast, lunch

DAILY LIFE
Before- or after-school care: 7:30–9:00 AM, 12:00–6:00 PM
Food allergy policy: Peanut- and nut-free, teachers trained in CPR and first aid
Resource specialists: Music & movement
Summer programs: 9-week summer camp
Special features: N/A

FACILITIES AND LONG-RANGE PLANS
Three campuses

HISTORY AND PHILOSOPHY
Began in 1970, grew to 3 campuses serving 150 families. Focusing on the whole child, developmentally appropriate practices and learning through play.

NOTE: This data applies to the 2009–2010 school year.

WHITE FLINT CHILDREN'S HOUSE   est. 1994

Margaret Akatu, Head of School
11810 Parklawn Drive
Rockville, MD 20852
301-230-9720
www.wfchm.com

Judy Sylvester
wfchedu@yahoo.com

2–6 years
Wheelchair accessible

Governance: Proprietary
Accredited by: MSDE
Memberships: AMS
Religious affiliation: Nonsectarian

PROFILE
Total enrollment: 140
Number of faculty: 26
Number of teaching assistants: 12
Schools three or more children attend next: Beauvoir, Green Acres, Holy Cross, Maret, Montgomery County Public Schools, Norwood

APPLICATION PROCESS
Birthday cutoff: 2 by time of enrollment
Deadline: Ongoing enrollment
Fee: $50
Testing required: None
Steps: Parent tour/classroom observation, application, student visit

COSTS
Average additional fees: $500 enrollment fee
Financial aid: No; 4 scholarships
% of children receiving aid: N/A

NOTE: This data applies to the 2009–2010 school year.

Age	Days	Hours	Tuition	Openings	Class size	Teachers per class	Food provided
2	5	9:00–12:00	$10,900		12	2	Snacks; hot catered lunch option
2	5	9:00–3:00	$12,050		12	2	Snacks; hot catered lunch option
2	5	7:30–6:00	$16,900		12	2	Snacks; hot catered lunch option
3–6	5	9:00–12:00	$8,300		28–30	3	Snacks; hot catered lunch option
3–6	5	9:00–3:00	$9,650		28–30	3	Snacks; hot catered lunch option
3–6	5	7:30–6:00	$14,620		28–30	3	Snacks; hot catered lunch option

DAILY LIFE
Before- or after-school care: 8:30–9:00 AM, 3:00–6:00 PM
Food allergy policy: Peanut butter–free; case-by-case for all allergies
Resource specialists: Admission testing associates, CDS Early Childhood Services, Expressive Therapy Centre LLC, PEP parenting classes, Montgomery County Infants and Toddlers Program, music therapist
Summer programs: 4 weeks (mid-July–mid-August)
Special features: Montessori 2-year-old program, extended school calendar (August–July), indoor gym, optional hot catered lunch, high staff retention rate; field trips, in-house guests; foreign languages, art, music, drama

FACILITIES AND LONG-RANGE PLANS
11,000–square foot indoor space, auditorium, gallery, indoor gym, library. Long-range plans: Attain accreditation by the American Montessori Society.

HISTORY AND PHILOSOPHY
Our mission is to provide an academically sound early learning environment that is dedicated to excellence and stimulating individual growth for children ages two through six. With a well-prepared environment designed to provide nurturing, creative, artistic, and developmentally intellectual experiences for the toddler, preschool, and kindergarten child, we are committed to instilling in each child a natural and ongoing curiosity toward learning. We believe in Dr. Maria Montessori's methods of encouraging the natural development of the whole child.

NOTE: This data applies to the 2009–2010 school year.

Preschool Maps and Table

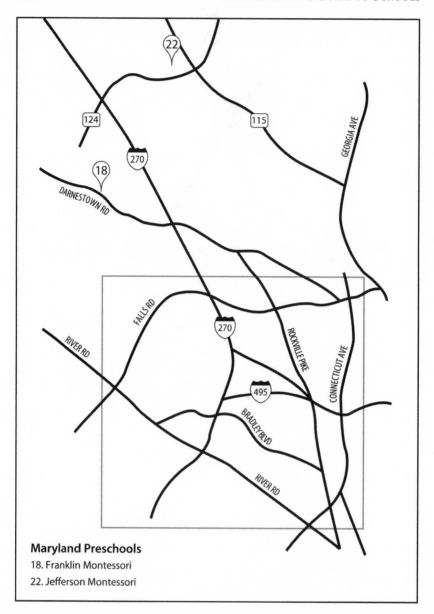

Maryland Preschools

18. Franklin Montessori
22. Jefferson Montessori

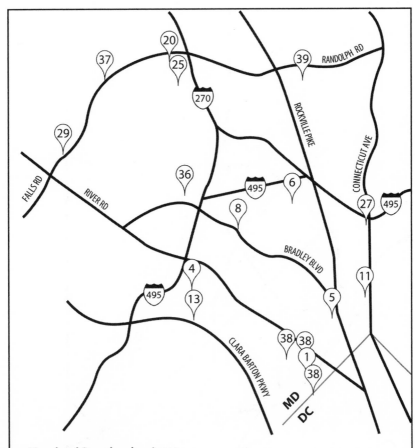

Maryland Preschools—Inset

1. Abingdon Montessori
4. Apple Montessori
5. Bethesda-Chevy Chase Cooperative Nursery
6. Bethesda Country Day
8. Bradley Hills Presbyterian Church Nursery
11. Chevy Chase United Methodist Church Preschool
13. Clara Barton Center for Children

20. Geneva Day
25. Maddux
27. Outdoor Nursery
29. Potomac Glen Day
36. Walden Montessori Academy
37. Washington Hebrew Congregation Early Childhood Center
38. Westmoreland Children's Center (3 sites)
39. White Flint Children's House

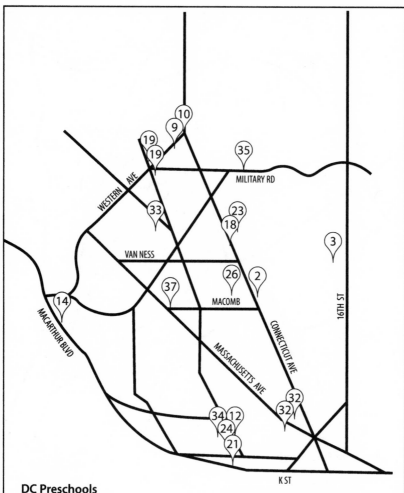

DC Preschools

2. Adas Israel's Gan HaYeled
3. Amazing Life Games
9. Chevy Chase-Bethesda Community Children's Center (CCBC)
10. Chevy Chase Presbyterian Church Weekday Nursery
12. Children's House of Washington
14. Community Preschool of the Palisades
18. Franklin Montessori
19. Friendship Children's Center (2 sites)
21. Georgetown Montessori

23. Jenny Waelder Hall Center for Children
24. Little Folks
26. National Child Research Center
32. School for Friends (2 sites)
33. St. Columba's Nursery
34. St. John's Episcopal Preschool
35. Temple Sinai Nursery
37. Washington Hebrew Congregation Early Childhood Center

Virginia Preschools

7. Beverley Hills Church Preschool

15. Country Day

16. Dolley Madison

17. Emmanuel Lutheran

28. Peter Piper

30. Reston Children's Center

31. Ridgemont Montessori

Table 2.1 Alphabetical List of Preschools with Age Range in Years

Name of School	State	Infant	1	1.5	2	2.5	3	4	5	6	End	Page
Abingdon Montessori School	MD					●	●	●	●	●		286
Adas Israel's Gan HaYeled	DC			●	●	●	●	●	●			288
Aidan Montessori School	DC			●	●	●	●	●	●	●	6th	48
Amazing Life Games	DC					●	●	●	●	●		290
Apple Montessori School	MD				●	●	●	●	●	●		292
Barnesville School	MD						●	●	●	●	8th	54
Barrie School	MD				●	●	●	●	●	●	12th	56
Beauvoir	DC						●	●	●	●	3rd	58
Bethesda-Chevy Chase Cooperative Nursery School	MD						●	●	●			294
Bethesda Country Day School	MD				●	●	●	●	●	●		296
Beverley Hills Church Preschool	VA					●	●	●	●			298
Bradley Hills Presbyterian Church Nursery School	MD				●	●	●	●				300
British School of Washington	DC						●	●	●	●	12th	64
Browne Academy	VA						●	●	●	●	8th	68
Burgundy Farm School	VA							●	●	●	8th	72
Butler School	MD						●	●	●	●	8th	74

Key: "End" = grade at which the school ends, if beyond 6 years

Name of School	State	Infant	1	1.5	2	2.5	3	4	5	6	End	Page
Capitol Hill Day School	DC						●	●	●	●	8th	76
Chevy Chase-Bethesda Community Children's Center (CCBC)	DC			●	●	●	●	●	●			302
Chevy Chase Presbyterian Church Weekday Nursery School	DC		●	●	●	●	●	●	●			304
Chevy Chase United Methodist Church Preschool	MD				●	●	●	●	●			306
Children's House of Washington	DC					●	●	●	●	●		308
Children's Learning Center	MD	●	●	●	●	●	●	●	●	●	5th	78
Christ Episcopal School	MD				●	●	●	●	●	●	8th	84
Clara Barton Center for Children	MD				●	●	●	●	●			310
Community Preschool of the Palisades	DC					●	●	●				312
Concord Hill School	MD					●	●	●	●	●	3rd	88
Congressional Schools of Virginia	VA						●	●	●	●	8th	90
Country Day School	VA				●	●	●	●	●			314
Dolley Madison Preschool	VA					●	●	●				316
Edlin School	VA						●	●	●	●	8th	96
Emmanuel Lutheran Preschool	VA					●	●	●	●			318

Key: "End" = grade at which the school ends, if beyond 6 years

Name of School	State	Infant	1	1.5	2	2.5	3	4	5	6	End	Page
Evergreen School	MD					●	●	●	●	●	6th	104
Flint Hill School	VA						●	●	●	●	12th	108
Fourth Presbyterian School	MD						●	●	●	●	7th	110
Franklin Montessori School	DC/MD				●	●	●	●		●		320
French International School (Lycée Rochambeau)	MD					●	●	●		●	12th	114
Friendship Children's Center	DC	●	●	●								322
Geneva Day School	MD				●	●	●	●	●			324
Georgetown Day School	DC						●	●	●	●	12th	116
Georgetown Montessori School	DC				●	●	●	●				326
German School	MD				●	●	●	●	●	●	12th	122
Grace Episcopal Day School	MD						●	●	●	●	8th	126
Grace Episcopal School	VA						●	●	●	●	5th	128
Green Acres School	MD							●	●	●	8th	130
Green Hedges School	VA						●	●	●	●	8th	132
Harbor School	MD							●	●	●	2nd	136
Highland School	VA						●	●	●	●	12th	140
Holy Trinity School	DC						●	●	●	●	8th	146

Key: "End" = grade at which the school ends, if beyond 6 years

Name of School	State	Infant	1	1.5	2	2.5	3	4	5	6	End	Page
Ivymount School	MD							●	●	●	12th	152
Jefferson Montessori School	MD				●	●	●	●	●	●		328
Jenny Waelder Hall Center for Children	DC						●	●	●	●		330
Jewish Primary Day School	DC							●	●	●	6th	154
Julia Brown Montessori Schools	MD					●	●	●	●	●	3rd	156
Katherine Thomas School	MD							●	●	●	12th	158
Langley School	VA						●	●	●	●	8th	166
Little Flower School	MD							●	●	●	8th	168
Little Folks School	DC					●	●	●	●			332
Loudoun Country Day School	VA							●	●	●	8th	170
Lourie Center School	MD							●	●	●	5th	172
Lowell School	DC						●	●	●	●	6th	174
Maddux School	MD						●	●	●	●	age 7	334
Melvin J. Berman Hebrew Academy	MD				●	●	●	●	●	●	12th	184
National Child Research Center	DC					●	●	●	●			336
National Presbyterian School	DC						●	●	●	●	6th	188
Nysmith School for the Gifted	VA						●	●	●	●	8th	196

Key: "End" = grade at which the school ends, if beyond 6 years

Name of School	State	Infant	1	1.5	2	2.5	3	4	5	6	End	Page
Oneness-Family School	MD				●	●	●	●	●	●	8th	202
Outdoor Nursery School	MD					●	●	●	●			338
Peter Piper Preschool of McLean	VA					●	●	●	●			340
Potomac Glen Day School	MD				●	●	●	●	●	●		342
Primary Day School	MD							●	●	●	2nd	212
Reston Children's Center	VA	●	●	●	●	●	●	●	●	●	age 12	344
Ridgemont Montessori School	VA			●				●	●	●		346
River School	DC			●	●	●	●	●	●	●	3rd	216
Sandy Spring Friends School	MD							●	●	●	12th	218
School for Friends	DC				●		●	●	●			348
Seneca Academy/Circle School	MD						●	●	●	●	8th	220
Sidwell Friends School	DC/MD						●	●	●	●	12th	224
St. Andrew's Episcopal School	MD				●	●	●	●	●	●	12th	230
St. Columba's Nursery School	DC						●	●	●			350
St. John's Episcopal Preschool	DC				●	●	●	●	●			352
St. Patrick's Episcopal Day School	MD						●	●	●	●	8th	236
St. Stephen's and St. Agnes School	VA							●	●	●	12th	238

Key: "End" = grade at which the school ends, if beyond 6 years

Name of School	State	Infant	1	1.5	2	2.5	3	4	5	6	End	Page
Stone Ridge School of the Sacred Heart	MD							●	●	●	12th	242
Temple Sinai Nursery School	DC				●	●	●	●	●			354
Wakefield School	VA					●	●	●	●	●	12th	244
Walden Montessori Academy	MD				●	●	●	●	●	●		356
Washington Episcopal School	MD						●	●	●	●	8th	246
Washington Hebrew Congregation Early Childhood Center (Bindeman)	DC/MD				●		●	●	●	●		358
Washington International School	DC						●	●	●	●	12th	248
Washington Waldorf School	MD					●	●	●	●	●	12th	250
Westmoreland Children's Center	MD				●	●	●	●				360
White Flint Children's House	MD				●	●	●	●	●	●		362
Woods Academy	MD						●	●	●	●	8th	254

Key: "End" = grade at which the school ends, if beyond 6 years

Alternatives

CHARTER SCHOOLS

Charter schools are a type of public school designed to provide a choice of schools. They are for children entering preschool through twelfth grade; not all serve the entire age range. They operate under different standards and accountability than typical public schools, and the laws that govern them vary from state to state. A concept that began in the 1970s, the charter school's mission is designed to provide parents, students, and teachers the opportunity to choose a school with high academic standards and innovative teaching methods. These schools have grown dramatically in number and popularity in recent years and increasingly serve economically diverse communities. A charter school can be started by any group of committed citizens. An elaborate contract (or charter) is made between the responsible citizens and a public school board or its representatives. This charter provides a standard of excellence with a set of expected results, but there is no specific required model or system for achieving the results. If the charter school cannot demonstrate that it is successful according to the terms of its charter, it can be closed.

Each school can create its own curriculum, hire and fire its staff, adjust the length of the school day, and require uniforms and other features more consistent with independent schools. Some are designed like public magnet schools and focus on language immersion, the arts, science, or technology.

As you tour charter schools, look for the same attributes that apply to independent schools, including the appropriateness of each for your child. Websites will provide admission procedures and deadlines. It is important that you understand the financial plan and facilities information, including the budget and the length of the lease or plans to own a building. Since the significant rise in the number of these innovative schools is relatively recent, their overall success is still being determined. Some have already had their charters canceled; however, many students have greatly benefited from charter school opportunities.

Parents must submit an application, and students are admitted on a first-come, first-served basis or by lottery. No tests or record of achievement are required, and students may present with the entire range of academic or social or emotional needs; however, a school can define its mission in a way that gives it a specialty. For instance, a school may seek students who have emotional or behavioral issues and design a program that is focused on healing as well as educating. At another school, students live on campus during the week. Most charter schools want to offer a curriculum that is exciting, challenging, and flexible, involves experiential learning, and supports each student appropriately. Parental involvement is also important, and siblings are sometimes given a priority in admission.

Attendance at charter schools is free. Once a student leaves a public school system to attend a charter school, the money allocated for the education of that child follows him or her to the charter school. Additional funding comes from federal and private sources.

Washington, DC, has about one hundred charter schools; none are currently located in northern Virginia or Montgomery County. Useful websites are www.focusdc.org, www.mdcharternetwork.org, and www.virginiacharterschools.org.

HOME SCHOOLING

For years, expatriates home schooled their children when they lived in areas where schools were not available. Now, home schooling is growing in popularity all over the country among parents who seek this alternative for a broad range of reasons. Christian parents mobilized the home-schooling movement in order to provide religious coursework and to avoid the secular culture in public schools. In increasing numbers, other parents want a more flexible schedule to meet the extracurricular demands of intense practice in the arts or serious athletes in competitive sports; the standard school day may preclude full participation in travel sports, swimming, skating, gymnastics, dancing, or acting for aspiring young people. Other parents think their child or children need a focused curriculum with the ability to work in depth at an advanced level; for still others the need is for a slower pace. Parents sometimes home school their children when they travel for a year or more.

Within the home schooling movement, parents can develop their own materials and curricula for coursework, or they can buy texts and curricula from companies who cater to home-schooled children. Some materials address religious beliefs; others are secular. Parents might develop a curriculum that is highly experiential, or is focused on global issues like the environment and calculated to whet the interests and creativity of the student. Music lessons are often a vital part of home schooling.

Schooling at home may be conducted one-on-one with a parent and child and possibly siblings or in a small-group setting with other home-schooled students. Different parents may teach subjects in their expertise, or they may hire teachers for certain subjects such as foreign languages. Individuals or small groups may assemble periodically for field trips or other activities like physical education at a gym. Some school systems allow home-schooled students to participate in extracurricular activities. Scouts and other similar organizations provide positive activities for home-schooled children.

Every state has home-schooling laws that include providing the department of education with curriculum, goals, and objectives for each grade, hours in class, and sometimes lesson plans, student work, tests, and requirements for graduation. More and more older students are taking courses online; these online courses often provide transcripts, which can be useful when applying to college.

By seventh grade, courses should have titles (for example, pre-algebra or physical science). Work should be graded by the time the college-bound student enters high school, and even earlier if a student wishes to enter a public or independent school. In eighth and ninth grades, the family should start to browse college websites to see what courses and how many years of each subject the colleges recommend. Many colleges have specific requirements for home-schooled students. Science requirements are of particular importance, since without adequate laboratories, proficiency in these subjects can be more difficult to assess. The logistics of taking standardized tests such as the PSAT, SAT, and SAT II and the ACT need to be considered, along with the possibility of taking AP exams. Some colleges require the General Education Development (GED) exam. Contact the admission department if a school's policy is unclear. All students, but especially home-schooled students, should plan interesting summer activities to meet new friends and perhaps spark a new interest. Being involved in religious organizations or community activities or holding a job or an internship in an area of interest provides additional socialization with peers and life experiences.

If a child is to be home schooled successfully, the parents need to be well organized, plan ahead carefully, and commit the significant time and resources required.

A Conversation
with Georgia

There are no formulas or easy answers to the questions that I am asked every day. What works in one family may not work in another. The approaches to parenting and decision making that follow have helped many of the parents and children with whom I have worked. Understanding that each child has his or her own specific needs, please use what I have learned to help determine what is best for your child and family.

KINDERGARTEN READINESS

Is My Child Ready for Kindergarten?

Being bright or "smart" has little to do with a child's readiness for kindergarten. Social and emotional development are the tools children need to be able to use their intellect and function in a group. Children of the same chronological age may develop at different paces, and pushing a child ahead can impede this vital part of development, which is best acquired in the early years and is important to both future success in school and long-term emotional health. In determining kindergarten readiness, educators look for progress in the following areas that, under normal circumstances, improve with age:

- Memory—Ability to repeat nursery rhymes, sing songs, follow directions with three or more steps, recall three or more digits
- Attention span, impulse control, concentration
- Ability to remain quiet, listen attentively, follow a storyline, persevere through an activity without distraction
- Multitasking skills—Ability to perform two or more tasks simultaneously, such as talking and putting on mittens, move from one activity to another with minimal frustration and in a timely manner
- Social skills—Ability to cooperate, accept correction, share objects and attention, take turns, be a friend, work in a group, modify rough play
- Speaking skills or language development—Ability to be understood by those other than parents, speak in complete sentences, listen to others, ask questions, make needs known, know his or her name and birth date, modulate voice
- Interest in reading—Ability to remain seated, follow a story, predict what is going to happen, ask the meaning of words or ideas, supply an omitted word, enjoy listening to a story
- Visual discrimination—Ability to begin discerning differences in symbols such as letters ("B" and "P," "E" and "F") and numbers ("6" and "9"), recognize own name in print
- Fine motor skills—Ability to use a crayon, markers, pencils, scissors; fold a piece of paper
- Gross motor skills—Ability to climb, hop, jump, skip, ride a tricycle, throw and catch a ball
- Independence—Ability to separate from parents, try new things, communicate with other adults, enjoy play dates, demonstrate age-appropriate self-help skills

Most children enter and are successful in kindergarten before reaching all of these developmental milestones, but it is important that you be aware of your child's level of development and remain vigilant and supportive to ensure that these basic skills are acquired in a timely manner.

Children born with low birth weight may take up to five years to catch up with their peers. Prolonged illness, medical trauma, persistent ear infections, and other health-related problems may lead to excessive separation anxiety or delayed development of speech and language.

All families experience change, but some events can be more traumatic than others. The birth of siblings, a death or serious illness in the family, moving, divorce, remarriage, and new stepsiblings may contribute to delayed development. We also know that the neurological and psychological development of boys is often slower than that of girls.

HELPING YOUR CHILD BE SUCCESSFUL IN SCHOOL

What to Do with a "Gifted" Child?

Defining the word *gifted* is not easy. Personally, I believe every child is gifted in some way; teachers should teach to those gifts, whatever they may be. In reality, students who acquire skills quickly and do not need repetition can find much greater success in magnet programs or in schools with other accelerated learners. Teachers with command of the subject and knowledge of how children learn can provide maximum opportunities for these children to fulfill their potential.

From an early age, some children evidence the ability to excel beyond their peers. Young children who easily develop excellent verbal skills have an early advantage, but sometimes the child who learns spoken language more slowly will gradually surpass those who were more advanced. Other children will show an amazing aptitude for numerical thinking. Parents must be careful not to send messages to these young children that they are "the smartest." This sense of being more talented than others can create self-doubt when the child encounters tasks that are hard and at which other children may excel. While every parent needs to appreciate his or her child's talents, in these early years it is better to applaud effort than achievement. Many educators subscribe to the theory of educating the "whole child," and that is especially important for gifted children.

In my experience, the most telling attributes of a child who is precocious are:

- Understanding the nuance of language and having a love of words.
- Having a burning desire to read and comprehend.
- Ability to see patterns and relationships in shapes and numbers.
- Ability to concentrate and persevere in subjects and tasks that are not of his or her own choosing.
- Superior short-term and long-term memory.
- Active curiosity and desire to fathom the answers.
- Excellent problem-solving skills.
- Ability to understand abstract ideas and draw inferences.
- Ability to organize information and learn through trial and error.

The degree of giftedness may vary, but these children need to be engaged in the learning process by teachers who understand them and who have time to provide additional challenges. Faculty in many independent schools have experience teaching intellectually talented students. I always hope that these children have a "soul mate," or another child in the class who shares common interests and abilities and from whom he or she can learn and share a love of learning. Opinions vary on the subject of skipping grades, but most of the local schools keep students with their peer group while providing additional academic challenges. The National Association for Gifted Children provides helpful information at www.nagc.org.

Should My Child Repeat a Grade?

When considering grade placement for a student, be careful not to use the words "hold back" or "repeat." I prefer "take an extra year." Deciding whether your child needs to take an extra year can be difficult, but it is important to approach this issue with confidence and to frame discussions positively. You need to talk to your child's current teachers and pediatrician, and to other professionals who know how children learn and mature and who have some understanding of the age range of students in independent schools in this area. You should have sound reasons to believe that an extra year will help your child and realistic expectations about what can be achieved. It is wise to consider educational diagnostic tests, which can often help to confirm or identify what is best for the child.

An extra year will not help a child with average ability, as determined on intelligence tests like the Wechsler Intelligence Scale for Children (WISC-IV), sustain a superior performance over the years; however, it may ensure that he or she performs up to his or her ability. The critical point is that parents not expect more from the child than can be achieved by taking an extra year. A child who has superior ability and is not performing at that level may experience superior achievement with the "gift of time," as noted child psychologist David Elkind discusses in his book *The Hurried Child*. Children develop at different rates, and children of all ability levels may need more time to master basic skills such as reading and writing. Keep in mind that delayed development in these areas may have more to do with physical maturity or genes than intellectual ability. If either parent experienced difficulty acquiring basic skills, it may indicate that your child would be well served by taking an extra year.

Never threaten a child by saying, "Unless you do better or work harder, you will have to repeat." If you decide to have your child take an extra year, have someone else (an educational consultant, the director of admission of the new school, or a friend or relative who took an extra year) also talk to your child if possible. Most children realize when school is not going well for them and can be led to understand the reasons for making this change; nevertheless, no matter how you frame it, this news hurts. Try not to be the sole perpetrator of the pain because that may deprive your child of a loving shoulder to cry on.

If you decide to give your child an extra year, it is always best if he or she can move to another school. This helps avoid the social implications of perceived failure. Among other benefits of being one of the oldest instead of among the youngest is the ego boost of being one of the first in the class to get a driver's license. Also keep in mind that taking an extra year does not mean that your child has to change grade levels in scouts, sports leagues, or religious activities.

What Should I Expect from Tutoring?

I think of tutoring as a short-term, supplemental educational service designed to ultimately enable a child to work independently. It is not a cure-all. Tutoring is most effective when your child recognizes his or her need for it, and the extra work does not interfere with activities that boost self-esteem. Like taking an extra year, tutoring does not enable a student with average ability to sustain a superior level of achievement. However, for the child who is frustrated or failing, tutoring can provide different methods or techniques to master a subject and build the self-confidence that he or she needs.

You may seek tutoring in one subject or in skills applicable across subjects, such as organizational skills. Select a tutor qualified to provide the help your child needs and whom your child likes. You, your child, and the tutor should agree on specific, realistic goals. When the goals are reached, the tutoring should end. Otherwise, a child can become dependent upon tutoring, refuse to take risks or do the work on his or her own, and become more discouraged. Too much support can make a child feel "broken" and in need of being "fixed." One boy told me that he felt his parents were dissatisfied with him because they were always trying to "fix" something.

If your child is not progressing toward the tutoring goals, consult a physician about possible medical issues. Attention deficit disorder, thyroid imbalance, allergies, or depression may be contributing to the problem. Diagnostic tests can determine if learning disabilities or sensory integration or auditory processing issues are interfering. Possible alcohol or drug use must be addressed in older children. You might also consider other alternatives such as changing schools or taking an extra year.

The Homework Struggle

Most children want their parents to know and care about their homework; however, no parent should become the homework police officer who is dreaded or even feared as the "homework laws" are enforced. Beware of implying, "You need me because I don't think you can do it alone." This only makes a child feel inadequate, inferior, and, invariably, angry. You can be most helpful by saying, "If I can help you, let me know" or "Can I help?" Dignify the work, and reward the effort more than the finished product. Children may become resistant to accepting help with their homework if they want and need reassurance and support and instead receive a harsh judgment.

How can you be helpful? Recognize and show respect for your child's needs. Some children are disorganized and forgetful and need help developing a checklist that parents can review. The best help a parent can give a child is to empower him or her to work independently.

Be careful not to start every conversation with, "Have you done your homework?" or "What grade did you get on the test?" Many children believe that the only thing their parents care about is grades. They get the impression that their own value as a human being is based upon the marks they receive in school. An "A" grade means you are an "A" person; a "C" implies you are not a really good person; an "F" means you are worthless. If you make good grades, you are loved; if the grades are poor, you are unloved. Some will cheat to make an "A" in order to please their parents, while others who make an honest "C" may feel they have failed. I never want a child to fail, but grades are not my standard of personal worth, and I trust they are not yours.

Fear of failure and perfectionism haunt many children. Some students allow themselves to fail, with the subconscious belief that if they had tried, success would have been impossible. These same children usually make sincere promises to "do better," but get trapped in their subconscious, self-defeating method of managing fear of failure by failing. Their parents respond with a sincere, "All I want you to do is try," but to try hard and receive a poor grade is intolerable to the child. Children who suffer from perfectionism are intolerant of their own mistakes and become easily upset if an assignment is difficult. They are inefficient and procrastinate because they may fear the inability to meet their own high standards. Often these children are highly verbal and have been told many times and in many ways how bright they are. Because they have often been the first to succeed at many of the linguistic tasks, they seem to feel they should already know whatever is being taught.

Being first to finish can be viewed as being the smartest, but it also can be an avoidance technique. Perhaps the child reads well, but has a difficult time with math. Perfectionist students cannot understand why, if they are so bright, they cannot accomplish the work in every subject area with equal ease. Self-doubt begins to erode the will to try, or fosters rushing through work as an attempt to minimize the fear of failure.

How do parents help these children? Gently reassure them that it is all right not to know in advance what the teacher is teaching. Remind them that if they already knew it, they would not have to go to school. Surprisingly, this appears to be a new idea to some children, who seem relieved at the thought. Parents can exacerbate the problem of perfectionism by being intolerant of their own mistakes or the mistakes of others. Children observe how their parents react to errors. Let your child know that you make mistakes, but you also learn from them. Show respect for those who try hard. Make sure your children are aware that you understand what it means to be wrong: it can be disappointing, but it is no reason to give up. It takes time to help children realize that they will be respected if they do not perform perfectly, but it can be done. Sometimes a therapist or counselor can identify and clarify the parents' concerns and expectations and the child's perceptions and needs.

How Can I Maximize My Child's Potential?

I am concerned about sleep deprivation and the constant fatigue I observe in many children. I am also concerned about the absence of opportunities for families to listen to and to help resolve the anxieties that keep some children awake at night. Children should go to sleep early enough to enable them to get up with ease. Try to set a good example, then set firm boundaries about how the evening hours are used. There should be no overstimulation from sweet foods, TV, or the Internet; the ideal is to have a quiet family time in the evening as often as possible. Only when the environment is conducive will your child reveal worries to you.

The goal is to help your child identify ways to solve his or her own problems. From the moment of birth, parents are conditioned to solve their children's problems and to make life as happy and comfortable as possible. Children learn and gain confidence in their own abilities when we listen to their problems and let them devise acceptable solutions. Just as we learn from our mistakes as adults, as parents we must allow children to experience some trial and error. Children are empowered and comforted when parents are good listeners. Allow them to find their own ways to respond to situations, and show respect for their capacity to make some decisions and to solve problems themselves.

It has been said that the greatest gift we give our children is the gift of *our* time. It is important to find time every day to play with your children. If you have young children, get down on the floor and play their games at their level. For older children, find time to share an interest or hobby— not just homework.

I am adamant about the importance of eating breakfast. While breakfast does not have to be a sit-down meal, every child needs to eat something (preferably not sweet) before going to school. Eating breakfast is like putting gas in the car; it provides children with the energy to keep going. Studies have shown that good nutrition plays a role in children's performance in school by improving stamina and concentration. Set a good example by eating a nutritious diet, including breakfast. All of this is easier said than done, I know, but your efforts will pay off.

Being successful in school is hard work for most children, and it consumes a great deal of time and energy. Children are often tired when the school day is over. On occasion, they take on more activities than they can accommodate without feeling stress and exhaustion. You may need to help your child define and limit his or her involvement. Children with many interests often require a great deal of parental support such as driving to and from activities, having meals at special times, and being exempt from some household chores.

Should I Be Involved in the School?

Schools depend on the interest, time, and financial resources that parents contribute. Studies indicate a positive correlation between parents' personal involvement in the school and the motivation and achievement of their children. Being involved, even if your time is limited, is a meaningful way to show a child that his or her education is important. It also gives you more opportunities to meet classmates and other parents, to get to know the teachers, and to observe the social and academic climate of the school. Fathers who volunteer are especially welcome as role models for boys because the faculty of many schools are predominately female. At a minimum, attend school meetings. Your involvement is an investment in your child, not just in the school, and reduces the likelihood of problems arising. Often, parents who complain about a teacher or situation have not made a sustained effort to communicate with faculty or school administrators. Teachers appreciate thoughtful parents who participate in an honest and respectful dialogue. Many communicate through e-mail with parents and older students. Parent organizations in independent schools sometimes sponsor programs that address parenting skills and offer help in responding to the issues that confront children at different stages of development.

The years in which children rejoice in their parents' presence in school are limited. Little ones love having Mom or Dad come to class, but at about sixth grade a parent's presence becomes more awkward for the child, and in high school parents are generally *persona non grata*. Seize the moment and enjoy those years when parents who visit or work with the school are heroes to their children.

Should I Consider an Independent School? When?

I think a child needs the best possible education in the early, formative years. Children who have had the opportunity to acquire a love of learning and a good work ethic can make the best of almost any school. I have seen too many children who did not receive the attention necessary to maximize their potential in the early years; as a result, their performance in school declined annually. Some parents saved their money for an independent middle school, upper school, or college, only to discover that the child was not adequately prepared for an accelerated curriculum requiring a high level of motivation. On the other hand, many of the public elementary schools are excellent, and some of the public middle and high schools also provide excellent quality. I am perfectly comfortable advising parents to enroll their child in a public school as long as the child is in a social and academic environment that enables learning at a level consistent with his or her academic potential and is feeling good about himself or herself, and parents are satisfied with the nonacademic culture.

You must weigh the relative merits of a neighborhood public school and an independent school based on your own values, priorities, and financial resources and the needs of your child. Please do not use your own educational experience as the only criterion. Both public and independent schools have changed in recent years.

When a child enters an independent school, the family often gives up the advantages of a neighborhood school, which in most cases include economic, racial, and cultural diversity, a sense of community, close friendships with children who live nearby, and even parents' relationships with neighbors.

Regarding the optimum time for enrollment, schools begin at many different grade or age levels (see tables 1.2 and 2.1, starting on pp. 266 and 370, respectively). Most schools increase the class size at certain grades. These grades with openings are sometimes called *enrollment windows*. I often hear concerns that acceptance in an independent school becomes more difficult at each advancing grade. That is not always true because, in this city, often the largest number of applicants relative to the total number of spaces is at preschool and kindergarten. In fact, there may be fewer applicants at the enrollment windows than at the beginning grade levels. There are relatively fewer places available in area schools at second, fifth, eighth, and eleventh grades because class size at those grades is rarely increased; spaces are a result of attrition. Unless a student has a strong academic record and extracurricular interests, acceptance is unlikely for the senior year.

Schools in the area end at varying grade levels (see tables 1.2 and 2.1). There are advantages to each of the age combinations. A primary school or a junior school invests all of its financial resources in a limited age group; children can experience leadership opportunities and a sense of belonging in a cozy environment that promotes confidence and a sense of well-being. A school for ninth through twelfth grades can focus exclusively on age-appropriate opportunities for that age group. Schools that span the primary through high-school years offer students many opportunities to grow within a consistent educational philosophy.

Over the years, schools have refined their ability to make admission decisions with increasing astuteness, but the fact remains that the needs of a child are more evident as he or she gets older. Making a decision for the educational future of a child who is less than a thousand days old is difficult at best, but this is necessary for children entering preschools. Parents should be open every year to the possibility that a change of schools is advisable. This is not to say that the match of student to school will likely be amiss and that you may have to go through the tedious admissions process again, but you need to be vigilant and make sure that your child's school is the best available place for him or her at any given time.

There is an unfortunate misperception that enrollment in any one school is a ticket to a specific, possibly prestigious secondary school, college, or university. A high level of success in a fine school is a way to maximize future school options and does increase the opportunity for scholarships, but it is the child's achievement, not simply your investment, that makes the ultimate difference.

LEARNING ISSUES

What Is ADD? ADHD?

Attention deficit disorder (ADD) is not uncommon and takes different forms. Generally, it is not officially diagnosed until at least age six. We think of children with attention issues as being fidgety and impatient, but the child who daydreams excessively and cannot concentrate or complete work in a timely manner also has issues with attention. Among other characteristics of attention deficit hyperactivity disorder (ADHD) is behavior that is inconsistent with the child's age for a period of more than six months. This includes being easily distracted, impulsive, and in constant motion or having difficulty focusing, following instructions, and completing tasks. If you notice your child exhibiting these behaviors, try to determine what might be a contributing cause. Might these behaviors indicate depression, anxiety, or evidence of stress? Could they be triggered by diet, environmental factors, or overstimulation at home or at school? Consult your pediatrician, who may refer you to a psychologist or psychiatrist for a diagnosis. Work with professionals who will design and implement a plan to address the problems. Whenever feasible, I first encourage alternatives to medication such as exercise, yoga, changes in diet, and an examination of stress in the family, but there are medicines that provide hope and relief to children in need. The options in medications are increasing, and if one medication does not work, be aware that others are available.

What Is a Learning Disability and What Does It Mean for My Child's Future?

The term *learning disabled* describes a child with average to very superior intelligence who shows a significant discrepancy between academic achievement and intellectual potential as measured on standardized tests. The consequences are mild to severe difficulty in reading, math, or written or oral expression. Some students instinctively learn how to compensate for their inadequacies, and may use a good memory or perceptual reasoning or verbal skills to camouflage their problems until the work becomes more difficult or exacting. Significant progress has been made in helping children overcome or compensate for disabilities. Research in the field confirms that intelligence is not the issue; many of the world's most brilliant people are learning disabled. A child with a learning disability in math may write magnificently. Every child needs to feel competent, and learning disabled children need to be encouraged in their areas of strength, which often include the arts or athletics.

The most severely affected children need *remediation* that is best provided by specially trained teachers. Usually, a wide range of materials and techniques are used. The teacher/student ratio must be very low, even one-to-one. A child with a severe learning disability needs special education daily and probably regularly scheduled social skills classes as well as occupational, physical, and speech and language therapies. Special education is expensive because children receive intense personal attention from teachers with enhanced teaching techniques.

A second approach is *accommodation.* Here the student is taught like all others in the class. The teacher or teachers may not have had the additional training to provide the expertise that may be needed. In this environment, special exceptions are made. Students may be given additional time on tests, use of calculators or computers in class, abbreviated assignments, or a waiver of a foreign language requirement. A specialist may work with the student for a class period each day, either within the mainstream class or in a resource room. It can be emotionally more difficult for a child to be barely surviving in a school providing accommodation than to be in a special needs program with remediation; however, if the disability can be managed effectively and the student's self-esteem, emotional well-being, and academic success are not compromised, accommodation is an appropriate choice.

Being learning disabled is neither a character fault nor a sign of mental incompetence; to the contrary, it may be a sign of greater creativity and sensitivity. To fail to use a special needs program or school when it is appropriate for fear of being stigmatized is like failing to put a cast on a broken leg. If the cast is never applied, the child may limp forever.

Some children with learning disabilities do not want to acknowledge their own condition. Often they have been teased or taunted and are afraid of further humiliation. You cannot let these fears prevent your child from getting remediation. I am gratified when parents tell me that, contrary to their expectations, their child found relief and comfort in a place where he or she was able to progress and relate to others with similar challenges. What a cause for celebration when a child who has never enjoyed success becomes one of the best in the class! Being ahead instead of behind is a welcome respite and is often necessary if the child is to gain energy and confidence for future challenges.

What does a learning disability portend for the future? To be honest, it means that high school may be stressful. Most college-bound students must take all the required courses, even if their disability makes foreign languages, math, or the humanities difficult. Once in college, however, students may select courses at which they can succeed and avoid the classes in which their disability will preclude success. Children who have grappled with learning disabilities may have better study skills than others and may excel. Graduate school can be even more rewarding. Future success is far more likely if the child receives academic help and if parents keep fragile egos intact during difficult times.

USE OF TIME

The Trials of Technology

In this era of technological toys, it is extremely difficult to find the balance between the positive and the harmful use of the Internet. Children (and adults) seem obsessed with mobile phones, social networking sites, texting, TV, and video games, which are ever-increasing in number and variety. They are often used as an escape from distress and can become addictive. You should not apologize for setting limits on how much time your children spend on these activities. Try to involve your child in defining a reasonable amount of computer, gaming, or TV time, but know that the final decision is yours. At the time of day when your child is most apt to be on the Internet, watching television, or playing games, provide an activity that you can do together. Begin by sharing an activity that you hope he or she will continue independent of your participation. Shoot baskets or walk the dog. Make it a policy to play video games together for a short period. Read aloud to one another. Parents tell me they read or reread their children's assigned books so they can discuss them. I like to see fathers and sons read the same novels or biographies. Book clubs for parents and children are thriving. Your best defense against abuse of technology is to set clear limits, stick to them, and establish acceptable alternatives.

Ideally, your child's passion requires engaging with peers and adults, working hard, and stretching himself or herself physically and mentally. Some activities are more solitary and these need to be respected. You do need to worry if your child does not relate well to peers, seems more lonely and isolated than rewarded by an activity, or exhibits characteristics that signal an angry, addictive, or self-destructive personality. In these situations, you should seek help from professionals.

Summer Plans

There is a summer camp or summer program that addresses almost any conceivable interest. I urge parents to insist that their children engage in activities that introduce new ideas or cultivate abilities. For children about nine years old and older, a sleep-away summer camp can be a wholesome adventure that teaches independence and self-reliance and enhances self-esteem and confidence. At camp, other adults reinforce the importance of participating and being responsible, without any of the judgments that are common in a parent–child or teacher–student relationship. Children learn they are capable of being successful away from family. They make new friends, take safe risks, learn new skills, and explore their own possibilities under the watchful eye of caring adults and young counselors who often become role models. They survive their homesickness and return with glorious memories and a vigor and self-confidence that can carry over into the classroom.

I am not as enthusiastic about solely remedial academic summer schools; I prefer to see students experience success in a nonacademic arena that energizes them. Some boarding schools have excellent remedial and enrichment academic programs combined with organized sports and other activities in which students can have fun and be rejuvenated.

For older children, too much leisure in the summer is not advisable. Hanging out in the city or at the beach can be an accident waiting to happen. Older children need constructive programs that enhance their physical skills as well as develop other interests. Most summer jobs do not require a sufficient number of hours at work to keep older children fully occupied; ideally, a child with a summer job is also involved with sports or other organized activities with others whom their parents know and trust. If you begin to ask your child to account for his or her use of time and money at an early age, you may avoid future problems. Tips on Trips (www.tipsontripsandcamps.com) is a resource for summer camps, social service opportunities, and foreign language enrichment programs. Students who have attended camps and their parents are another fine source of information.

Colleges are interested in how students use their leisure time, especially in the summer. Challenging activities are considered evidence of curiosity, discipline, motivation, initiative, and independence.

THE TROUBLED CHILD

Depression and Substance Use

All children, especially adolescents, undergo stress. They are often moody and disagreeable; however, for some, their emotions overwhelm them. Serious distress may occur after a trouble-free childhood. Adolescents may suffer from anxiety, depression, posttraumatic stress, low self-esteem, grief, or drug and alcohol use, as well as various neurological disorders affecting behavior. When moods and attitudes interfere with your child's ability to function, seek medical advice. Do not ignore the signals even if the child protests that he or she is fine. You cannot wish away depression, substance use, or other serious problems that manifest in different ways at different ages. Any one of the following behaviors should be carefully monitored and, if persistent, treated by competent professionals.

Young children who are depressed may cry excessively, be overly fearful, angry or violent, engage in shoplifting or other antisocial behaviors, exhibit addiction to the Internet or computers, complain of physical ailments, become withdrawn and prefer to be alone, or exhibit decreased interest in school. Look for defiance, rebelliousness, lying, cheating, excessive fatigue, excessive passivity, loss of interest in activities, and negative thoughts. Older children may also evidence these behaviors as well as eating disorders, self-mutilation, sexual promiscuity, and self-medication by using drugs and alcohol. These behaviors seriously disrupt the life of the child and of family members, and must be addressed.

The Therapeutic School or Wilderness Option

Until recent years, students who were experiencing emotional and behavioral difficulties had limited options if conventional psychotherapy was not effective. Today, there are excellent programs or combinations of programs that are significantly different from anything that existed even ten years ago. *If local options are unsuccessful,* consider the many exceptional therapeutic schools and wilderness experiences that address depression and self-destructive behaviors in children from seven to eighteen years old. The programs that consultants recommend are not as they are usually portrayed in the media. Qualified clinicians have respect and compassion for the participants; they are not punitive.

There are hundreds of these programs. An official governing body does not supervise the industry of therapeutic programs. A parent cannot tell which ones are excellent and which ones are questionable. If you believe that your child needs this type of intervention, I strongly urge you to work with an educational consultant. Go to www.iecaonline.org or call the Independent Educational Consultants Association (IECA) at 703-591-4850 for the names of educational consultants who visit these programs, get to know the therapists who work in them, and understand which programs are appropriate for the specific problems of your child.

Some valuable resources are Dr. Paul Case's book, *What Now? How Teen Therapeutic Programs Could Save Your Troubled Child,* and the website for the National Association of Therapeutic Schools and Programs (NAT-SAP) at www.natsap.com.

Therapeutic wilderness programs employ techniques that are psychologically sound and insightful, but are distinctly different from traditional psychiatric models. "Mother Nature," the outdoors, teaches children respect and natural consequences, while therapists establish a trusting relationship with children who are removed from the stimulation and distractions of their home environments. With a small group of fellow campers and field staff, in the high desert or forest, therapists help children evaluate their lives to date, gain insights about the effect of their behaviors, design new patterns for dealing with stress and temptations, and build self-esteem through mastery of wilderness survival skills. In individual and group counseling sessions, they begin the journey to emotional health. Parents are involved through regular telephone communication with the therapist and sometimes by going into the wilderness with their child. The duration of the program can be four weeks to three months. Students usually return from the wilderness thanking their parents for "saving" them, and parents often report feeling profoundly rewarded.

In some instances, a therapeutic wilderness program is sufficient to enable a child to examine his or her choices and values and to experience a "wake-up" call. More often, it is the beginning of a longer healing process. Few students can sustain the dramatic improvement that occurs in these programs by returning to the same school and conditions that contributed to their problems. Children can continue to gain emotional health by attending therapeutic schools. These schools rely on a combination of individual, group, and family therapy, highly structured days and evenings, positive peer culture, academics, and physical activity to continue to restore the young person to emotional health and responsible citizenship. Successful students emerge from these schools accountable for their own actions and possessing resources for dealing with temptation, frustration, sadness, or other emotional issues that beset them. The length of stay in any of these schools or programs depends upon the seriousness of the student's condition at the time of entry and his or her ability to make progress.

Unlike more conventional academic settings, therapeutic programs continue throughout the year and admit students on a rolling schedule as space permits. Students who refuse help may need a professional escort who is skillful, compassionate, knowledgeable, and reassuring to take them to the program site.

With the specialized training of the staff, high levels of supervision, and lower faculty/student ratios, costs are considerably higher at therapeutic institutions than at conventional schools. A program that lasts for a few weeks can cost $300 per day or more, and a program that lasts several years can cost $5,000 per month or often more. Graduates and parents often comment on the incredible value of the experience.

LOOKING AHEAD

How will education change in the coming years? I already see independent schools using Skype or similar options to interview students who live all over the world. Distance learning is a viable option in every subject area, and a student can learn a foreign language from a native speaker in any country via the Internet. Students can take classes online that are not available in their school, and home-schooling programs are increasing their use of distance learning. There are those who think that the research and personal commitment that a student needs to invest in online courses balance the advantages of the individual attention of a classroom teacher. It seems reasonable to think that independent and public schools will increase use of the Internet and other technologies, in ways yet undetermined, to enhance the depth and breadth of academic opportunities for students of all ages.

A FINAL NOTE

When asked what I want children to gain from their education, I think of this quotation from John Ruskin:

> The entire object of true education is to make people not merely to do the right things, but enjoy them; not merely [to be] industrious, but to love industry; not merely [to be] learned, but to love knowledge; not merely [to be] pure, but to love purity; not merely [to be] just, but to hunger and thirst after justice.

This is a lofty ideal but a worthy one. My answers to questions are influenced by this ultimate goal that I hold for all children.